Current Research in Ethnomusicology
Outstanding Dissertations
Volume 3

Edited by
Jennifer C. Post
Middlebury College

LONDON AND NEW YORK

CURRENT RESEARCH IN ETHNOMUSICOLOGY
JENNIFER C. POST, *General Editor*

1. NEWLY COMPOSED FOLK MUSIC OF YUGOSLAVIA
Ljerka V. Rasmussen

2. OF MERMAIDS AND ROCK SINGERS
Placing the Self and Constructing the Nation through Belarusan Contemporary Music
Maria Paula Survilla

3. "MARACATU ATÔMICO"
Tradition, Modernity, and Postmodernity in the Mangue Movement of Recife, Brazil
Philip Galinsky

"MARACATU ATÔMICO"
Tradition, Modernity, and Postmodernity in the *Mangue* Movement of Recife, Brazil

Philip Galinsky

LONDON AND NEW YORK

Published in 2002 by
Routledge
711 Third Avenue,
New York, NY 10017

Published in Great Britain by
Routledge
2 Park Square, Milton Park,
Abingdon, Oxfordshire OX14 4RN

First issued in paperback 2015

Routledge is an imprint of the Taylor and Francis Group, an informa company

Copyright © 2002 by Taylor & Francis Books, Inc.

All rights reserved. No part of this book may be reprinted or reproduced or utilized in any form or by any electronic, mechanical, or other means, now known or hereafter invented, including photocopying and recording, or in any information storage or retrieval system, without permission in writing from the publisher.

Tropicalia by Caetano Veloso © 1968 (Renewed) Warner Chappel Edicoes Musicais Ltda (UBC). All Rights administerd by Warner-Tamerlane Publishing Corp. (BMI) All Rights Reserved. Used by Permission, Warner Bros. Publications U.S. Inc., Miami, FL. 33014. *Pau de Quiri* by Zé Neguinho do Côco and *Eu Tenho Pressa* by Cannibal, Neilton, and Celo used by permission of BMG Music Publishing Brazil Ltda All rights for the US obo BMG Music Publishing Brazil Ltda. Administered by BMG Songs, Inc. (ASCAP). *A Cicade, Monologo Ao Pe Do Ouvido*, and *Da Lama Ao Caos* by Chico Science ©1995 Sony Music Brazil (UBC). All rights administererd by Sony/ATV Music Publishing LLC, worldwide. Reprinted with permission. *Mateus Enter* and *O Cidadão Mundo* by Chico Science et al. ©1996 Sony Music Brazil (UBC). All rights administererd by Sony/ATV Music Publishing LLC, worldwide. Reprinted with permission. *Free World*, by Zero Quatro, Tony Regalia, and Fabio Malandragem. ©1995 Universal-Songs of Polygram Int., Inc., on behalf of Mercury Prod. E Ed. Musicais Ltda. All Rights reserved. Reprinted with permission. *Destruindo A Camda de Ozônio* by Zero Quatro, Fabio Malandragem, Tony Regalia, Otto Fuleragem, and Bacteria Maresia. ©1995 Universal-Songs of Polygram Int., Inc., on behalf of Mercury Prod. E Ed. Musicais Ltda. All Rights reserved. Reprinted with permission. *Vô Imbolá* by Seca Baleiro. ©1995 Universal-Songs of Polygram Int., Inc., on behalf of Mercury Prod. E Ed. Musicais Ltda. All Rights reserved. Reprinted with permission.

Library of Congress Cataloging-in-Publication Data
Galinsky, Philip.
"Maracatu atômico" : tradition, modernity, and postmodernity in the mangue movement of Recife, Brazil / by Philip Galinsky .
  p. cm. — (Current research in ethnomusicology ; v. 3)
Originally presented as the author's thesis (Wesleyan University)
Discography: p.
Includes bibliographical references (p.   ) and index.

  1. Mangue (Music)—History and criticism. 2. Popular culture—Brazil—Recife. I. Title.
II. Series.
ML3487.B78 R43 2002
781.64'0981'34—dc21   2002002501

ISBN: 978-0-415-62790-0 (hbk)
ISBN: 978-1-138-90404-0 (pbk)

To my parents, Norman and Ellen Galinsky, and my grandmothers, Leora Osgood May and, In memoriam, Hilda Galinsky

To the memory of Francisco de Assis França (Chico Science) and to the França family

Contents

Acknowledgments	*ix*
Preface	*xiii*
Chapter 1. Introduction	1
My Introduction to *Mangue* and the "New Music Scene" of Recife	1
The Objective, Scope, and Basic Findings of The Research	3
A Review of Literature on Brazilian Popular Music	5
Theoretical Orientation	10
Research Methods and Fieldwork Synopsis	17
Organization of the Dissertation	21
Some Background on Recife	22
Chapter 2. "Da Lama Ao Caos" (From Mud to Chaos): A History of the *Mangue* Movement and "New Music Scene" of Recife	27
Introduction	27
Setting the Scene: Recife in the 1980s	29
The Emergence of Chico Science and Nação Zumbi	30
Mundo Livre S/A (Free World Ltd.)	37
Fred Zero Quatro's First Bands and the Early Years of Mundo Livre S/A	37
Fred Zero Quatro and Chico Science Meet: the Making Of *Mangue*	40
The Beginnings of a "New Music Scene"	42
The *Manifesto Mangue*	43
The Consolidation of Recife's "New Music Scene"	44
Mangue to the World	45
The Recife Scene Loses Its "Greatest Exponent"	47

Chapter 3. *Mangue* In The Context Of Brazilian Pop Music History: A Comparison With Other Movements   49

Introduction   49
Tropicália   49
Pernambucan Precedents to *Mangue*   56
Rock Brasil: The 1980s Boom in Brazilian Rock   63

Chapter 4. "*É Do Caralho Ser Pernambucano, Pôrra!*" ("It's Damn Cool To Be Pernambucan!"): An Ethnography of the Recife Music Scene   67

Introduction   67
Folklore and Recife's Middle Class: New Folkloric Associations   69
"Regional Rhythms Bands": Bands that Work Predominantly with Regional Folk Styles   73
Regional Folk Artists and Associations   80
Rock, Rap, and *Mangue*   86

Chapter 5. *Mangue*, Postmodernity, and the Global Culture Debate   101

Introduction   101
Mangue Style and Ideology   104
The Local within the Global and the Global within the Local: A Postmodern Challenge to National Identity   113
Mangue and the Global Culture Debate   119

Appendices

1. The *Manifesto Mangue*   127
2. Musical Transcriptions and Analysis   131
3. Song Notes   157
4. Fieldwork Account   163

Notes   167
Glossary   199
Discography   213
Bibliography   217
Index   225

Acknowledgments

Although I take full responsibility for this dissertation, including any errors it may contain, the work is in large part the result of many relationships I have developed with people in Brazil and the United States. Thus, the text that follows would not have been possible without the help and contributions of many individuals. To all of these people—those mentioned here and those that must remain anonymous—I grant my most sincere gratitude for their remarkable time, generosity, friendship, and assistance.

First, I must acknowledge all of my gracious interviewees in Recife, whose information and ideas formed the backbone of my data, providing me with many insights. In order of interview date, these are: DJ-journalist Renato Lins; producer Zé da Flauta; folklorist Dr. Mário Souto Maior and anthropologist Eduardo Fonseca of the Joaquim Nabuco Foundation; Éder Rocha (Mestre Ambrósio); producer-impresario Paulo André Pires; Pupillo (Nação Zumbi); Fred Zero Quatro (Mundo Livre S/A); Mestre Bernardo (Nação Pernambuco); Maureliano Ribiero and Hamílton Tenório (Via Sat); Alessandra Leão (Comadre Florzinha); Dito D'Oxossi (Ilê D'Egbá); Jorge Martins da Silva (Cascabulho); Gilson Santana (Daruê Malungo); Secretary of Culture Ariano Suassuna; Oni (Faces do Subúrbio); Maciel Salu and Rodrigo Costa (Chão e Chinelo); folk musician Mestre Salustiano; Valter Ferreira de França ("Mestre Valter" of Maracatu Nação Estrela Brilhante); journalist José Teles; Dona Rita, Seu Francisco, and Jefferson França (family of Chico Science); producer Sílvio Romero Costa Lima; José Severino Vicente (a.k.a. Zé Neguinho do Côco); and DJ José Antônio de Souza Leão Filho. (See Appendix 4 for a list of these interviews.)

In addition, I am highly grateful to the following people in Recife for their generous help, participation, and friendship: Neide Alves; Tânia Lima and Benedito; Cristina and Virgínia Barbosa; Ana, John, Andrea, and Márcia; Queen Marivalda and the Maracatu Nação Estrela Brilhante; the other members of Cascabulho—Silvério Pessoa, Wilson Farias, Marcos Lopes, Kléber Magrão, and Lito Viana; Professor Carlos Sandroni; Pácua and the other members of Via Sat; the members of Comadre Florzinha and Chão e Chinelo; Ortinho, Hélio,

Adelson, and the members of Querozene Jacaré; Felipe Santiago of Nação Pernambuco; Garnizé and the other members of Faces do Subúrbio; Hélder Aragão and Sérgio; Antônio Gutierrez (Gutt); Marcelo and Andrea Soares; Isabel Pessoa Raposo; Anna Cristina, Cinthia, Gilva and Aguinaldo Cordero; Lars Skroder; Júnior; Michelle de Assumpção (*Diário de Pernambuco*); Flávia de Gusmão (*Jornal do Commércio*); Pedro Rampazzo (*Jornal do Commérco*); Manuel do Nascimento and the Sítio do Pai Adão in Água Fria; Rachel do Melo Pessoa Leite and her family; Roberta Queiroz of TV Jornal; Didier Bertranc of TV Viva; Professor José Amaro Santos da Silva; Max Carneiro; Ricardo and Fátima Barbosa; Elcy Oliveira of CD Rock; Fred Lasmar; Paulinho Macedônia; Bete e Beto; Francisco Accioly; José Renato Accioly; Josuel Barbosa; Luciana and the family of Jorge Martins da Silva on the Morro da Conceição; Daniel Marcus; Maria José Teodózio; Paula and Poliana Lopes; Cristina Fernances; Cybele Bion; Kelly Regina Timótio dos Anjos; Bárbara Heliodora; Tatiana Germano Martins and Isabel Soares Chaves; the owners and staff of the Portal dos Arrecifes hotel in Boa Viagem; the staff of Soparia; and all the others whom I have neglected to mention.

In Recife, I am pleased to acknowledge the Joaquim Nabuco Foundation, where I was a visiting scholar in the Department of Anthropology, under the direction of researcher Tânia Lima, beginning in March until my departure from Recife on June, 25 1998. I am particularly grateful to Tânia for her arranging this position for me. In a similar vein, I wish to thank my colleague, fellow ethnomusicologist Carlos Sandroni for inviting me to his ethnomusicology forum (*núcleo de etnomusicologia*) of the Music Department at the Federal University of Pernambuco to discuss my research; I also wish to thank the other members of the forum for their comments, support, insights, and camaraderie.

In the United States, many people have contributed to the development of my scholarship before and during the research process as well as during the writing period. First, I want to express my deep appreciation for Gage Averill, my academic advisor since my entrance into the Wesleyan University music program as a master's student in 1993 through the completion of this doctoral dissertation. In this time, he has given me unwavering encouragement, support, and advice in my research and studies; he has been a great advocate of my professional growth; and most of all, he remains a cherished mentor and teacher. I am also grateful to my two readers and professors, Mark Slobin and Su Zheng, for their having opened up my knowledge of the discipline, for their solid support and encouragement, and, of course, for their helpful comments. I am grateful to these three professors for helping me to create a path for myself in ethnomusicology. In a general sense, I want to acknowledge all of the professors at Wesleyan who, through their commitment to excellence and critical thinking, have contributed to my growth as a scholar. Thanks go also to my colleagues and friends in the Wesleyan Music Department for their support. In particular, Heather Dea Jennings and Madras Viswanathan Gandhimohan deserve a special

Acknowledgments

note of gratitude for their having generously provided me with some initial and highly useful contacts in Recife prior to my research trip.

In addition, the following people deserve mention for stimulating my thinking in general about Brazilian music and ethnomusicology, for their friendship and support, and for their teachings: Mestre Jorge Alabê, David Rumpler, Eddie Rosenthal, Ellen Azorin and Dionísio Santos, Michael Grossman, Steve Travers, Frederick Moehn, John Murphy, Eric Galm, Justino Rogers, Dennis Waring, David Yih, Mestre Efraim Silva, Billy and Lília Newman, Gordon Gottlieb, Ticco da Costa, Marty Lipp, Aochan and Mari, Wanderley Pereira and Susan Davis, Umberto Martins dos Santos and Elizabeth Shaler dos Santos, and many others. A special thank you goes to Abby Farber for her technical computer assistance.

Finally, I want to give my deepest thanks to my family for their unyielding love and support. In addition to Norman, Ellen, Leora, and Hilda, I want to thank my sister Lara Galinsky, my aunts Sally Ruth May and Betsy Rowe, my cousins Sasha Rau and Page Rowe and my cousin Ryan Rowe in memoriam, my uncles William Rau and Carl Rowe, and my "second mother" Simone Durandisse. I also want to express a very special gratitude to Valerie Corbia and to her family—Artonio Corbia, and Josiane, Robert, Stephanie, and John Cabrera.

Preface

Originally written as a dissertation in ethnomusicology (1999, Wesleyan University), "*Maracatu Atômico*" is the first academic work in English to treat at length the influential *mangue* movement and related "new music scene" of Recife, capital of Pernambuco state in Northeast Brazil. Hailed as the most important trend in Brazilian popular music since the late 1960s *tropicália* movement of Caetano Veloso, Gilberto Gil, and others, *mangue* was formed in Recife in the early 1990s as a cultural response to a debilitating socioeconomic situation. Indeed, Pernambuco, and the Northeast generally, has long suffered greatly from poverty, unemployment, inadequate health services, and socioeconomic marginalization. Moreover, Pernambuco's rich culture has until recently occupied a peripheral (albeit important) role in the nation's self-image. Taking its name from the ubiquitous mangrove swamps on top of which the city of Recife is built, *mangue* addressed this predicament by placing a renewed value on local traditions as it absorbed foreign influences. The goal was, in the words of the movement's "manifesto," to "engender an 'energetic circuit' capable of allegorically connecting the good vibrations of the mangue [mangrove swamp] with the world network of the circulation of pop concepts," and as such to "stimulate what still remains of the fertility in the veins of Recife" (quoted in Teles n/d: 5-6).[1]

Articulated primarily in popular music but also later expressed in theater, dance, cinema, fashion, and the plastic arts, the *mangue* project symbolically involved planting a satellite antenna in the mud of the region and picking up signals from the rest of the world. In the work of Chico Science & Nação Zumbi, one of the most original and influential bands to surface in Brazil in recent years, this led to the reinvigoration of neglected regional genres and costumes allied with an assortment of global pop styles and imbued with an active dose of technology. The other pioneering *mangue* band, Mundo Livre S/A also embraced global pop influences, but combined them with samba and the samba-soul-funk sounds of Brazilian musician Jorge Ben. With the exposure of these two bands, *mangue* garnered attention and critical acclaim throughout the country and internationally, putting Pernambuco onto the map of world pop

xiii

music and leading to the increasing visibility of other local artists. Out of this musical activity, the so-called "new music scene" of Recife emerged in the 1990s, marked by a diversity of sounds and approaches, allegorizing the biodiversity of Recife's *manguezais* (mangrove swamps). One of the principal transformations in Recife since *mangue* has been a dramatic increase in self-esteem in the population; many people credit this resurgence directly to Chico Science, regarded as the leading figure in the *mangue* movement. A local cultural hero, Chico Science died in a tragic car accident in 1997 at the age of 30.

There are two basic arguments contained in "*Maracatu Atômico*." One is that the relation between and among traditional and modern, local and global, and domestic and foreign elements in *mangue* and the Recife scene is fluid, overlapping, and symbiotic. Just as the regional Pernambucan genre *maracatu*, for example, has greatly informed the contemporary pop fusion of the *mangue* movement, *mangue* has provided a boost to the perceived cultural and social value of previously marginalized and embattled traditions such as *maracatu*. Similarly, while folk artists serve as inspiration for young musicians on the scene who rework traditional elements into contemporary fusions, many of these same folk artists have seen their audiences grow along with the popularity and expansion of the *mangue* movement. Musicians on the Recife scene of various musical and social backgrounds not only engage such regional folk genres as *maracatu de baque virado, maracatu de baque solto, côco, ciranda, baião,* and *embolada* as important elements of their traditional heritage with links to their past. They also see these genres as modern emblems of their identity that speak to their present condition and orient them toward the future. These same local ingredients become more "global" as they are associated with global genres and flows and are injected into hypersyncretic popular music that reaches international audiences. At the same time, musicians on the scene not only embrace global genres such as heavy metal, hardcore, funk, rap, *raggamuffin*, and electronic dance music, as well as imported technology such as samplers and the Internet, as universal symbols of modernity. They also absorb and indigenize these global influences, making them ever more "local" and "traditional." Indeed, Recife music makers establish various global trends as an increasingly integral part of local Brazilian music practices, arguably transforming them into genres as "Pernambucan" as *côco* or *maracatu*. This fluidity of cultural identity (a sort of blurring of Self and Other) is embodied clearly in the music and behavior of Chico Science, for whom black urban sounds and gestures from the U.S. were just as important cultural vocabulary as more traditionally Pernambucan idioms. Part of the brilliance of Chico Science and other bands and artists on the Recife scene is the way in which they highlight intimate connections and elide boundaries among various local and global influences.

The other major argument of the dissertation is that, in contrast to older ideologies that define Brazilian genres within a national framework, *mangue* represents a postmodern shift in emphasis away from the nation-state and toward the region or city as the primary vessel of cultural identity in Brazil. Indeed, *mangue* positions Recife as the foremost locus of its identity, just as, for example, the *axé-music* trend privileges Salvador, Bahia, or as Brazilian pop artist Fernanda Abreu conceptualizes Rio de Janeiro as the primary point of departure for her music. Aided by technology, local musicians in Recife symbolically bypass the nation-state of "Brazil" to interact directly with the rest of the planet; in the process, the notion of what Brazilian music constitutes expands beyond established categories. Unlike the urban samba, bossa nova, and *tropicália* before it, the *mangue* movement is a resolutely regional initiative that is associated most strongly with one city—Recife—and that does not depend on a national identification. Instead, Brazilian music is given a particular regional interpretation in *mangue*. As Chico Science revealed in an interview with José Teles in the Recife newspaper *Jornal do Commércio* in 1995:

> We revisit the samba, which is an African thing that spread throughout Brazil, in a wider conception: there's the samba of the maracatu, of caboclinho, of cavalo-marinho, of the morro, of the bumba-meu-boi, with elements of the Arabs, Dutch, Spanish, indigenous, all the Brazilian miscegenation. (Quoted in Teles 2001: 330, 332)

This passage points to the fact that, through the work of Chico Science & Nação Zumbi and other Recife bands, Pernambuco is in one sense claiming its own space within a Brazilian national identity: Chico Science broadens the boundaries of Brazil's foremost "national" genre, samba, to include various regional rhythms. But beyond this, musicians in Recife absorb and mix regional, national, and international influences, projecting the resulting sounds and ideologies out to the globe as not only Brazilian, but also even more particularly as Pernambucan. Refining this locality further still, some bands on the Recife scene (i.e., Devotos of the Alto Zé do Pinho) position their own neighborhood as the primary emblem of their identity. These findings support other studies (see, for example, Averill 1995, Bilby 1999) that regard globalization not as mere cultural imposition but as a complex process of local synthesis.

In the four-and-a-half years since his death, Chico Science has become a pop icon in Brazil, and there has been a growing national and international interest in his work and in the other folk and pop sounds coming from Recife and Northeast Brazil. In the two years since the "defense" of this dissertation in September 1999, two books and four academic articles that treat *mangue* and the "new music scene" of Recife have come out. The most extensive of these publications is journalist José Teles's *Do Frevo Ao Manguebeat* (Editora 34, 2000), written in Portuguese. Teles's earlier booklet entitled *Meteoro Chico* (Editôra Bagaço, n.d.), which compiles press articles on the movement, offers original commentaries by Teles, and features testimonies by musicians and producers on the importance of Chico Science, served as a major source for the *mangue* history contained in "*Maracatu Atômico*." Teles's latest effort has a wider scope, outlining a selected history of Pernambucan popular music that spans from the production of *frevo* (the state's most characteristic Carnival genre) to the region's bossa nova and rock excursions of the 1960s, he experimental pop and erudite trends of the '70s, the rock scene in the '80s, and finally, the diverse sounds of *manguebeat* and the "new music scene" of Recife in the '90s. The book's strength is its rich historical narrative replete with anecdotes, into which Teles embeds his opinions and insights about the significance of the musical trends he discusses. *Do Frevo Ao Manguebeat* is clearly intended for readers already interested in and somewhat informed about popular music in Pernambuco, and in that capacity, it serves as a useful source of information for scholarship on *mangue*.

Whereas Teles's book privileges a historical narrative over theoretical musings, Moisés Neto's short book, *Chico Science: A Rapsódia Afrociberdélica* (Recife: Editora Comunicarte, 2000), also written in Portuguese, is a free-flowing esoteric literary reading of the work of Chico Science. Like *Do Frevo Ao Manguebeat*, Neto's book presupposes a strong interest in and knowledge about the music of the *mangue* movement. But unlike Teles's work, it is of limited use to someone who is not already intimately familiar with the music of Chico Science, Northeastern Brazilian culture, and various academic discourses such as postmodernity. Even so, the book does not seem to offer a clear position and reads more like a poem than an informational or narrative text.

Scholarly treatments of *mangue* and the Recife scene have also begun to appear in more English-language publications. The newly released book, *Brazilian Popular Music & Globalization* (edited by Charles A. Perrone and Christopher Dunn, Routledge, 2001) contains three chapters that address aspects of *mangue* and the "new music scene" of Recife. In their respective articles ethnomusicologists John Murphy and Frederick Moehn write about Mestre Ambrósio and Brazilian pop artists such as Chico Science, Fernanda Abreu, and Carlinhos Brown, offering insights about globalization and identity that I incorporated into "*Maracatu Atômico*" via drafts of these articles. In his chapter for the same volume, Larry Crook examines the urban, Afro-identified *maracatu de baque virado* and its connection to the music of Chico Science & Nação Zumbi. Crook's brief essay highlights the importance of the *maracatu* tradition to *mangue*, placing *maracatu* within a context of black cultural practices and racial politics in Brazil. Notably, Crook emphasizes the role that Afro-Bahian trends played in Recife in both reinvigorating a sense of black pride and in stimulating some middle-class Pernambucan artists (such as Nação Pernambuco) to return to their own local folk musics. It would be worth examining further the different ways in which musical groups in Recife have received Afro-Bahian music.

Although I have left "*Maracatu Atômico*" in its original form as much as possible, I have updated references (e.g., Moehn 2001, Murphy 2001a), directed readers to new sources (e.g., Teles 2001, Dunn 2001, Harvey 2001) at a few points in the text, made some minor textual changes, and revised the discography and bibliography. In addition, in Chapter Four I have added a very brief segment commenting on the burgeoning music scenes in Peixinhos and especially the Alto José do Pinho, with a special focus on the remarkable social transformations that the latter neighborhood has experienced in the 1990s.

In addition to the five new works just mentioned, several other *mangue*-related works are forthcoming. An article based on this dissertation has been published in the book *From Tejano to Tango: Latin American Popular Music* (Routledge, 2002). John Murphy, who wrote his Ph.D. dissertation on the *cavalo-marinho* (a folk play of Northeast Brazil), is preparing a manuscript for a book on cultural politics and regional identity in the current Recife music scene. Several masters' theses on topics related to *mangue* and the Recife scene are already coming out (see, e.g., Sharp 2001).

It remains to clarify a few points related to *mangue* and its discussion herein. In a recent interview for the web magazine *Manguenius*, DJ-journalist and *mangue* pioneer Renato L. (Lins 2001) explains the modifications that the name for the movement underwent. The original name for the cultural initiative was simply "*mangue*," he maintains, but after the release of the song by Fred Zero Quatro called "Mangue Bit" (on *Samba Esquema Noise* by Mundo Livre S/A), the press began to refer to the movement as "*mangue bit*" (as in computer bit). From there, Renato L. says, "it was also easy to confuse this with 'beat.' And the thing left our control." The term "*mangue beat*" (or "*manguebeat*") thus became the most common label for the movement. In keeping with the original terminology, however, I generally refer to the movement here as "*mangue*," as opposed to "*mangue bit*" or "*mangue beat*."

In the same interview, Renato L. suggests that the media was responsible for labeling the release that they sent the press in 1991, *Caranguejos Com Cérebro* (Crabs With Brains), a "manifesto." Renato L. reveals that, contrary to what is believed, Fred Zero Quatro wrote this release alone, not in collaboration with Renato L. Renato L. even contends that "We never wanted to call [*mangue*] a movement, we thought the term very pretentious." Indeed, the word "movement" is not included in *Caranguejos Com Cérebro*, although subsequent interviews with Chico Science reveal his adoption of the term (see Teles n.d.).

All of these points highlight both the important role of the media in shaping this, and any other, popular cultural project as well as the ongoing investment that *mangue*'s creators retain in shaping public perceptions about the movement. Using the media outlets available to them and those that they create, Fred Zero Quatro, Renato L., and other *mangue* pioneers maintain a critical stance toward what is written and said about *mangue* in the press. For example, they continue to emphasize the diversity of the label "*mangue*," which was one of the original concepts of their project, fighting against the notion that the identity of the movement can be captured by any particular combination of sounds and images (see Lins 2001).

Finally, I would like to comment briefly on the current state of the Recife music scene. In a recent paper for a panel that I chaired at the Society for Ethnomusicology, John Murphy (2001b) reveals some of the results of his latest research on the scene. Contrary to the optimistic sense, which I witnessed in 1998, that the Recife scene would soon explode with commercial opportunities for its bands, this situation has not happened. As Murphy states in his paper:

> While I was aware that popular music vanguards are not typically commercially successful, I was nevertheless surprised by the limited circulation of the music that had drawn me back to Recife. . . . Live performances by the best-known bands were infrequent. Recent CDs by local alternative bands were available in specialized downtown record shops, and a few showed up in larger record chains, but some of the most important recordings of the Recife scene are available only in the form of rental CDs at one downtown shop, CD Rock. (Murphy 2001b)

This is the exact same situation that I observed in Recife in 1998. Murphy goes on to explain the continued lack of airplay of music from the Recife scene. He suggests further that "Festivals and other single events that attract tourists and media attention are not helpful in creating a sustainable musical scene, which requires the formation of new bands and a steady increase in quality" (ibid.).

Hélder Aragão (a.k.a. DJ Dolores) evokes a sense of disappointment in this predicament. He sees upcoming popular musicians on the scene as, in Murphy's words, "subject to a glut of musical information that crowds out the reflection and critical thinking that give rise to creativity" (Murphy 2001b). Drawing from his interview with Aragão, Murphy relates a nostalgic view of the early *mangue* scene, when "information about musical developments elsewhere was more difficult to get. . . . The scarcity of information increased its value and its impact on creativity" (ibid.). Whether this point of view is widespread or not, it presents a marked contrast with a more pervasive sense of optimism that I observed among musicians in Recife in 1998 toward globalization, toward creative growth, and toward the prospects of commercial exposure. I saw the question of creativity hotly debated during my field research (mostly centered around the originality of a given band or trend), and people such as Fred Zero Quatro and Paulo André Pires were already lamenting about media exclusion, in particular with respect to radio. What appears to be new here in Aragão's comment is a jaded attitude toward globalization and its role. Is there an oversaturation of globalization on the Recife scene as Aragão suggests? To be sure, combined with the lack of more opportunities for musicians, too much globalization (i.e., a kind of flow where much more information is coming in than is going out) can have a negative effect on a local music scene. On the other hand, Murphy (2001b) sees cause for optimism in the increased support by local government and globalized corporations of festivals such as Abril Pro Rock.

The full effect of these developments in Recife remains to be seen, and questions concerning globalization, local agency, cultural values, and creativity will continue to encourage debate in Brazil and elsewhere. In the meantime, "*Maracatu Atômico*" examines what is widely regarded in critical circles as one of the most innovative popular movements and music scenes in Brazil in recent decades. In its most optimistic moments, *mangue* contended creatively with modernity and globalization, offering a new perspective on the meaning of place. The highly self-aware pioneers of *mangue* and the "new music scene" of Recife have helped to give wider exposure and value to a diversity of new and old musical styles, providing a fresh outlet, voice, identity, and sense of self-worth to communities that have suffered disproportionately from poverty and marginalization.

Philip Galinsky
June 2002

BRAZIL

PERNAMBUCO

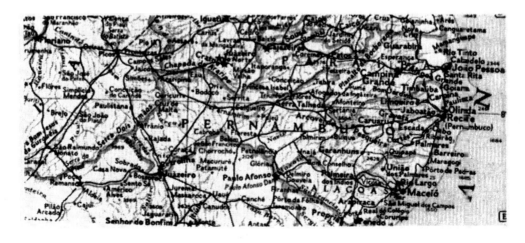

Chapter 1
Introduction

My Introduction to *Mangue* and the "New Music Scene" of Recife
I first heard the music of Chico Science & Nação Zumbi (Chico Science & The Zumbi Nation) in either late 1994 or early 1995 on the National Public Radio program Afropop Worldwide as part of an episode that featured new sounds from Brazil. At the time, I was completing my masters thesis on the *pagode* samba of Rio de Janeiro and was on the lookout for topics for my Ph.D. dissertation. This fresh Brazilian band caught my attention with their fusion of heavy metal guitars, funky grooves, rapping vocals and technology with elements of regional Brazilian folk music. Indeed, I had never heard any music from anywhere this decade that managed, in my mind, to encode in such a striking and convincing fashion a "rootsy" regionalism within a cutting-edge, transnational sound.

Beyond their innovative sound, however, the band's conceptual basis intrigued me. Nação Zumbi hail from the city of Recife in Brazil's very poor northeastern state of Pernambuco, which is acknowledged for its ample-but still-not-widely-disseminated, folk heritage. According to its vocalist and leader Chico Science, Nação Zumbi's project symbolically involved planting a satellite antenna in the mud of the region (Recife is built on swamps) and picking up signals from the rest of the world. Musically, this translated into the recuperation of regional northeastern styles such as *maracatu*, *côco*, *ciranda*, and *embolada* within a varying base of heavy rock, funk, soul, rap, Jamaican *raggamuffin*, electronic dance music, and other influences.

As I learned, Nação Zumbi is the foremost band in a citywide pop culture initiative—the so-called *"mangue"* movement—named after the vast mangrove swamps of Recife. Reminding me somewhat of the intentions of the *tropicália* movement of the late 1960s of Caetano Veloso and Gilberto Gil, this new Pernambucan band's work seemed to me the latest attempt in 1990s Brazil to inform the nation's popular music with the most up-to-date global sounds while simultaneously asserting and valorizing its most regional and particular character. Indeed, both *tropicália* and *mangue* make use of the modernist Brazilian concept of *antropofagia* (anthropophagy, or cultural cannibalism) in which foreign elements are "cannibalized" in Brazilian art and recontextualized within local frameworks.[1] Open to information from the rest of planet earth, *mangue* affirms a strong local grounding in a region of Brazil that has long remained at the margins of the nation's socioeconomic development and identity. Fascinated with the interplay of the "traditional" and "modern" in Brazilian pop, and with the ways in which musicians there negotiate with international influences in their constructions of cultural identities, I soon resolved to center my dissertation research around the *mangue* movement in Recife.

Two performances of Chico Science & Nação Zumbi in New York City (at Central Park's SummerStage in the summer of 1995 opening up for Brazilian pop star Gilberto Gil and at Brooklyn's Prospect Park in the summer of 1996 as part of The Brazilian Music Festival) further confirmed my interest in this project. The band's live performance was, for me, nothing short of amazing. First, there was the sheer power of three large *bombo* bass drums culled from the Afro-Pernambucan *maracatu* tradition combined with heavy rock guitar and hip-hop attitude. This alone struck me as a dynamic union of "resistant" sounds across the two Americas. Then there was Chico Science's singular stage presence. At one moment, he was full-fledged rapper with sunglasses and hip-hop mannerisms mastered to the letter; the next he had dressed himself as the *caboclo de lança*, a popular spear-thrower figure in a magnificent headdress from the Pernambucan Carnival, and was executing its enchanting dance. Critically, these personae did not come across as imitations; rather, Chico Science embodied all of them with complete and utter conviction, the result of having lived these various cultural expressions. The band's style of dress—such as, for example, Rayban sunglasses and the straw hats worn by Pernambucan fishermen—also embodied a cross-cultural identity. Similarly, Chico Science's name affirms the fusion of the local and traditional ("Chico" is a common nickname for Francisco in Portuguese) and the modern and global (the word "Science" in English).

At the 1996 Brazilian Music Festival, I also had the opportunity to hear Mundo Livre S/A (Free World Ltd.), the co-pioneering band in the *mangue* movement. More quietly avant-garde than the bold sounds of Chico Science & Nação Zumbi, Mundo Livre adopted elements of the Brazilian national samba and the samba-soul-funk fusions of Jorge Ben (as opposed to regionalisms) into a base of punk and new wave musics.

While still preparing for a trip to Recife, I learned that Chico Science had died in a car accident at the age of thirty in early February 1997. Saddened and shocked by this news, I decided to push on with my research plans. Although Chico was indisputably the leader of the *mangue* movement, I heard from sources that his band would continue and that there were many other interesting musical projects alive in Pernambuco. Indeed, the work of Chico Science & Nação Zumbi, Mundo Livre, and others had made feasible a "new music scene"

Introduction 3

in Recife (the so-called *nova cena musical do Recife*), representing the wide diversity of music in the city.[2] The music of this scene ranges from regional folklore to various international pop styles and fusions of these, sometimes referred to as *mangue beat*.

I was able to experience some of the diversity that the *nova cena* had to offer before going to Recife. In the summer of 1997, Central Park SummerStage in New York featured an unprecedented Brazilian Music Festival of five days that sampled some of the nation's most vital, current folk and pop performers and genres; the entire multi-day festival was dedicated to the memory of Chico Science. Some of the highlights of this line-up included two of the most acclaimed acts from Recife's scene: Cascabulho, which specializes in *forró* (a term for a variety of local dance musics of the Northeast) and other regional rhythms; and the band Mestre Ambrósio, which presented a dramatic interpretation of rural and urban folk sounds of Pernambuco, combined at times with rock and other global sounds. In addition, the folkloric Banda de Pífanos Dois Irmãos de Caruaru, a typical drum and fife band from the interior of Pernambuco, opened up for Mestre Ambrósio. The sheer energy, diversity, and quality of all this music reinforced my conviction that Recife was the center of one of the most dynamic and important music scenes in Brazil.

The Objective, Scope, and Basic Findings of the Research

In late January 1998, I arrived in Recife and subsequently embarked on five months of fieldwork. My original research proposal aimed to compare the Afro-Brazilian *maracatu* and music of the *mangue* movement, since the former is one of the main local sources for the latter. The comparison of a folk idiom with a related hybrid pop music, I thought, would help to illuminate the interplay between tradition and modernity in the Recife context. Although I did investigate the *maracatu*, and I do discuss its relation to *mangue* here, my project did not end up being a comparison of *mangue* and its folk sources per se, but rather a focus on *mangue* in its wider sociocultural context of Recife's diverse "new music scene." As such, I sought to learn about how domestic and foreign, local and global, and traditional and modern influences are theorized and negotiated in Recife's scene and in the construction of what could be considered a refashioned cultural identity.[3] The ultimate objective was to discover what *mangue* and Recife's *nova cena musical* might tell me about the interaction of these domains in contemporary Brazil.

The writing up of any ethnographically based work involves a high degree of selection. This selection process becomes more problematic when one considers the vast diversity and high number of important bands and artists on Recife's scene. In no way is this dissertation meant to be a representative survey of that scene. In fact, I have purposefully left out, or only mentioned in passing, many significant groups, locales, and events. This is because my aim here is to use *mangue* and this scene as a springboard into more theoretical issues. I have chosen to speak about particular aspects of the scene insofar as they contribute to the story that I wanted to tell, based on my experiences. Many times, the inclusion of other important data or group stories would have contributed too much ethnographic detail for the balance between data and theory that I wanted to achieve.

Given the remarkable diversity of the folk culture alone in Pernambuco, this dissertation does not attempt to supply a comprehensive explanation, in terms of sociocultural context or musical analysis, for any one particular genre. Even though this folk culture provides much of the source material for *mangue* and the "new music scene," my intent here was less to document these genres than to investigate how they are used and conceptualized vis-à-vis international pop music and fusion. However, I do provide a brief history of the *maracatu* tradition and discuss this and other regional styles in relation to Chico Science & Nação Zumbi; Appendix 2 provides a series of transcriptions and musical analyses of various songs and styles discussed in the dissertation. Along the same lines, there are many aspects of culture in Recife that are fundamental but that I do not discuss in detail. Carnival and the *Festas Juninas* (*São João*, etc.), for example, are two of the biggest seasonal parties in Pernambuco that I feel should merit full attention elsewhere.

My focus here is on the *mangue* movement, Recife's *nova cena musical*, and more specifically on the work of Chico Science and his band. By the same token, I do not suggest that this is the final word on the work of Chico Science (or on rock and rap in Recife, for that matter).[4] Not only was Chico a pioneering figure in the "new music scene" of Recife, but he was also, in my opinion, a pivotal musician in the history of popular music in Brazil. Emblematic of simultaneous localizing-globalizing tendencies in Brazilian music in the 1990s, Chico Science not only has helped to bring MPB (*Música Popular Brasileira*) up-to-date with global youth culture; but also his work has contributed immensely to a revalorization and revitalization of some of the nation's underappreciated local folk musics. Chico embodied in his music and personality, possibly more than any other current Brazilian performer, the meeting point between the folkloric and pop, the traditional and modern, the local and global, and the domestic and foreign. More than that, I argue here that the movement of which he was a central figure reinforces the fluid, blurry, and symbiotic relationship among these elements.

In its fusion and juxtaposition of modern genres and technology with once obscure regional music, *mangue* has helped revitalize the traditional folk culture of the region while also having spawned and influenced a host of rock and other *mangue*-fusion groups. I argue that in Recife, for specific reasons, a more fluid interaction between "traditional" and "modern" influences and musicians was able to develop, whereby in a sense the "tradition" has become more "modern" and the "modern" more "traditional." In general, my data suggests a coming together or synthesis of elements and social groups in the construction of a workable music scene and renewed cultural identity. I saw a remarkable

Introduction

confluence of men and women of various social classes, races, and musical/cultural backgrounds linked through friendships and working relationships.[5] Indeed, many people of various musical affiliations in Recife—from folk artists and bands that reinterpret folk traditions to *mangue* musicians, rockers and rappers—seemed to accept and appreciate each other's work. This condition has helped to create a situation where the relation between categories such as "traditional" and "modern" could be one of affinity, symbiosis, and overlap rather than one of opposition.

The very blurring of such categories is accompanied by a blurring of discrete roles among the people involved in research. If this research project has shown the overlapping of domestic and foreign, for example, it has also presented the overlapping of researcher and "native." In my affinity for and participation in the scene, I have adopted some aspects of the native Pernambucan culture as my own (not the least of which is a residual Pernambucan inflection in my speech, even in English). By the same token, members of the Recife scene are as well versed—or more so—in certain aspects of U.S. and European pop culture as I am. This is a kind of blurring of the domestic and foreign.[6] Moreover, as I take on certain aspects of native culture, the consultants in my project adopt the role of researchers, analyzing for *me* what their culture and social situation are about. Although some of this self-reflection may have been occasioned by my presence, everyone on the Recife scene was already in one way or another a researcher of his or her own music and sociocultural milieu. This was, in fact, one of the most remarkable discoveries of my fieldwork—that as they shape their sociocultural scene and identity (or identities), the members of the scene also research the various aspects of their journey, from their folk heritage to information from the world. All of the consultants with whom I spoke were particularly self-aware and analytical about their situation.

But no one, neither the Pernambucans I worked with nor I are detached, completely objective researchers. Nor should we be, since it is through our deep involvement with others that we grow and learn. As such, I see fieldwork as a constant dialogue among the various people involved, from foreign and native researchers to native members of the social milieu under study. This methodological approach—as the very results of my research—reveals an overlapping and blurring of boundaries and a continual process of cultural exchange and evaluation. In the end, I am hopeful that such a process and ethos of exchanges and interpenetrations (musical, cultural, social, etc.) may contribute to a bridging of the gaps in understanding among peoples of various backgrounds across the globe.

A Review of Literature on Brazilian Popular Music

Much of the literature on Brazilian popular music (as opposed to folk music) has tended to focus on the city of Rio de Janeiro, the metropolis whose syncretic cultural products have long served as most emblematic of Brazil as a nation.[7]

Principally the urban samba, and to a lesser extent the bossa nova, are inextricably linked to the sociocultural environment of Rio, thus functioning as powerful symbols of the Brazilian nation for Brazilians and foreigners alike. A large body of literature treats variously these two musical forms or older popular styles from Rio such as the *modinha, lundu, maxixe, marcha,* and *choro* (or *chorinho*). Another sometimes-overlapping group of texts examines various aspects and strands of MPB (*Música Popular Brasileira*), a "catch-all" category for a highly eclectic assortment of post-bossa nova popular music (mid-1960s onward). Taking its cues from diverse artists and regions of the country and embraced as national music, this contemporary movement creatively incorporates and mixes various domestic and foreign styles.

A foundational base of literature written in large part by Brazilians has engaged these established popular forms and movements and their corresponding sociocultural contexts from mostly descriptive and historical perspectives. Some works on national popular music from Rio have been descriptive from the perspective of folklore (see, e.g., Carneiro 1974, Alvarenga 1982). Many texts offer summaries and sociohistorical trajectories of musical forms and movements (see, e.g., Muníz 1976, Appleby 1983, Tinhorão 1986, Cáurio 1988, McGowan and Pessanha 1998). Others provide detailed, narrative historical accounts of popular institutions, movements, or the lives of important artists (see, e.g., Cabral 1996 and n/d, Castro 1990, Calado 1997, Teles n/d).

Some works select aspects of these musical traditions for expanded historical exploration and analysis. Several projects focus on the musica traditions and social histories of black popular music in Rio. Based on written and oral historical data and his analysis of song texts, Nei Lopes (1992) charts various folk influences on, and transformations within, the traditional music repertoire of Afro-Brazilians in Rio, particularly the samba. Roberto Moura (1995) examines a key figure in the early Afro-Bahian samba community in Rio, revealing this community's relation to the city's popular culture and to Brazilian modernity. Anthropologist Hermano Vianna (1995) provides a detailed argument for the urban samba of Rio's status as a national music being a social construction facilitated by links among a wide variety of social groups. At the same time, Vianna contributes to academic discussions about cultural homogeneity and heterogeneity, transculturation, and nationality.[8]

Some scholars have combined approaches from history, musicology, anthropology, and other disciplines to trace the origins and/or development of Brazilian movements, styles, and traits. In this vein, ethnomusicologist Gerard Béhague (1973) summarizes several developments in Brazilian popular music (especially bossa nova, early Brazilian rock, and the *tropicália* movement). Gerhard Kubik (1979) and Kazadi wa Mukuna (1979) attempt to link Brazilian folk and popular traits and traditions to Angolan and Bantu African sources. Another line of work interprets the aesthetics of Brazilian popular music. Supported by textual analysis, biography, history, and musical description,

Charles Perrone (1989) provides an exemplary critique of several of MPB's most enduring artists.

Probably the most significant recent trend in literature on Brazilian popular music (which extends to include the Northeast and particularly Afro-Bahian musical and cultural movements from the 1970s onward, as well as various international genres in Brazil such as rap and funk) critically examines race, class, and gender, jointly with other intersecting issues as they are manifest in musical and cultural production. Some of these issues include cultural identity and the question of foreign influence, power and politics, co-option and resistance, and so on. This group of texts represents scholarship by both Brazilian and non-Brazilian authors. Because of the importance of this trend—and because this dissertation engages with and at times departs considerably from some of the theoretical orientations embodied in its texts—I will briefly run through some of the works that follow this general approach.

In Brazilian musical scholarship, specific urban music trends have traditionally been understood as "belonging" to specific groups defined primarily by socioeconomic (and, by association, racial) criteria. The Marxist-derived idea that class determines musical style is an underlying presumption in some studies. The preeminent scholar of Brazilian popular music, José Ramos Tinhorão, for instance, regards the evolution of a popular musical genre such as the samba as representing a struggle for control and development by various social classes and groups with certain a priori aesthetic interests.[9] Indeed, in Marxist fashion, Tinhorão attributes the eventual proliferation of urban samba types to the coexistence of various social conditions and their corresponding social classes in the country, from industrial progress to residual feudal conditions (1986: 131).

Whereas in many works class has been understood simply as a static, reified marker of musical style and affiliation, some more recent studies politicize the concept of class, examining both the unequal power relationships inherent in music-making within the class system as well as aspects of class and group identity. For example, Tiago de Oliveira Pinto (1994, 1996), a Brazilian scholar residing in Berlin, emphasizes the severe limitations placed on traditional Carnival groups in Recife, Pernambuco from the poorest sectors of society by governmental and official organizations. Stressing both racial and class factors, Alison Raphael (1990) paints a similarly bleak picture of Rio de Janeiro's Carnival "samba schools." She argues that these largely black, lower-class clubs went from being genuine vehicles for the expression of popular culture to "profit-seeking microenterprises" that have become co-opted by the dominant middle and upper class white society. In a third example, unequal power relationships, if not social class per se, are highlighted early on by Tinhorão (1969) in a historical study of the "misrepresentation" of Brazilian music abroad. For Tinhorão, the practice of marketing forms of music that already conform more closely to international taste as opposed to more traditional Brazilian forms is intimately tied to power dynamics, both within Brazil and between Brazil and the more dominant United States.

Discussions and perceptions about race in music scholarship, as well as in Brazil generally, have undergone a dramatic change in recent decades. Whereas both class and race were (and still are) taken for granted and left undiscussed by many, they have been treated in notably different ways. Given Brazil's overt and openly acknowledged class hierarchy, assumed class distinctions have been upheld as fundamental, even if only implicitly, while racial difference (as opposed to cultural difference) has traditionally been elided and ignored for a whole host of sociopolitical reasons. The end result has been the widespread adherence to the idea of a "racial democracy" in which all races are valued for their cultural contributions and in which racial differences (as opposed to class differences) purportedly do not matter.[10]

In light of widespread evidence of racism and disproportionate poverty among non-whites, a host of literature since the 1950s has attacked the notion of the racial democracy. However, only with a series of far-reaching changes in the 1960s and '70s—including the black pride movement emanating from the U.S., the emergence of Jamaican reggae, the independence of former Portuguese colonies in Africa, and the opening to democracy leading to the return of a Brazilian civil government in 1985—have race and racial identity become politicized with an upsurge of overt racial conflict and consciousness (Winant 1994: 140-147). These changes have had important manifestations in the realm of popular music, most explicitly in the Afro-groups (*blocos afro* and *afoxés*) of Bahia, but also more generally in a wide range of popular music forms (on the Bahian groups see, e.g., Risério 1981, Crook 1993). While literature in other fields has taken account of these changes in the perception of race and identity more consistently, writings on popular music have been lagging (although the few works in this area have been highly intriguing).

Nei Lopes, an esteemed composer, performer, and scholar of samba and Afro-Brazilian music, has been one of the most vocal writers—and one of the few Brazilian writers—active in this area of Brazilian popular music studies. An uncompromising black activist and strong proponent of Brazilian popular traditions, Lopes has both critiqued elite views on race and shown how the bearers of Afro-Brazilian culture have resisted co-option, oppression, and internationalization through music. Following Tinhorão's perspective, Lopes sees international influences, supported inside and outside Brazil, as threatening to (black) Brazilian tradition. His excellent article on the *pagode* samba movement of Rio de Janeiro (1986), for instance, positions this upsurge of the samba tradition within a long line of black cultural resistance against the imposition of international taste in the country.[11]

Other work into popular music focuses on creative alternatives to established or dominant views on racial, class, and gender identities. A sub-set of these works is concerned with the incorporation of international—particularly black North American and Caribbean—cultural influences by young Afro-Brazilians, a practice which has only begun to be explored in the literature. Examining the overtly political music of the Afro-Bahian Carnival groups, Larry

Crook (1993) argues that the *samba-reggae* (samba with Jamaican reggae and other influences) of the *blocos afro* provides alternative viewpoints on Brazilian history and black identity, while musically articulating a link with other blacks in the African diaspora and debunking the racial democracy myth. And the urban Brazilian funk and rap movements as depicted by George Yúdice (1994) are characterized as a means of establishing "new forms of identity, but not those premised on Brazil's much-heralded self-understanding as a nation of nonconflictual diversity" (197).[12]

Treating the Bahian Carnival as well as Rio samba, *Candomblé*, and *capoeira*, dance scholar and literary theorist Barbara Browning (1995) unravels a sophisticated and insightful investigation into the complex interplay of identities in Afro-Brazilian culture—including the relationship between African and Indian identities, and between racial and gendered ones.[13] She sees Bahia's Carnival as exploding any fixed notion of "Brazilianness," "Indianness," and "Africanness," while offering alternative notions of power and gender relations (1995: 157-159). In the Rio samba tradition she explores the relationship between race and gender, urging that "samba *is* a racial history lived in the modality of sexuality. Gender *is* constructed in specifically Afro-Brazilian terms" (1995: 159).[14] Coming from a very personal perspective, Browning sees the samba dance as allowing an underclass Brazilian woman—regardless of color—the chance to express resistance to her situation (1995: 34).[15]

Little research has been done in theorizing models of racial identities and popular music in Brazil. For the case of Afro-Brazil, José Jorge de Carvalho's contribution to the landmark book, *Music and Black Ethnicity: The Caribbean and South America* (1994), is a pioneering first attempt at an overview. Here, Carvalho presents four distinct models of Afro-Brazilian identity, ostensibly corresponding to the main types of Afro-Brazilian music in the country: the Afro-Brazilian cult model (e.g., *Candomblé*); the Black-White Conciliation model (*congadas* and similar folk groups); the Syncretic Cult model (e.g., *Macumba, Umbanda*); and the Affirmation of Black Pride (e.g., *blocos afro, afoxés*, related commercial styles). While for various reasons the first three models obscure a clear articulation and resolution of black ethnicity vis-à-vis the dominant society, the last model makes race explicit and positively affirms black Brazilian pride. However, as Carvalho contends, even this model faces some of the same difficulties in communicating its message as the other three models, although here the problem stems largely from the music's commercial, mediated contexts.[16]

Finally, the examination of indigenous Brazilian racial/ethnic identity has, compared with the avid interest in Afro-Brazilian culture, received scant attention. Anthony Seeger's article (1994) in the same volume is a notable exception. Here, Seeger analyzes two indigenous Brazilian communities vis-à-vis music and identity, providing some valuable theoretical insights. Three points he wishes to challenge are: (1) that the identification of groups with musical forms is enduring over time and that each group has its own typical style; (2) the idea that ethnic and musical identities can be analyzed without regard for the sociopolitical and historical contexts which affect them; and (3) that researchers themselves assume they do not influence people's ideas about music and ethnicity, even though they are social actors in the cultures they study. One of his main points, which I firmly uphold in this study, is that while the fusion of musics and cultures in the Americas is confusingly "mixed up," social actors use musical performances in clear, purposeful ways that are not mixed up at all—and these purposes may change over time. This article, more than most, points to the flexibility and contingency of identity, while rightfully acknowledging the researcher's own biases in studying, and indeed affecting notions about, music and ethnicity.

Several recent articles (Moehn 2001, Murphy 2001a) expound on both the interplay of local and global elements in Brazilian popular styles and related issues of style, identity, and ideology.[17] Murphy discusses the members of the Recife band Mestre Ambrósio's relation to both their folk culture heritage and imported international influences, while Moehn explores the relations of certain cutting-edge MPB artists (including Chico Science) to globalization.[18]

Theoretical Orientation

The theoretical orientation of this dissertation departs considerably from most of these previous trends in Brazilian popular music studies on several key criteria. First, my topic of study, a pop culture movement in Recife, is itself not typical in a body of literature that has overwhelmingly privileged music produced in Rio de Janeiro and Salvador, Bahia (and, to a lesser extent, São Paulo).[19] As such, I see my work as contributing to a more well-rounded depiction of Brazilian popular culture, helping to give due to a culturally abundant and influential region of the country now coming into its own.

My theoretical orientation borrows in part from the range of literature cited above. As such, Chapters Two and Three offer a historical account and an analysis of the movement vis-à-vis other Brazilian popular trends, respectively, although I have not attempted to create a full-fledged social history of *mangue*. Likewise, while I do engage in an aesthetic interpretation of *mangue* in part, my primary aim is not to elucidate the oeuvre of any one artist or band (or the movement as a whole) in sociocultural, musical, and historical context, as Perrone (1989) has done remarkably with some classic MPB performers. Third, I place *mangue* in a musical and historical context and provide extensive musicological analysis; but I am not primarily concerned here with pinpointing the origins and charting the developments of musical styles or phenomena, as other authors have done from a variety of disciplinary perspectives (see, e.g., Andrade 1937, Guerra-Peixe 1980 [1955], Béhague 1973, Carneiro 1974, Kubik 1979, Mukuna 1979, Alvarenga 1982, Real 1990, Oliveira 1991, etc.).

Finally, and most importantly, I do not focus here on issues of race, class, and gender identity as they relate to power, politics, co-option, and resistance—a current trend in the literature on Brazilian popular music. My own masters thesis and related articles (see Galinsky 1994, 1995, 1996) indeed treat the *pagode samba* of Rio de Janeiro from this basic perspective, highlighting issues of black cultural identity and ideology as they relate to co-option, resistance, tradition, modernity, commercialization, international influence, and Brazilian nationalism. I examine some of these same issues here, but I do not privilege a model of co-option and resistance and I do not engage in a predominantly racial perspective.[20] This is due to my own current theoretical direction, to the nature of the research topic, and to my particular fieldwork experiences.

In my earlier fieldwork on the samba of Rio, race was one of the most salient organizing factors. The members of the *pagode* groups I studied were largely black or mixed-race musicians of lower-class background whose music and discourse were firmly connected with issues of Afro-Brazilian identity. A focus on race in that project was further bolstered by the people I interviewed, by the issues circulating on the scene, by the more divided racial situation of Rio, and, as always, by my own intellectual framework. That earlier research topic comfortably led me to issues of co-option and cultural resistance organized around Afro-Brazilian racial and cultural identity.

My Recife experience, however, led me in another theoretical direction. Race, class, and gender are important factors there—as anywhere—and I certainly do not wish to suggest that more emphasis on these factors could not prove illuminating. Nonetheless, these three factors, or at least conflicts surrounding them, were less central to this project. For one thing, the racial and class profiles of Recife's groups are much more diverse than Rio's *pagode* groups, lending a more ambiguous character to these factors.[21] Racial, gender, and especially class issues do emerge on the Recife scene, and I do raise some of these important issues in this work. Differences between social classes and races (as well as between men and women) are an indelible aspect of *mangue*, of Recife, and of Brazil as a whole. But rather than representing a particular racial or class identity, *mangue* has enabled various groups and social classes to unite in their critique of the Recife and Brazilian sociopolitical situation, and it has provided a new, important social space for both lower-class and better-off Pernambucans on local and supra-local levels.

Indeed, the most intriguing aspect of *mangue* for me was how Pernambucan musicians of diverse backgrounds were coming together to reinvigorate—and refashion—aspects of their local traditions while they embraced elements of global technology and culture. The ideological basis of the *mangue* movement itself is in precisely this vein. Hence, both my theoretical proclivities and -*emic* preoccupations led me to investigate some of the same phenomena treated in earlier literature (tradition and modernity, foreign influence in Brazil) but using the local and global as guiding tropes.

Much like Moehn (2001) and Murphy (2001a) in their respective articles, I am interested in how specific popular artists and movements engage with both local heritage and globalization in their formation of renewed ideologies and identities. For this, I needed to use slightly different lenses than are customary in the bulk of Brazilian popular music scholarship; and I needed to engage with other bodies of literature that treated popular music, ideas of the local and global, and modernity and postmodernity. Even so, I must acknowledge having derived much influence particularly from the work of writers such as Tinhorão (1969, 1986), Lopes (1986, 1992, 1993, n/d), Moura (1995), Vianna (1995), and Pereira (1993) (among others), who have contributed to a nuanced understanding of popular music and the various social groups involved in its production vis-à-vis international influence and a modernizing Brazil. The work of these authors collectively functions like one, albeit diverse, intellectual tradition from which I both borrow and depart. Likewise, the various other approaches in the literature on Brazilian popular music outlined above find some expression here, as I have indicated. As such, I see my work as interacting critically with these predominant currents in Brazilian popular music studies while making a contribution to this body of literature by theorizing a Brazilian topic from perspectives that are only beginning to be applied to Brazilian music in the academy (such as local and global, postmodernity).

A considerable body of literature that addresses popular musics of the world (sometimes called "world music" or "world beat") and local-global interactions has emerged (for a very small sampling, see, e.g., Slobin 1992, Guilbault 1993, Feld 1994, Averill 1995, Erlmann 1996, Monson 1999, Bilby 1999, etc.). I have engaged these discourses here in my efforts to understand *mangue* and the "new music scene" of Recife.[22] Below, I critically review some contributions to globalization and popular culture discourses, providing a general sense of where my own work fits into this intellectual tradition.[23]

Scholars writing in the social sciences have contributed to a recent ongoing debate about how to map what has been recognized as the reconfiguration of the modern world into a strikingly new interactive global system (Appadurai 1990: 1). For music scholars, one of the basic objectives has been to understand music and the dynamics of its production, reception, use, and imaging in this global system. Specifically, this endeavor has centered on questions of ethics, politics, and aesthetics: How do various components of this global system intersect and interrelate in the creation and circulation of music and identity? Where can we fit human agency into such a system, and whose agencies are being represented? What in music can be said to represent local identity (however perceived or constructed) and what represents other aspects of this global network?

In his *Subcultural Sounds: Micromusics of the West*, Mark Slobin (1992) borrows Appadurai's (1990) notion of various "scapes" (ethno-, media-, techno-, finan-, and ideo-) to propose a multi-dimensional picture of the interaction among three basic organizing elements: superculture, interculture, and subculture. In this picture,

> There is no overall sense to the system, no hidden agency which controls the flow of culture. No one parameter is paramount—not populations, money, ideology, media or technology—and each factor is only partly dependent on the

Introduction 13

other. Things are highly kinetic and extremely volatile, not only because of economics, but also because the "imagined community" . . . of an individual or group is itself an actor on the world stage. (1992: 5)

Slobin's depiction of a highly contingent, fragmentary, and complex interplay of factors does not ignore the powerful forces impinging on local musicians while it simultaneously leaves room for a range of personal and group expressions through music:

Music is at once an everyday activity, an industrial commodity, a flag of resistance, a personal world, and a deeply symbolic, emotional grounding for people in every class and cranny the superculture offers. . . . It is not that music has nothing to say [as Bordieu argues], but that it allows everyone to say what he or she wants. It is not because music negates the world, but because it embodies any number of imagined worlds that people turn to music as a core form of expression. (1992: 77-78)

In short, Slobin regards the interactions among factors in this globalized system as so complex that the possibilities for what or whom music means and represents are context-dependent and highly numerous.

In an article entitled, "The Aesthetics of the Global Imagination: Reflections on World Music in the 1990s" (1996), Veit Erlmann offers a contrasting reading of the global musical economy to that of Slobin. Erlmann questions Slobin's privileging of disjuncture, multiple viewpoints, and multivalence (1996: 471), proposing instead a "global cultural totality" based on Jameson's idea that "the production of difference is inherent in the logic of capitalism itself" (ibid.: 472). In this more menacing, pessimistic vision, recent forms of world music never attain the role of "an antidote to the venom of Western consumer culture and cultural imperialism" (ibid.: 469) simply because any difference they purport to assert is itself a part of the system. Borrowing Niklas Luhmann's systems theory in which each subsystem becomes a replication of the larger picture, Erlmann maintains that

The omnipresence of commodity production is the roof, as it were, under which differentiation and homogenization now comfortably reside as members of the same family. . . . Difference . . . is no longer an antithesis to the system, it is drawn back inside the system. (ibid.: 473)

According to this perspective,

World music, then, is not the new music of the "non-Western world," let alone of the disenfranchised "lumpen proletariat". . . . [In world music] the forces and processes of cultural production are dispersed and cut loose from any particular time and place, even if local tradition and authenticity are what the products of the global entertainment industry are ostensibly about. World music, in this reading, appears to be the soundscape of a universe which, underneath all the rhetoric of roots has forgotten its own genesis. (ibid.: 475)

More emphatically, Erlmann posits world music as "an attempt by the West to remold its image by localizing and diversifying itself through an association with otherness" (ibid.: 470):

> The equalizing logic of commodity exchange also makes it possible for a particular form of local identity—the West—to conceal its own hegemony. . . . The local, then, is not the historical antecedent to modernity, but essentially a myth produced by the growing differentiation of society. (ibid.: 479)

Compared to Slobin's refusal to privilege any one of his variables in the global system in the allowance for a multitude of possible roles for music, Erlmann rather portrays almost every aspect of what music could represent as being subsumed under the hegemony of the West and its disguised and localized association with the Other. Indeed, in such a perspective, the tentacles of the dominant group leave no realm of the system untouched, undercutting the ability of the "Third World" (or any community?) to represent itself through music. I put "Third World" in quotes here to indicate that the categories of "First" "Second," and "Third" Worlds should not be taken as reified ones. Indeed, parts of the so-called "First World," for example, contain some aspects of the so-called "Third World" and vice versa.

Although Erlmann's arguments are persuasive, his theoretical approach problematically presumes that products in a kind of global music arena, even when firmly situated and grounded in local sociocultural contexts, realities, times and spaces, cannot truly represent the people who create these products. Although it is important to acknowledge the hegemony of the West in the global economy, I would not go so far as to say that the West therefore, in some form or another, speaks for any community that participates in this economy. I would not argue in response to this that subsystems of difference (such as any kind of "world music") necessarily stand outside of the system. Rather, my understanding of local and global relations owes much to Gage Averill's (1995) analysis, which posits that

> Global systems are in an ongoing relationship with local systems, which are neither independent of the global systems nor fully incorporated in them. Local music systems are created and recreated by aggregates of individual decisions and behavior, and thus individuals cannot be written out of the equation, nor can they be presumed to be perfectly subservient to the systems in which they are located. (1995: 356)

In this interpretation, which proposes a dynamic relation between local and global systems, popular music then comes to embody both "local" and "global" identities:

> The global circulation of expressive culture doesn't render it incapable of addressing identities, nor does it assign all the signifiers to the category of pseudo-difference. Rather, these cultural symbols better represent identities that are at once local and supra-local. (ibid.: 357)

Local musics themselves, as Averill reminds us, already "embody multiple historical layers of global cultural flows" (ibid.: 356). My own fieldwork supports and adds to these contentions; I portray the music of the *mangue* movement as embodying a simultaneous localization and globalization of identity. And as I pointed out above, my findings also reveal the fluid, overlapping, and interpenetrating nature of the local and global.

Slobin's portrayal of the global musical economy also highlights a dynamic interaction among various factors, ideologies, and human agents that appropriately speaks to the multivalent nature of musical production. In line with this, I do not see *mangue* as essentially speaking for any one social class, for example, but as representing—though not in any fixed, essentialist way—the product and process of a complex relation of groups and individuals. I do not regard *mangue* as a platform for the ideological and aesthetic battles of various social groups (see Chapter Five), but rather a coming together and cooperation among them (see Chapter Four). *Mangue*'s role in an international circuit (which I do not focus on here) should also not be essentialized, since it, like any cultural symbolic nexus, surely could mean many things to many people.

In terms of their position on whether commercial music can serve as a tool of resistance, some writers are much less cautious in awarding music an oppositional role as a marker of difference. George Lipsitz, for instance, counters the sort of argument made by Erlmann by appealing to the ability of local musicians to utilize commercial culture "to build coalitions capable of circumventing the political and cultural constraints of any one nation state" (Lipsitz 1994: 153). Particularly in Chapter Five, I examine *mangue*'s role vis-à-vis the nation-state, arguing that the movement places an emphasis on the ever more specific locale (state, city, even neighborhoods) that challenges somewhat the primacy of the "nation-state" (itself a confluence of ideological currents and human actions) as the dominant shaper of musical identity. At the same time, I reveal how a "Brazilian" identity is still highly relevant for musicians on the Recife scene. In other words, this is not an "either-or" situation, but instead a relative shift in favor of more local (and global) symbols, combined with some nationalist discourse and ideology. Moreover, *mangue* helps reveal the diversity of a Brazilian national culture.

Although I uphold the new emphases on the local and recent challenges to nationalism that have been proposed in postmodern theories, I am reluctant to do away with the ideological power of the nation-state. In short, my various fieldwork experiences in Brazil do not allow me to see an immersion in global culture (and an appeal to international styles) as a clean "opting out" of a national cultural framework (see Yúdice 1994). More specifically in Yúdice's (1994) case, his article problematically opposes domestic and foreign musics in Brazil in a way that ignores the often fluid interaction of such boundaries in the Brazilian arena (I provide much evidence for this mutual relevance in Chapter Four).[24] *Mangue* may very well constitute part of a recent widespread challenge to the sociopolitical aspects of what Yúdice calls the "consensus culture." However, in its ideology the movement does not reject either the notion of the nation-state or national traditions such as samba and Carnival that often embrace a nonconflictual picture of Brazil. As such, I see *mangue* as part of a recent sociopolitical critique of the nation but not of "national" cultural forms, as Yúdice's position would have it.

In this dissertation, I understand *mangue* and the Recife music scene as representing a critical reworking of aspects of local cultural tradition within an embraced global modernity, and vice versa. I do not see *mangue* as embodying all aspects of postmodernity by any means, especially a supposed radical dislocation from history, time, and space (see Chapter Five); in fact, I dispute the notion here that any music can truly be detached from social, spatial, and temporal contexts. Instead, I present *mangue* as postmodern in very specific ways. Some of the postmodern aspects of *mangue* that are relevant here include: an emphasis on the so-called "margins" of the world system and on subaltern groups, and particularly their cutting-edge appeal and universal cultural role (see Buell 1994); the opportunities afforded to peripheral groups and communities in general by new economies and technologies (such as the Internet and computers); a sensitivity to class difference; an embrace of globalization or interconnectedness among traditions and peoples across the globe (see Buell 1994: 342); an explicit use of collage and syncretism; a refashioning of tradition and a sense of history; the relative decline of the state ("Brazil") as the primary conduit for cultural representation; a recent importance placed on the local and locality; and a new relation between the local and global.

As Frederick Buell maintains, with its basis in syncretism, postmodernism s more empowering for the "Third World" than the idea of (Western) modernism, in which the "Third World" has had to play a game of "catch up" (1994: 327). Indeed, in light of a postmodern identification on the part of the West with aspects of the subaltern world, I suggest here that in the process of globalization the subaltern and "Third World" have come to take on an increasingly special role. I do not regard this Western identification as either an undiluted triumph of the Other, or, on the other hand, as a disguised form of Western hegemony per se. Rather, more optimistically, I see *mangue* as, in the best of circumstances, allowing for a sharing of a sense of history and culture across the planet and even a blurring of Self and Other. Whereas Edward Said has pointed out that Orientalism, in fact, distances oneself from the Orient (i.e., the Other) (1979: 21-22), I see *mangue* as allowing for a closer relation, and even a breakdown of rigid cultural boundaries between, peoples and places. But at the same time, firmly uphold the salience of discrete locales within the global network (see Averill 1995, Monson 1999, Bilby 1999).

I argue here for the ability of people and communities in specific locales in the (subaltern) world to express their views through music and culture, even if these views are not explicitly political or accompanied by a substantial increase in socioeconomic power. Agreeing with Averill's conclusions about Haitian music in an international arena, I would be cautious about portraying *mangue* as a "source of difference per se" or as a veritably "authentic" form of culture any more than any other. Instead, *mangue* highlights the ways in which global culture is indigenized in specific locales, allowing for its creators' stories to be told and giving them a voice in a global network:

> I do want to suggest that global flows are continually domesticated, reinterpreted, and reconstructed locally and that these are intimately related to emergent identity formations. I also propose that these texts (understood not just as the lyrics but the totality of a musical product) be interpreted as voices of these emergent identities in the developing world. (Averill 1995: 357)

In a similar way, I see *mangue* as the emerging and potential success of a peripheral region in the world system within certain limits discussed above. And I, too, maintain that this movement can be seen as representing local voices who have reinterpreted tradition, history, and global flows to speak to their particular situation—which may have increasing relevance for the rest of the world.

Research Methods and Fieldwork Synopsis

The methods I used in my fieldwork consisted primarily of participant-observation and formal interviews and informal communications. I supplemented these with video and audio documentation, private lessons and classes, and some performance. Not all of the latter activities directly pertained to my research topic, but in a general sense they gave me a better understanding of the local culture and provided the foundations for further research into other areas of Pernambucan music. In addition, I read and collected articles on the music scene from Recife's two main newspapers (the *Diário de Pernambuco* and the *Jornal do Commércio*), conducted some library research on folk music, and obtained videos from TV Viva in Olinda and CD and vinyl recordings of a variety of music from music shops. For a list of some of my main fieldwork activities, refer to Appendix 3. Below I describe some of these activities in more detail.

For most of my five months based in Recife, I lived in a small, cramped single room of a modest hotel in the neighborhood of Pina, on the border of Boa Viagem, one of the most upscale districts of the city. Situated across the street from Boa Viagem Beach, my hotel was, by good fortune, a ten-minute walk from Soparia ("Soupery"). This small, unassuming bar with a collection of kitsch art in the Pólo Pina strip was *the* spot for local bands and artists of various types on the scene. These acts ranged from local folk music to fusion to straight rock 'n' roll, blues, and other international styles. The juxtaposition of these styles not only from day to day but even during the same night embodied for me the general sense of camaraderie and mutual affinity among diverse musics and people on the scene at large. Many groups, of course, brought their own followings, which may have tended toward one kind of music or one side of the socioeconomic spectrum; but on many, if not most, nights, there appeared to be mixed crowds—people of different races, class backgrounds, and musical predilections. This is not to say that all of these people interacted among each other without regard for these differences; in fact, at times, I could readily distinguish small clusters of people of different classes, for example, socializing separately. But at the same time, what struck me was how much these lines were crossed at Soparia through conversations and social interactions and sometimes within the bands themselves. Perhaps Soparia's function as the foremost, indeed one of the only, steady commercial venues on the scene even helped reinforce these connections, partly out of necessity.

I made many contacts, heard and danced to much music, hung out with friends and colleagues, and ate soup and drank beer at this locale throughout my time in Recife. In this sense, I was a participant (as a researcher) in the local culture. Soon after I arrived in Recife, a contact of mine, Marcelo Soares, wrote a short article about me and my research that was included in the cultural section of the *Diário de Pernambuco* as part of a special edition dedicated to *mangue* and Chico Science on the one-year anniversary of Chico's death. From that piece and from word-of-mouth, I became known by many members on the tight-knit scene and was even sought out.[25]

I had the opportunity to see Zé Neguinho do Côco (an expert performer of the *côco*, an Afro-Brazilian style of Northeast Brazil), a *maracatu* group from the Daruê Malungo (a grassroots cultural educational center for poor youth in the Chão de Estrelas neighborhood), and Comadre Florzinha and Chão e Chineo (two spectacular bands that perform folk styles from Pernambuco and the Northeast, the former an all-female group) at Soparia. In addition, I saw many *mangue*, rock, blues, and pop groups there.

A majority of musical performances on the Recife scene takes place not at clubs but outdoors or in designated indoor spaces as festivals or events sponsored by some combination of local or international business and/or the state and city government. Besides Soparia, I attended many such events and festivals throughout the city during my stay. Of particular note was the three-day music festival Abril Pro Rock (April For Rock) held in the convention center of Olinda (April 3-5, 1998). Presented by MTV and funded by many companies and the state of Pernambuco, this landmark annual event features a wide range of acts from the Recife scene as well as other regional, national, and international pop and rock bands. In addition, I attended several Todos Com A Nota (All With A Note) performances at the Animal Exhibition Park of Cordeiro, which were part of a government-supported program featuring free-of-charge music and other cultural events. Some of the local talent I saw at these shows were the aforementioned Cascabulho, the *mangue*-type bands Via Sat and R.D.A., the rap group Faces do Subúrbio, and the hard-core band Devotos do Ódio. A similar, outdoor government-sponsored program during the Carnival season in the neighborhood of Recife Antigo (Old Recife) featured folkloric music, films, and other activities. At one of these events, I saw the Nação Pernambuco and folk legend Mestre Salustiano. Toward the end of my stay, I attended *Maracatu Atômico* (Atomic Maracatu), another official, free outdoor party in Recife Antigo (May 29, 1998) featuring the Maracatu Estrela Brilhante (one of the most prominent traditional *maracatu* "nations") and Selma do Côco (the most visible traditional performer of the *côco* in Pernambuco). I also attended a large party at the airplane club of Pina as part of an international association of journalists taking place in the city; aside from several DJs (including *mangue* mover Renato L), the party featured the roots folk music of the young band Chão e Chinelo and the fusion sounds of Via Sat. The *Mercado Pop* (Pop Market) is an alternative market for art, clothes and jewelry that often had music and was frequented by members of the *cena musical*. I attended many private parties where DJs played a variety of local and international music, and I visited several groups—such as Cascabulho, Via Sat, and the Pernambucan-flavored rock band Querosene Jacaré—in their formal rehearsals. Through these and other activities, I established ongoing relationships with members of bands and other participants on the scene, with whom I exchanged information and ideas. Beyond the events mentioned, I witnessed countless traditional parades and performances during Carnival in Recife/Olinda and the *Festas Juninas* (June Festivals) in both Recife and Caruaru (interior of Pernambuco).[26]

Study of the folk culture and music of the region was one of my main personal objectives during fieldwork, which clearly supported an understanding of my topic. Since I discuss very little about the folk music aspects of my research, I will provide a synopsis here. As one of my colleagues in Recife remarked to me, "To understand *mangue* you have to understand all of the music of Pernambuco." While I've only begun a process of understanding the music I experienced (and there were many kinds of music I had only limited exposure to) I feel like much of this music has become an indelible part of me. The well of music of the region is so vast that I regard this research as an exciting first step. Also, my endeavors were restricted mostly to the coast; music and culture in the region vary greatly from the coast (*litoral*) inward to the *zona da mata* and from there to the *agreste* and *sertão*.

Of all the folk music I experienced in Pernambuco, the Afro-Brazilian *maracatu* is the one that I have learned the most about. During the Carnival in Recife and Olinda I had the chance to make contact with and accompany the Maracatu Nação Estrela Brilhante (Shining Star Maracatu Nation) for several of its performances. I documented some of these on video both for my own research and to assist Cristina and Virginia Barbosa, two colleagues at the Federal University of Pernambuco who were playing in and conducting research on Estrela Brilhante. Following this, I came to accompany the Maracatu in its post-Carnival schedule, establishing a relationship with several of its members, particularly those who were studying at the Federal University as well as with Jorge Martins da Silva (also of the band Cascabulho) and Percussion Director Mestre Valter. Furthermore, my private study with Estrela Brilhante members Neide Alves and Jorge Martins da Silva on the percussion of *maracatu* has greatly refined and reinforced my understanding and love of this music, bred from an immersion into it over the course of my stay.

Another cherished connection was the one I formed with Zé Neguinho do Côco, a master of the *côco* and I believe a national treasure, whose band at the time comprised mostly the same young musicians on the scene who studied at the Federal University and played with Estrela Brilhante.[27] I was able to attend a rehearsal of Zé Neguinho's band as well as interview him and record some of his original compositions.

Another fundamental aspect of my research into the folk culture involved my connection with Dito D'Oxossi, an authority in the *Candomblé* Afro-Brazilian religion. Along with several other members of the Recife scene, from researchers to musicians and other enthusiasts (many of them, again, associated with the Federal University), I attended classes on the *Candomblé* taught by Dito at his home in the Alto José do Pinho neighborhood. As a part of this course, I was able to attend and record a ceremony at the Sítio do Pai Adão *terreiro* (house of worship) in the neighborhood of Água Fria. Dito is also the founder of an *afoxé*, a type of group that adapts music from the *Candomblé* into a secular context. His group, Ilê D'Egbá, was performing the *afoxé* and other Afro-Brazilian genres at a club in Olinda every Sunday night, which I attended several times.

I was also able to benefit greatly from my status as Visiting Scholar at the Joaquim Nabuco Foundation of Recife (a local governmental organization that studies the people of Northeast Brazil) in the Department of Anthropology. There, I worked under the guidance of Tânia Lima, who was also conducting research into *mangue* and its environmental ramifications. My partnership with Tânia was highly valuable in the exchange of ideas. At the Foundation I was also able to exchange with other scholars such as the esteemed folklorist Dr. Mário Souto Maior and anthropologist Eduardo Fonseca.

In addition, I made a connection to the Federal University of Pernambuco Department of Music. There, I met and exchanged ideas with a group of musicians and researchers (including those who were associated with Estrela Brilhante and Zé Neguinho do Côco). During my stay, this group formed part of an informal ethnomusicology forum to discuss research issues and concepts, headed by my colleague, ethnomusicologist Carlos Sandroni. Carlos invited me toward the end of my stay to head a lecture/discussion for the forum about my research. I worked very closely in my research into folk music with one member of this informal group, Neide Alves. At the time, Neide was performing with Estrela Brilhante, Zé Neguinho, and the erudite ensemble Sa Grama, and she was

Introduction

conducting her own research on the *maracatu* and the *côco*. We worked together on various joint endeavors that have been applied to our respective research projects.

Organization of the Dissertation

Chapter Two provides a history of the *mangue* movement and "new music scene" of Recife. It is based on the interviews I conducted, the written sources I had available to me (particularly local journalist José Teles's book, *Meteoro Chico* [n/d]), and the particular experiences I happened to have—all of this filtered through my own biases and proclivities. I focus on Chico Science & Nação Zumbi and Mundo Livre, the twin pioneers of the movement, over and above other groups that subsequently may have been referred to as *mangue*. Some other groups on the scene (*mangue* or otherwise) are covered in Chapter Four.

Chapter Three compares *mangue* with some other previous trends in Brazilian pop that have also blended local and global sounds in experimental fusion; here, I attempt to arrive at *mangue*'s unique place in the history of Brazilian popular music. Rather than representing a radical break from Brazilian tradition, *mangue* is treated here more as the latest innovation within a long practice of self-aware, experimental musical miscegenation in the country. I see the movement's peculiar role to be in its updating of foreign ingredients, and a general immersion in a global network of information, coupled with its reassertion of regional characteristics.

Chapter Four is a selective ethnographic account of Recife's "new music scene." Here I examine some of the main tendencies on the scene—folk music of various guises, *mangue* fusion, and straight rock or rap—in light of the musicians' relation to both their folk heritage and international influences. In short, I attempt to understand the interrelationships among the scene's diverse musics and musicians, suggesting what these relationships might reveal about the interplay of tradition and modernity, the local and global, and the domestic and foreign. Chapter Five examines a *mangue* style and ideology, supported by some analysis of the music and lyrics of Chico Science & Nação Zumbi and correlated to some of the modernist and especially postmodernist aspects of the movement. Of the latter, I emphasize in particular the relative decline of the nation-state in the representation of cultural identity and the ways in which *mangue* both reasserts a more local identity and engages more fully with global culture. In the end, this chapter offers a reading of *mangue* as it pertains to recent debates over politics, aesthetics, and globalization.

The title of this dissertation makes reference to a song in the MPB tradition called "Maracatu Atômico" (Atomic *Maracatu*). Composed by Jorge Mautner and Nelson Jacobina, the song was reinterpreted by Chico Science & Nação Zumbi on their *Afrociberdelia* CD (Sony Latin CDZ-81996 2-479255). I chose this piece to be part of the title primarily because it juxtaposes the idea of modern global technology ("Atomic") with a symbol of rustic local tradition ("Maracatu"). A seamless integration of high technology and modernity with Nature and traditional cultural practices is one of the foundations of the *mangue* ideology. Furthermore, the importance of the *maracatu* in *mangue* makes this song particularly apt as a kind of symbolic reference for the movement. (See Appendix 3, Track 2 for a discussion of the *maracatu* and funk rhythmic influences in the *mangue* version of this song.) Finally, my use of this song title is meant to highlight that while they reclaim their regional heritage and embrace modern technology and culture, *mangue* musicians are also engaging with the work of their national forebears, affirming their place within a history and tradition of self-aware, hypersyncretic Brazilian pop music.

Some Background on Recife

In the 1530s, the Portuguese established Olinda, turning its surrounding fields into sugar plantations and importing the colony's first Africans to work them. A player in the sugar trade and eager to stake a claim in Brazil, the Dutch established the Dutch West India Company in 1621. By 1630, Dutch forces had driven the Portuguese settlers out of Olinda, rebuilding a new capital in neighboring Recife. By 1640, the Dutch had secured control of a large portion of the Northeast, and in the first effort at city planning in the hemisphere (Page 1995: 190), they transformed Recife into the first bourgeois commercial city in the colony. By 1654, the Portuguese planters who had taken arms regained control of Recife, forcing the Dutch—the last European threat to Portuguese Brazil—to surrender.

With the help of the Portuguese crown, the economically superior Recife came to prevail over Olinda, which was home to the established planter aristocracy. Olinda has since declined in political importance to become one of the largest and best-preserved colonial cities in Brazil. Recife's dependence on the declining sugar-cane economy (with its inefficient production modes) allowed the northeastern city to be eclipsed economically by Rio de Janeiro and São Paulo in the South. But Recife still developed into an important regional capital and port city that could boast Brazil's first newspaper, a distinguished University, and a lively intellectual life (Page 1995: 190). However, desperate socioeconomic conditions for the vast majority of Recife's population have continued to plague the city into the present.

When I was making plans for my doctoral research in Brazil, I tried to imagine what Recife was like. In my two previous trips to Brazil (1993 and 1994) I had stayed in Rio de Janeiro and Salvador, Bahia. Only Salvador, with its location in the country's Northeast and consequent widespread destitution, provided a clue about what to expect in Recife. But compared with the wealthier southern city of Rio, Recife, capital of Pernambuco, one of the most impoverished states in Brazil, seemed to me like another world. Boasting a large, developed South Zone of chic beachfront neighborhoods and a sizable middle and upper class, Rio offers at least a façade of "First-World" glamour that masks

Introduction 23

the slum conditions under which hundreds of thousands of *cariocas* (residents of Rio) live. Recife's poverty, by contrast, is more encompassing, covering all but sporadic pockets of wealth and comfort: Candeias and Boa Viagem in the southern part of the city along the beach; neighborhoods such as Boa Vista, Madalena, Torre, and Casa Forte further inland and to the north; and parts of neighboring Olinda, in the extreme north of Greater Recife, among other areas.

To be sure, in recent years, the face of Recife has undergone drastic changes.[28] High-rise apartments now line an Atlantic beach that twenty years ago contained only three large buildings, while hotels, restaurants and shopping centers have popped up all over Boa Viagem, once a "sleepy seaside neighborhood on the outskirts of the city" (Page 1995: 193). A major sign of recent "progress"—and a powerful symbol of modernity—is the heavily air-conditioned Shopping Recife complex in Boa Viagem, purportedly one of the largest malls in South America and a paradoxical monument in a city with the nation's highest levels of unemployment.

Beyond its recent development, the beachside city is blessed with a special architectural and natural charm. Located close to the equator, Recife bristles with hot sun year round (except for its rain spells), its colorful colonial-era buildings recall a glorious past, and its location at the confluence of three rivers that flow into the Atlantic Ocean has led some to call the city the "Brazilian Venice." However, Recife's natural and architectural assets and recent development nonetheless belie a harsher reality: the fact that the vast majority of *recifenses* (Recife residents) live in underprivileged, even detrimental, conditions—a situation which any resident of this regional capital, rich or poor, or any visitor can do little to ignore. Since the 1950s and '60s Recife came to be known by another nickname: the "Calcutta of the Western Hemisphere," and in the 1980s it was ranked as the fourth worst city in the world to live in (according to an institute of population studies in Washington D. C.). Thus even in a country where the majority of people are poor, Recife "came to develop a distinctive kind of wretchedness not found anywhere else in Brazil" (Page 1995: 191). The sight in 1998 of dozens of little boys forced to hawk, among other things, tiny quantities of water tied up in plastic bags in the center of the city, or packs of underage girls selling their bodies all along Conselheiro Aguiar Avenue in Boa Viagem, is testament to Recife's grave social and economic legacy.

At the same time that it is distinguished by a virulent brand of misery, Pernambuco State is considered within Brazil to possess one of the nation's richest and most diverse expressive cultures. Brazilians in general have a keen sense for what they have to offer the rest of the planet; for Pernambucans, it's their ample folk, and more recently pop, cultural heritage that is projected on regional, national, and international levels as a fundamental characteristic of their identity.

The local government and official culture's relation to both the regional folk culture and to *mangue* is a crucial condition of the sociocultural situation of Pernambuco in the 1990s. With respect to *mangue* in particular, there is a complex official connection that simultaneously involves support and disregard or even unambiguous opposition. In a 1997 article, Mundo Livre S/A frontman Fred Zero Quatro speaks out against the local cultural establishment:

> There is in Recife a hegemony of a certain regionalist, folkloric, traditionalist aesthetic, which is totally suffocating. The public organs, the channels that would be able to promote a certain cultural rebirth, since the economy was totally destroyed, were and are all immersed in the official regionalism, which has an academic and erudite arm, the Movimento Armorial, and a more folkloric branch, which I am accustomed to call macumba [a Brazilian syncretic religion] for the tourist. The dominant cultural politics in Recife always were this, to folklorize, to stagnate or else surround itself with the erudite, as the Movimento Armorial does. It judges itself the proprietor of the regional folk culture. Nobody else could want to drink from this fountain. (Quoted in Abramo 1997: 75)

One of the most outspoken critics of *mangue* is the current Secretary of Culture of the State of Pernambuco, writer Ariano Suassuna, founder of the above-mentioned *Movimento Armorial*. According to Fred Zero Quatro, *mangue* and other contemporary bands constructed Recife's current scene independently and in spite of the state and city government: "Only now, because it doesn't work anymore to deny the strength of the movement, they've begun to provide some support here and there" (Quoted in Abramo 1997: 75). Aside from an unambiguously anti-*mangue* interview from Suassuna, my research experience in 1998 revealed an official support of both folk and pop fusion music. As a counterpart, the local mass media has served as one of the strongest allies of *mangue*. Despite their importance, the peculiar ramifications of these governmental and mass media connections in Pernambuco's culture are not addressed at length in this dissertation but surely could be the subject for future research.

Beyond its local cultural dynamics, at the national level, Pernambuco is claiming its space in the Brazilian cultural identity. A prominent commercial for the Brazilian national tourism agency, Embratur, which promotes internal tourism in the country, has several familiar visual references to Pernambuco and Bahia, for example, among other areas of the country. Although the theme music is a samba, in the middle of the piece is a sort of *forró* with rap, serving as an assertion of northeastern culture and an appeal to visit the region based on cultural references (within a framework still dominated by Rio de Janeiro). The rap-*forró*, if not a direct nod to *mangue*, certainly points to the new kinds of music coming out of Recife and Northeast Brazil.

To understand this dynamic between regions of Brazil, one has to consider the great socioeconomic differential cited above between northern and southern Brazil, the significant cultural divisions among the diverse regions, and the traditional dominance particularly of Rio de Janeiro in representing the cultural identity of the country. Suffice it to say that *mangue* both reflects and embodies a

Introduction   25

current assertion of pride in being a northeasterner and a Pernambucan specifically. *Orgulho de ser nordestino* (Proud to Be a Northeasterner) was a common car sticker I saw in Recife. Several consultants emphasized the value of northeastern culture and how *mangue* relates to a recent surge in self-esteem in being Brazilian, and particularly in being from the Northeast (e.g., Interview: Zé da Flauta 1998).

Considering the growing importance of *mangue* and the Recife scene nationally and internationally, perhaps *mangue* (as the huge success of Bahian popular musics in the 1980s and '90s)[29] marks a shift in the dynamic of the cultural image of Brazil, which for long has had its center in Rio de Janeiro, back toward the Northeast.[30] The Northeast is regarded by many as the cultural heart of Brazil, the region where the nation's most influential cultural traditions (including the samba) were first manifest. Furthermore, in light of *mangue* and other trends ranging from the Afro-Bahian cultural renaissance in the 1970s, '80s, and '90s to *tropicália*, the Northeast is also acknowledged as a source of some of Brazil's most innovative musical and cultural developments. But while it reconnects with what many may regard as the " true essence" of Brazilian national culture, *mangue* can also be seen from another perspective as a salient example of how Brazil is becoming more consciously pluralistic and decentralized. It shows how, in part through alliances to global music, technology, and other cultural practices, certain established Brazilian nationalistic images and identities have been challenged.[31]

Chapter Two

"Da Lama Ao Caos" (From Mud to Chaos)
A History of the *Mangue* Movement and "New Music Scene" of Recife

Introduction

The *mangue* movement is one of Brazil's most vital pop culture trends of the last thirty years. Formed in Recife in the early 1990s as a cultural response to a debilitating socioeconomic situation, *mangue* reinvigorated activities in pop music and later theater, dance, and the plastic arts. The movement takes as its namesake and point of departure the geography of Recife—specifically, the ubiquitous swamps on top of which the city is built. Providing sustenance for local fishing communities, the *manguezais*, as they are called, comprise one of the planet's most diverse and fertile ecosystems; for the movement's creators, the *manguezais* serve as a metaphor for the cultural richness of their native region.

On the musical front, *mangue* was led by two bands—Chico Science & Nação Zumbi (Chico Science & The Zumbi Nation) and Mundo Livre S/A (Free World Ltd.).[1] These bands, and others that followed them or that were formed during the same time, make use of local and global musical elements in various proportions in creative hybrid forms. Chico Science & Nação Zumbi emerged as the most influential band in a new music scene—the so-called *nova cena musical do Recife* (new music scene of Recife)—that developed in the wake of *mangue* but that encompasses everything from local folk music to straight rock or rap.

Created by Chico Science of Nação Zumbi, Fred Zero Quatro (Fred 04) of Mundo Livre, DJ-journalist Renato L., and others as part of a cultural cooperative in the early 1990s, the *mangue* movement comfortably encompasses both straw hats worn by local fisherman and hip sunglasses, the distorted electric guitar along with the rustic *bombo* drums of the Afro-Pernambucan *maracatu*. In a nod to nutritionist Josué de Castro, who described the local life cycle of crabs and fisherman (see Castro 1970), the movement's 1991 manifesto imagines its adherents as "*caranguejos com cérebro*," or "crabs with brains," people in touch with and able to transcend their environment.[2] Symbolized by a parabolic antenna sunk in the mud (*lama*) of the city, picking up signals from the rest of the world, one of the movement's main objectives was to link the rich but neglected regional traditions of Recife (and national traditions such as the samba) with global pop currents, and in the process to revitalize the local culture.

Initially relegated to only two, albeit influential bands in Recife, *mangue* soon helped generate a dynamic local cultural scene, later inspiring musicians beyond Recife in the Northeast and other regions of Brazil. This scene has also garnered international renown, particularly through *mangue*'s most popular act, Chico Science & Nação Zumbi (hereafter referred to as CSNZ).

While its adherents uphold the cooperative aspect of their movement as fundamental, *mangue*'s undisputed frontman was Chico Science. A tremendously charismatic leader for a young, subcultural cohort in Brazil, Chico Science was arguably the most noteworthy pop musician of his generation in Brazil when he died in a tragic car accident in early 1997. Chico and his band not only updated the foreign soundscape of Brazilian pop—reworking such genres as soul, funk, rap, heavy metal, psychedelic rock, *raggamuffin*, and electronic dance music—but they also rediscovered and utilized old Pernambucan folk styles that were believed to be in danger of extinction. Chico assimilated and embodied in his dress, music, and behavior these local-global fusions, inspiring a legion of regional (and some national) rock and fusion bands, while simultaneously helping to reinvigorate Pernambucan folk music traditions. Indeed, such local genres as *maracatu, côco, embolada,* and *ciranda* are enjoying unprecedented popularity by people of all social classes in Recife in the 1990s. Serving as a local cultural hero, Chico paved the way for youth from Recife's underprivileged classes to enter a music scene that he helped create. Furthermore, in the midst of socioeconomic misery he provided a renewed self-esteem for Pernambucans and Brazilians in general, and, as his band traveled throughout Brazil and to Europe and the United States, they unequivocally put Pernambuco—one of Brazil's most musically abundant states—on the world musical map.

This chapter provides a history of *mangue* and *a nova cena musical* (the new music scene) of Recife.[3] It concentrates on the bands CSNZ and Mundo Livre S/A because the *mangue* movement was created around these two bands and because the "new music scene" that emerged along with *mangue* owes much to these groups—especially Nação Zumbi. But if CSNZ was the most influential and arguably the most original group to surface from Recife's *nova cena musical*, this scene has also been sustained on the strength of a diversity of notable groups and artists. These include, for example, Mundo Livre S/A, Mestre Ambrósio, Cascabulho, Devotos do Ódio,[4] Via Sat, Coração Tribal, Faces do Subúrbio, Eddie, Maracatu Nação Pernambuco, Dona Selma do Côco, Lia de Itamaracá, Zé Neguinho do Côco, Mestre Salustiano, Maracatu Nação Estrela Brilhante, Comadre Florzinha, Chão e Chinelo, and many more. (Chapter Four will cover a small sampling of these artists and the music scene as a whole in the form of an ethnographic account.)

Setting the Scene: Recife in the 1980s

Journalist José Teles[5] locates the origins of the *mangue* movement (which he prefers to call a scene) at the end of the 1970s or beginning of the 1980s. At the time, the military government, which had been in power since 1964, began to ease censorship, allowing for a tentative opening of the ports and consequently, a "timid but very important rebirth of pop art in the country." The author points to several manifestations of this pop culture such as a renewed interest in beat literature (*On the Road* received its first Brazilian translation in this period) and the availability of imported records in national editions (previously such records would be sold only in record import shops in the wealthier Southeast of the country).

In the 1980s there was a boom in Brazilian-made rock, centered in southern cities such as Rio, São Paulo, and Brasília.[6] Meanwhile in Recife, a group of middle class students at the Federal University of Pernambuco was introducing itself to beat literature, the cyberpunk fiction of William Gibson, and the sounds of Joy Division, New Order, the Smiths, Bauhaus, Siouxie and the Banshees, and PiL, among other groups. These students produced a program on the University radio called *Décadas* (Decades), on which "future manguegirls and mangueboys [the local term for adherents of the movement] began to tune into other sounds." Several of the *mangue* movement's figures, such as DJ-journalist Renato L. (Renato Lins), Herr Doktor Mabuse, and Fred Zero Quatro, formed part of the *Décadas* team. According to Teles, *Décadas* was important for the development of *mangue beat* because it showed the future proponents of the movement that "there was space to create a music outside of the parameters desired by the FM stations and multinational record companies, and even as such to make friends and influence people."

This cohort gravitated toward the music of "indie" (from independent record label), alternative, or underground artists mostly from England. Morrisey and Ian Curtis, as well as David Bowie, who, despite his major label affiliation "had an *indie* attitude" (Teles n/d: 14), were all notable influences, as was the Velvet Underground. An important source of such alternative sounds was the now extinct Stiletto label from São Paulo, which first introduced Durutti Column, Felt, and Joy Division to Recife listeners at the end of the '80s. Stiletto also had its own local acts; the underground Paulistano band Fellini was purportedly a major influence on Chico Science.[7] All of these groups had a cult appeal, as would later the *mangue* artists. According to Teles, "Of these albums [released by Stiletto], it could be said the same that was said of the first Velvet Underground LP [...]: only one hundred people bought the album, but all of them formed a band after listening to it."

Around 1987, dozens of rock bands spread throughout Recife, most of them playing heavy metal or hard-core.[8] *Mangue* pioneer Fred Zero Quatro of the band

Mundo Livre used to be a member of Câmbio Negro H.C. (Black Market Hard-Core). According to Teles, these bands had trouble finding places to p ay. Curiously, one of the most popular venues for this crop of '80s groups was at a dance academy directed by a rock enthusiast named Lourdes Rossiter: the Espaço Arte Viva, located in the chic beach neighborhood of Boa Viagem. Paulo André Pires, who later became the impresario for CSNZ and is today one of the foremost producer-impresarios on Recife's "new music scene," had just returned from living in the U.S. and opened a record store called Rock Xpress. In the early '90s, Pires began to produce shows featuring local rock bands and invited foreign acts, such as the German group Kreator and Morbid Angel from the U.S. (both played what is termed "thrash metal"), to perform in Recife.

Given the high proportion of rock—and particularly heavy metal, hard-core, and related styles—in *mangue*, and as represented by other current bands, the 1980s rock phenomenon was clearly an important precedent for Recife's "new music scene" of the 1990s. According to Teles, another significant influence on *mangue* was the so-called "world music" trend, particularly the musical fusions of U.S. and British pop stars such as Peter Gabriel and Paul Simon. Teles goes so far as to claim that this brand of music "made the guys [in Recife] wake up to the good little sounds that were simmering in the [sic] manguesal: cirandas, maracatus, caboclinhos." This assertion that the embrace of "Third World"—including Brazilian—sounds by Western pop musicians caused Brazilians in Recife to re-explore their own folk heritage is difficult to verify, especially since none of the people with whom I spoke in Recife cited "world music" so-defined as a formative inspiration for *mangue*. More likely, such "world music" fusions and *mangue* were parallel phenomena. However, there is at least one indirect connection between early 1990s "world music" and *mangue*: The Bahian *bloco afro* Olodum, which acquired international renown through its association with Paul Simon, was the model for a similar type of neighborhood group in Recife called Lamento Negro (as it was the model for dozens of groups throughout Bahia and Brazil). Lamento Negro in turn served as a springboard for the formation of Chico Science & Nação Zumbi, supplying the pioneering *mangue* group with its drummers as well as with a wealth of musical information and ideas.

The Emergence of Chico Science & Nação Zumbi

Chico's Formative Years

The concept of *mangue* came from Chico Science, a pivotal figure for whom the black urban style of late 1970s and early '80s New York was just as natural as the regional folk rhythms of his native Recife. Chico Science was born Francisco de Assis França in 1966 to a home of the lower middle class in the Rio Doce neighborhood of Paulista, a city on the periphery of Olinda. According to CSNZ's former impresario Paulo André Pires:

> [Chico] came from a poor family that only had the basic, never became needy, hunger, nor anything . . . it's that family that we call in Brazil middle class that lives with the dough that's only enough to eat and live on, they don't have a lot of comfort, money. [Chico] told me, for example, of a time that he would come to the center of the city and would bring some old books to sell so that he could buy the records that he wanted. And that he would see some shoes in the stores, like Adidas, which in the '70s became popular in Brazil also, and he wanted to have a pair. . . . (Interview: Pires 1998)

As a preadolescent and teenager Chico's musical taste was geared toward what is known in Brazil as "black music"—a term designating U.S. American black popular music, particularly of the 1970s and '80s. Chico favored the classic funk sounds of James Brown, Curtis Mayfield, and Funkadelic and the early hip-hop of Sugar Hill Gang, Kurtis Blow, and Grand Master Flash, among other groups (Teles n/d: 8,10). Such music was popular among youth in the poorer neighborhoods on the outskirts of Recife, and many, including a pre-teenaged Chico, would take part in the so-called *bailes funk* (funk parties). Paulo André Pires describes one of Chico's childhood musical rituals:

> He should have been between ten and thirteen years old when he was into this black American music of the '70s. He would put something underneath the bedsheet so his mother would think it was he sleeping, he would open the window and would go to the neighborhood party where they played this type of music. So there, since he didn't have money to buy records, there he began to see what was happening in the world also. (Interview: 1998)

As a counterpart to "black music," in the early 1980s the breakdance phenomenon arrived in Recife, and in 1984 Chico and his inseparable friend Jorge du Peixe joined the *Legião Hip Hop* (Hip-Hop Legion), one of the major street breakdance groups of the city (Teles n/d: 8).

Aside from international "black music," another crucial formative influence on Chico was the local folk culture (known in Brazil as *cultura popular*, or "popular culture," the culture of the lower classes). As Paulo André Pires recalls, "Across from [Chico's] house in the street there was a *ciranda* [a type of circle dance from Northeast Brazil]. So for him diversion was *cultura popular* and he had this in the soul really, in the blood as we say here" (Interview: 1998). Chico confirms this connection to the *ciranda* in a quote:

> When I was much younger, around twelve years old, I danced ciranda. The ciranda came from the interior [of the state], from the Zona da Mata [Forest Zone] to the coast. My parents had a ciranda. [The cirandas] were generally made in front of bars or grocery stores of the region. The guys paid the ciranda players to attract more clients. [The *ciranda* tradition] was proliferating more and more and reaching the coast. So I already danced ciranda on the beach. (Interview with Luís Claudio Garrido, April 30, 1994, *Jornal à Tarde*, Bahia, quoted in Teles n/d: 30)

Chico also recalls witnessing other folk traditions in his neighborhood, such as *maracatu* (in this case, the rural *maracatu* known as *maracatu de baque solto*):

> In my childhood I watched the *maracatus* doing the *acorda-povo* ["wake up people"], which happens during São João [Saint John's Day, an important regional festival in June], always around midnight. The people go out singing: Wake up people/Wake up people/Because the Saint John rooster/Woke you up. So I saw all these things that they taught us as folklore, as a past manifestation, but it isn't really in this way that you have to see it. (ibid.)

Indeed, Chico's early absorption of local folk music provided a foundation for the experimental fusions he later developed combining such regional styles as *maracatu* (both rural and urban types), *ciranda*, *embolada* (a type of street poetry), *côco* (an Afro-Brazilian dance from the Northeast), and a variety of world pop idioms.

Chico's First Bands and the Birth of Nação Zumbi

Rock music was a more indirect influence on young Chico, whose older brothers listened to such '70s bands as Led Zeppelin, Deep Purple, and Credence Clearwater Revival (Teles n/d: 28; Interview: Pires 1998). In 1987, Chico and Jorge du Peixe united their "black music" and rock interests by joining a rock cover band of guitarist Lúcio Maia, called Orla Orbe, which they inflected with a funk influence (Teles n/d: 10). Orla Orbe became part of Recife's late '80s rock scene, the principal point of which was the aforementioned Arte Viva dance academy; Orla Orbe made its debut at Arte Viva in February of 1988 but the band did not last (ibid.). In 1989 Orla Orbe was replaced by Loustal, named after a famous French cartoonist whom Chico admired. Loustal featured Chico as lyricist and singer, Lúcio on guitar, Alexandre Dengue on bass, and Vinícius on drumset (Teles n/d: 8). According to a 1993 press release, "The idea of the group was to rework rock of the 60s, but already thinking of incorporating elements of *soul*, *funk*, and *hip hop*" (in ibid.).

Loustal and other bands in the late 1980s already experimented with Pernambucan folk elements (Interview: Pupillo 1998; Interview: Zero Quatro 1998). However, it wasn't until Chico solidified a stronger musical link to the local Afro-*mestiço* culture and a social connection to the poorest communities of Recife that Nação Zumbi and a new musical movement were born. In 1990, Gilmar "Bola Oito" (Eight Ball Gilmar), a colleague at Chico's government agency job, introduced Chico to a *bloco afro*, a type of Afro-Brazilian drum corps, called Lamento Negro (Black Lament) of the Peixinhos neighborhood on the periphery of Olinda (Teles n/d: 8). At the time, Lamento specialized in the *samba-reggae*, a nationally popular musical hybrid formulated in Salvador, Bahia in the 1980s. They also worked on grass roots cultural education together-

"Da Lama Ao Caos"

with Daruê Malungo, a center for the support of poor communities based in nearby Chão de Estrelas under the direction of Mestre Meia-Noite (ibid.). Maureliano Ribiero, former member of Lamento Negro and percussionist for the band Via Sat (from "via satellite"), which was formed in the wake of Nação Zumbi, describes Chico's participation with the *bloco*:

> When Chico began music, he had a formal band of his own—drumset, bass, guitar. But he needed to do something new, different, for the sound he wanted to make. And he wanted to mix the culture, the "things of the culture"—in quotes, like this [makes quotation marks gesture]—as we did them [laughs]. So he went after Gilmar, who was a good friend of mine and such, we lived together in the same neighborhood, and he always asked Gilmar, "Let's do it like this: an exchange with the drums" .... He spent a year chasing after Gilmar. And I, stalling time, "No wait, Gilmar, wait." To see if he really wanted it, if it was only a—I let him spend a lot of time asking and searching. Until one day, "No, let's go". . . . And he insisted too much, he wants it [laughs]. He really wants it [laughs], so let's go. (Interview: Ribiero and Tenorio 1998)

Maureliano assumed an important didactic musical role in Nação Zumbi's formative period. He taught the future members of the band some local folk styles and created at least one of the band's signature rhythmic fusions (this and other aspects of the band's musical style will be discussed further in Chapter Five).

Chico and Jorge du Peixe began to attend Lamento Negro's rehearsals, which took place at Daruê Malungo in Chão de Estrelas (Teles n/d: 11). According to Maureliano, "We [Lamento Negro and Chico] . . . spent more or less one year [with] only percussion, without using electric guitar or bass. It was only this—only *tambor, caixa,* and *repique*" (Interview: 1998).[9] Deeply impressed with the sound of the *bloco afro*, Chico was inspired to form a band that fused the guitar of Lúcio Maia and bass of Alexandre Dengue from Loustal with drummers from Lamento Negro (Teles n/d: 9). Lúcio and Dengue were at first reticent—especially the bassist, who "didn't even want to hear about samba-reggae" (Teles n/d: 11). According to Teles, "Lúcio Maia ended up being convinced to take his guitar and a little amplifier to Chão de Estrelas. According to him, you couldn't hear his guitar correctly in the middle of the drums" (ibid.).

Featuring an erratic line-up in the beginning, the band that would become Nação Zumbi (originally called Chico Science & Lamento Negro) was formed. Only before the recording of their debut CD, in fact (released by Sony in 1994), did they narrow their members down from fifteen to eight: Chico Science on vocals; Alexandre Dengue on bass; Lúcio Maia on guitar; Gilmar Bola Oito, Gira, and Jorge du Peixe on *bombo* drum; Toca Ogan on percussion; and Canhoto on snare drum.[10]

The modest debut of the band occurred at the Espaço Oásis in Olinda on June 1, 1991 (Teles n/d: 11).[11] Only friends showed up for the gig, but according to Teles, "all confessed that they were surprised with [the band's] unusual [musical] alchemy" (ibid.). The first printed article about Chico came out in the local Recife paper that day, advertising the event as the Black Planet party It was to feature DJs Renato L., Dr. Mabuse, and Chico spinning black sounds such as soul, reggae, hip-hop, jazz, *samba-reggae*, funk, Jamaican *toast* and *raggamuffin*, and a new genre performed by Loustal/Lamento Negro called *mangue*. At the time, Chico defined the latter genre as "a mixture of samba-reggae rap [sic] ragamuffin and embolada," the latter being a musical-poetic form of Northeast Brazil (article reproduced in Teles n/d: 2). Describing his musical outlook, Chico comments: "It is our responsibility to recover the rhythms of the region and add them together with a musical vision of the world" (ibid.). Indeed, due to Chico's interest in reclaiming an unsung Pernambucan musical heritage, the influence of the Bahian *samba-reggae* was left behind in the band's efforts to couple regional sounds such as *maracatu*, *côco*, *embolada*, and *ciranda*, with heavy metal, rap, *raggamuffin*, soul, funk, psychedelic rock, electronic dance music, and samplers.

What Is Mangue?

As evidenced by this early article, the term *"mangue"* appears to have been adopted initially by Chico to describe the fusion of various styles he discovered with Lamento Negro. According to fellow *mangue* pioneer Renato L.:

> Chico was the guy who brought this label, it was he who discovered this magic word. He took this magic word from the day-to-day and brought it to our collective. . . . The first time that I heard this word from Chico's mouth, he arrived at a bar table; he had come from a jam session with the Afro group called Lamento Negro, a percussion group. And he had mixed hip-hop and house beats with the percussion of Lamento Negro, Afro percussion. . . . He arrived telling [us the story]: "Look, I made a mixture, I took the bass drum from rap and I put it with the I-don't-know-what of Lamento Negro. And damn, I'm going to call this story *mangue*!" So everyone at the table, "Wow, *mangue*! This label is too much." (Interview: Lins 1998)

But even though this label ostensibly referred to a new genre, it is not clear that there was any one rhythm or stylistic hybrid that could be pinpointed as "*mangue*," especially if we consider the development of Nação Zumbi. The definition of *mangue* at the Black Planet performance, for instance, encompasses the Bahian *samba-reggae*; the mature incarnation of Nação Zumbi, however, does not, instead emphasizing Pernambucan rhythms such as *maracatu* together with various other local and global ingredients. In fact, the stylistic repertoire of the foremost *mangue* band is diverse, varying from song to song.

In its initial stage, then, *mangue* could be said to reference a kind of musical fusion. It may have originally been applied to one beat with Lamento Negro (although this is not entirely clear), but soon admitted a range of possible influences, becoming a catchy label for the stylistically diverse sound of Nação Zumbi. In a general sense, "*Mangue* was the term that Chico used to baptize the mixture that he made between the traditional—the *maracatu* and the *ciranda*, the *tambores* [drums]—and the electric guitar and the influence of [international] pop music that he absorbed" (Interview: Pires 1998).

But even if at the outset *mangue* was a label for the fusion music of CSNZ, other members of what would become the *mangue* movement positioned the term as being defined less by particular musical characteristics. As DJ-journalist Renato L. explains it:

> Originally, when this whole story began here in Recife at the beginning of the '90s, *mangue* was a label that we used for a type of cultural cooperative . . . that united some bands [particularly Nação Zumbi and Mundo Livre S/A], some plastic artists, some journalists, some unemployed. And the idea—the label *mangue* emerged because Recife is a city that is constructed on top of the *manguezais* [mangrove swamps]. Our idea at the time [in the early '90s] was to try to create a cultural scene here in Recife that was as rich and diversified as the *mangue* swamps, because the swamps are perhaps the ecosystem that has the greatest biodiversity of the planet. So the idea was to create a cultural scene . . . that had the same diversity. That wasn't tied down to a single rhythm, a single style, or single fashion. So we made use of that label [*mangue*], it fit well with this idea. . . . A bit motivated by the work . . . of the cooperative . . . a musical scene was born here in Recife. And the press began to label the whole scene "*mangue*." So today there is a certain confusion between *mangue*, this cooperative . . . in the beginning of the '90s and the *mangue* that the press and the people call this new scene of Recife. (Interview: Lins 1998)

In summary, *mangue* initially referred to a kind of musical fusion, then came to apply to a cultural cooperative featuring two distinct bands (CSNZ and Mundo Livre) and most recently has come to cover, in its widest sense, a highly diverse range of music. As Renato L. recognizes, it would have been too limiting to restrict *mangue* to only one band:

> But as there were other bands involved in the story, and as there were other people who wanted to do activities in other areas, we thought, Why not, instead of calling *mangue* only one beat, we enlarge it to this cultural cooperative and then enlarge it almost as if it were a utopia, understand? And from there add this concept of diversity, because it gives us complete liberty, it gives us a very large margin to maneuver. And everything can be *mangue*, understand? (Interview: Lins 1998)

Despite these intentions of the *mangue* cooperative, however, there is some disagreement among members of the scene with regard to how widely to apply the *mangue* label. Paulo André Pires is quite restrictive in his conception of the term:

And when one speaks of *mangue*, people think that it's the whole scene of the city, and it's not. *Mangue*, specifically speaking, is only two bands; it came out of the idea of two band heads: Fred Zero Quatro of Mundo Livre S/A and Chico of Chico Science & Nação Zumbi. (Interview: 1998)

Even Renato L., who like the movement's other originators stresses the diversity of *mangue*, concedes that there is "a certain confusion" between the original collective in the early '90s and the entire "new music scene" of the city. Exactly what this "confusion" is is not clear. Perhaps this statement reveals some ambivalence on the part of the movement's pioneers in allowing a label that originally applied only to their collective to be used more indiscriminately to apply to any new Recife band. Even if the movement was founded on diversity (first by uniting two bands and then by allowing *mangue* to encompass other projects), it makes sense that the originators would still want in some sense to retain some ownership of the term and its usage. However, this remains speculation.

The members of Recife's music scene do make distinctions between *mangue* and other musical projects.[12] At times such distinctions are based on a similarity (or discrepancy) of vision or concept; at other times these distinctions are more concretely musical. Some of my consultants see *mangue* as any kind of fusion between local and global elements, while others articulate which kinds of fusion this could be applied to. Some regard particular ingredients as being central, such as the *maracatu*, while others identify the ways in which the various local and global styles are combined in *mangue*, specifying proportions among these elements.[13]

Still, given the emphasis on diversity in the *mangue* manifesto and in comments by its creators, it would seem to contradict the basis of the movement's conceptual framework to define precisely the boundaries of a *"mangue"* music. Indeed, as Renato L. told me, what unifies *mangue* is, paradoxically, diversity (Interview: Lins 1998). *Mangue* is a movement that was founded on certain principles. Some of these include working as a collective, bringing together the various influences of members of a band or group, stylistic fusion, diversity, reclaiming regional Brazilian heritage while embracing global technology and culture, etc.

Nonetheless, perhaps partly a result of Chico's initial use of the word to mean a particular beat or genre, the Brazilian press began to talk of a *mangue beat*—which was, in fact, a corruption of an earlier name for the movement *mangue bit*, in reference to a computer bit. The story goes that upon hearing of the movement, journalists in the South of Brazil heard the word "bit" as "beat"—since the two words have the same pronunciation in Portuguese—leading them to call the movement *"mangue beat"* (Interview: Zé da Flauta 1998; Interview Tenório 1998). This, in turn, not surprisingly, has compelled many to believe erroneously that there is one particular musical genre or rhythm called *"mangue beat."*

Mundo Livre S/A (Free World Ltd.)

The *mangue* movement's emphasis on diversity is highlighted perhaps nowhere more clearly than in the linking of its two foundational bands. If CSNZ is one half of the *mangue* equation, then Mundo Livre S/A is the other; but the two bands have markedly different histories. While CSNZ was formed just prior to the appearance in the early 1990s of Recife's "new music scene," Mundo Livre dates back several years before the proliferation in 1987 of rock bands in the city. And while CSNZ has become nationally and internationally acclaimed and has recorded two CDs for a multinational record company (Sony Music), Mundo Livre, even today, remains very much a cult band, known and appreciated by a more select group of listeners in Recife and other cities.

CSNZ and Mundo Livre come from different areas of the city and represent different social class configurations. CSNZ was based in Rio Doce, a poorer suburb in the extreme north of the city on the periphery of Olinda, and it comprised people from a variety of backgrounds. The band included the very poor (and darker-skinned) drummers from Lamento Negro of Peixinhos (Toca Ogan, Gilmar Bola Oito, Gira, and Canhoto); Chico Science and Jorge du Peixe, who were lower middle class and of intermediate racial appearance (*mestiço*); and Lúcio Maia, the guitarist, who is light-skinned and slightly better off (Interview: Teles 1998). Mundo Livre, on the other hand, is based in the neighborhood of Candeias in the extreme south of the city. According to José Teles, Candeias is a rich neighborhood that, along with Piedade and Boa Viagem, boasts the highest per capita income of Northeast Brazil (ibid.). While the members of Mundo Livre may not have been rich, they were at least middle class and were socially and culturally shaped by the environment of a more upscale neighborhood (Interview: Teles 1998). The sociocultural environments of most of CSNZ's members were markedly different.[14]

One of the primary figures behind the *mangue* movement, Fred Zero Quatro is the frontman of Mundo Livre S/A.[15] Fred Rodrigues Montenegro was born on May 26, 1962 in Recife, and he obtained a communications degree from the Federal University of Pernambuco before entering the world of music. His pseudonym dates back to his University days when he and some friends had a newspaper. Fred wrote one story for this paper in which all of the characters had numbers instead of proper names; in keeping with this idea, Fred would sign his story "Zero Quatro" (04), which comes from the last two digits of his identification number. Some friends thought this was funny and began to call him "Zero Quatro."[16]

Fred Zero Quatro's First Bands and the Early Years of Mundo Livre S/A

Fred's teenage musical experiences involved all night gatherings on the beach in Candeias in which he and some friends would drink wine and play rock with an acoustic guitar and percussion. Before Mundo Livre, Fred participated in two or three bands. His first band, Trapaça (Swindle), was formed in 1982 and was a "post-punk" group whose name was inspired by the Sex Pistols film *The Great Rock 'N' Roll Swindle*. Zero Quatro's friend and neighbor, future *mangue* mover Renato L. (Renato Lins), had just come back from São Paulo around this time, and he introduced the punk culture from the periphery of São Paulo to the members of Trapaça. Fred recalls one particular compilation album called *Grito Suburbano* (Suburban Cry): "Everyone from Trapaça was impressed and such. We thought, 'How is it that these guys could make such a rotten, dirty sound in Brazil?'"

Later that same year Trapaça disbanded and was replaced by Serviço Sujo (Dirty Service). At the time, there was a nucleus of three or four bands of this type in the city. According to Fred, they were "people who hardly knew how to play anything and only wanted to go out and make some noise and scream something." This punk phase lasted only about a year because there was no space for this kind of music in Recife and the bands had nowhere to play.

At the end of 1983, Fred helped found Câmbio Negro H.C. (Black Market Hard-Core). But in the beginning of 1984, Fred quit Câmbio Negro and reunited the old members of Trapaça (which included Fred on guitar, Fred's brother Fábio on bass, Neguinho on drumset, and Avron on *guitarra baiana*) and founded Mundo Livre S/A (Free World Ltd.) in March, 1984.[17] That same month, Mundo Livre made its debut at a *chopparia* (a place that serves *chopp*, beer on tap) in Candeias called Bebe Tudo (Drink Everything). Fred describes the concept behind the band:

> The idea was to make a sound that was at the same time new wave but with many ingredients of the samba. So . . . another brother of mine was always at the show [and] we invited him to play *tamborim*, *agogô* [percussion instruments typical of samba]. We wanted to make a fusion, a bridge between Johnny Rotten [of the punk band, the Sex Pistols] and Jorge Ben [a pioneering Brazilian pop musician who fuses funk, soul, and samba] and Moreira da Silva [a samba musician from the 1930s and '40s], understand? . . . . It would be a type of new wave but very Brazilian, really very Brazilian, that would be identified neither as rock nor as MPB [an acronym for *Música Popular Brasileira*, "Brazilian Popular Music"].

Fred compares Mundo Livre with the 1980s boom in Brazilian rock:

> Brazil passed through a time in the '80s that on one hand had the resurgence of the *pagode* [a kind of roots samba[18]] but on the other hand had the boom in what was called "Brazilian rock." At the time, there was the success of the Paralamas [the Paralamas do Sucesso, or "Mudguards of Success", a very popular Brazilian rock band] . . . and then RPM and Legião Urbana [Urban Legion] [two other successful Brazilian rock groups], and so on. And we [Mundo Livre] didn't identify with anything from that; we wanted to make a sound that was more radical, more rotten, and at the same time more ambitious and such, using samba instruments, too, and such.[19]

The kind of equipment the band used—poor quality instruments made in the periphery and a microphone stand improvised with a broom handle—also fit into their concept. The band's leader explains: "The idea was to make the most avant-garde sound possible with the most low-tech equipment possible. And so this was part of the concept of the band, as how an avant-garde of the Third World would be." Curiously, Mundo Livre's initial punk-influenced outlook toward technology is markedly different from the more techno-informed music of Mundo Livre's most recent work, of Nação Zumbi's concept, and of the *mangue* project generally, which embraces high technology in its quest to revitalize the local culture.

Although the band had no intentions of becoming professional in the beginning, Mundo Livre slowly built a name for themselves. In 1984 they played at friends' houses in Candeias and at a theater at the Federal University of Pernambuco. But as Fred maintains, the public was restricted. The few times they tried to play for a larger rock public in bars, they were booed:

> Because at this time not even this story of the new wave from Rio had arrived here yet. So rock, the rock public in Recife in '84 was still those people who enjoyed Led Zeppelin, Deep Purple, AC/DC . . . singing in English. There were even some bands at the time already that sang rock covers in Boa Viagem [a wealthy Recife neighborhood by the beach] with all imported equipment and the guys singing everything in English. . . . And we would do a show, and I even think there's a tape with us trying to play and the people [chanting]: 'AC/DC, AC/DC, AC/DC!!!' They wanted us to play a song by [heavy metal band] AC/DC. It was really funny, and we would go there with a *guitarra baiana* and *tamborim*, I don't know what. Because of that we only had the option of playing more restricted places really.

Until 1987, Mundo Livre never played for more than fifty people. In 1987, the band began to play for larger audiences. Fred attributes this change to the "first movement here in Recife of new bands sort of influenced by this [aforementioned] boom of Rio and São Paulo Brazilian rock." At the time, in middle class schools in Recife, many young boys began to form bands in the hopes of becoming millionaires like RPM, Legião Urbana, and Paralamas do Sucesso. According to Fred,

> They thought it was very easy to start a band and become rich. Because really it was something that happened with frequency at the time in Rio, São Paulo. Any old band recorded something more commercial and various one-hit bands exploded overnight.

Fred maintains that Mundo Livre fit into this nucleus of school bands in Recife and thus got to play for a larger public. But people still did not identify with Mundo Livre's sound since most rock bands of the period were copies of the Police, the Smiths, New Order, or other U.S. or English bands that were in fashion. Nevertheless, Fred concedes that some bands of the time did identify with his group and even played Mundo Livre covers at their shows.

But regardless of musical orientation, all of these rock bands in Recife were at a disadvantage in the 1980s. Fred describes the lack of any kind of infrastructure for bands of the period:

> Until 1988 more or less, '89, Recife was a place that had no [music] circuit. There wasn't any place to record a good tape, there wasn't any place to buy good instruments, no place to play, there was nowhere to rehearse, there were no sound engineers, no music producers, no impresarios, nothing!

Despite grim prospects, the band held onto the slightest hope that someday they would get a break. According to Fred, the bleak economic situation in the 1980s in Recife (which had, and still has the highest levels of unemployment in Brazil) was stimulus enough to maintain a band that at least had some name. Indeed, the alternatives were even less desirable.

Fred Zero Quatro and Chico Science Meet: The Making of *Mangue*

In 1988, the radio station in which Fred Zero Quatro held a job changed its formatting to *brega* (a pejorative word for tacky, romantic pop). Taking this opportunity to go on a vacation, Fred put Mundo Livre on hiatus and went south to São Paulo to learn about that city's pop music circuit (Interview: Zero Quatro 1998). In 1989, Fred returned to Recife and met Chico Science, who was about to embark on some innovative musical journeys. Fred describes his initial reaction to Chico's music and how he identified with it:

> In 1989 I returned [to Recife] and that was when I met Chico Science. At the time he was still Francisco França and [in] '89 Chico was stirring up a certain hip-hop movement here in Recife and I met him through Renato [Fred's friend and neighbor, DJ-journalist Renato L.]. Renato had already done some great parties with him and such. And at the time [Chico] had a hip-hop band [apparently referring to Orla Orbe] and then came to form this band Loustal, with Lúcio, Jorge [du Peixe]—no, Jorge was not yet in the band. Loustal was Lúcio [on guitar], Dengue—the bassist who is still with Nação Zumbi—and a drumset player named Vinícius. And when I saw Loustal's show for the first time, I thought, damn, I really identified [with them]. It had a lot in common with the sound of Mundo Livre because it was rock, there was an electric guitarist there and such, but the drummer was already adding heavy doses of *frevo, ciranda* [two popular regional folk styles]. And we [Mundo Livre] had this history with the samba, an idea from a long time ago and such. So I perceived that there was a possibility for the first time for a more cohesive scene to happen. (Interview: Zero Quatro 1998)

Fred goes on to describe how the geographic gap between his and Chico's band (first Loustal and then Nação Zumbi) was a useful condition for the forging of a citywide movement:

> Not to mention that they were from the extreme north of the city—they were from Rio Doce, Olinda—and we were from the extreme south, Candeias. So as such it's possible to form a certain circuit, to enlarge the public and such. And we even realized that, as there was this geographic distance, if we did shows collectively, produced shows of the two bands, uniting the audience of one band with that of the other, we could increase our public. And so since 1989 there was a desire to create a scene in the city, a movement. (Interview: Zero Quatro 1998)

Although at first many people did not understand the radical sounds of Nação Zumbi, Fred and his group of friends were immediately convinced of its huge potential, both in and outside of Recife. As Fred recalls:

> And with the passing of time, Chico met Gilmar, who was from Lamento Negro, and then there was this whole story of him doing rehearsals together with Lamento Negro, and that was when Chico Science & Lamento Negro was born. And from there, it was set! That was when we—Renato, Mabuse [a young computer genius involved in *mangue*], Hélder—the guys who were always together, helping things here in the city. We went to see this first experience of Loustal with Lamento Negro. We thought, damn! It was what was lacking to really give an *envenenada* [lit., a poisoning; fig., a corruption; here it means a big boost or injection] to the Recife scene. So we perceived also that there was a great potential of [this thing] exploding outside of Recife. I already knew how the São Paulo circuit functioned and such. (Interview: Zero Quatro 1998)

From the beginnings of the movement, the concept of the *mangue* served as both the local geographical setting on which the members of CSNZ literally lived and as a symbol for cultural and musical diversity that Recife could show Brazil and the world. As Fred Zero Quatro explains:

> So there was this story that Chico was from . . . Rio Doce, the people of Lamento Negro were from Peixinhos. It's that the whole area is in mud, the land of *mangue* and such. And when Chico went to do the promotion of a party, of a show, he would say, "It's going to be the greatest *lama* [mud], the greatest *mangue* [swamp]" and such. So this thing was created. Renato and I would meet with Chico and call him *"mangueboy"*. . . . [The sound of CSNZ] was a great musical formula, it was a great musical synthesis, very cool and irresistible, but it also had to be very well accessed so as not to come out of here as a thing, a band from Recife, something exotic like that. Because, damn, [it was] perfect to construct from there a scene based on diversity, because Recife has much diversity and such. And the thing would have much more weight united with Mundo Livre, because Mundo Livre has a totally different history, messing more with samba, to show that Recife really is something, that there

was a scene that even had a much bigger potential than something restricted just to Chico Science and such. And we knew there really was all this potential here in Recife. (Interview: Zero Quatro 1998)

Beginning in 1991, shows began to appear with the *mangue* label: "Viagem Ao Centro Do Mangue" (Journey to the Center of the *Mangue*) and "Mangue Feliz" (Merry *Mangue*, which was a play on Natal Feliz, or Merry Christmas) (Interview: Zero Quatro 1998). The *mangue* public began to grow, and, according to Fred, "everything was contributed spontaneously in the city to create a complex scene" (ibid.).

The Beginnings of a "New Music Scene"

Not to be confused with the entire music scene which it helped spawn—and of which it is a fundamental part—*mangue* (that is, the work and ideas of Chico Science and Fred Zero Quatro) appeared along with other bands and musicians in Recife in the early 1990s. Some of these bands derived from Recife's already extant rock scene, which was in place since 1987; others were developing concurrent projects integrating local and global influences; and others still were directly inspired by CSNZ. Paulo André Pires, who opened his record store, Rock Xpress, in December 1989 and began to involve himself in local music production "has accompanied, perhaps more than anyone, the evolution of this scene" (Interview: Pires 1998). Recalling its origins, Paulo André asserts that,

> At that time . . . in '90, '91 the pop scene of the city practically didn't exist. There existed a more underground scene of thrash and hard-core bands, and punk rock, too. The Devótos do Ódio [The Devotees of Hate, one of the most important bands on the current Recife scene], for example, dates back to this time. . . . Every little party, every little show, I would go. And sometimes it was even restricting because there were thirty people to see [the show]. So the majority of these shows lost money, the ticket counters didn't pay the costs of mounting a sound system. Because, as there weren't any bars that had their own sound systems—with the exception of Soparia [in the neighborhood of Pina, which in 1998 was still *the* spot for Recife's music scene], because all the bands passed through Soparia—the space was very limited like this, very limited (Interview: Pires 1998)

Suffering from its own insularity, this nascent scene began to benefit from the arrival in Recife of some new media, such as MTV at the end of 1991 and São Paulo's Rádio Rock, one of the biggest rock stations in Brazil, in 1992 (Interview: Pires 1998).

MTV brought information to the local bands and enabled them to see what was happening in other parts of the country; this was particularly crucial for Recife, which remains outside the country's circuit of international shows (Interview: Pires 1998). Rádio Rock, for its part, gave hope to the bands of playing some place. Because the local radio stations, in the great majority, ignored this music that is produced here. There were never great spaces for this music in its own state. (Interview: Pires 1998)

In time, this burgeoning music scene did garner more space, opportunities, and recognition, due in large measure to the launch of a vital new movement—*mangue*—which brought a fresh perspective on the sociocultural needs of the city. By confronting Recife's miserable socioeconomic conditions (which, among other things, prohibited the existence of a fully operational music scene), the lack of innovation on the pop music front, and the utter marginalization of the city's *cultura popular*, the *mangue* initiative has enabled a subcultural component of Recife and the nation both to feel pride in its local traditions and to re-engage fully in modern (or postmodern) global cultural discourse in Brazil's post-dictatorship era.

The *Manifesto Mangue*

As the modest beginnings of a new music scene were emerging in Recife, Francisco França (baptized by Renato L. with the pseudonym "Science" for Chico's predilection for mixing with the alchemy of sounds), Fred Zero Quatro, and Renato L. came out with the *Manifesto Mangue*, entitled *Caranguejos Com Cérebro* (Crabs With Brains). (See Appendix 1 for a full translation of the manifesto.) Written by Fred Zero Quatro (a journalist by trade) and distributed to the press in 1991, the manifesto consists of three parts (reproduced in Teles n/d: 5-6; see Appendix 1).

"Mangue - the Concept" discusses Recife's *manguezais*, swamps of tropical and subtropical plants that, as one of the most productive ecosystems in the world, are taken by scientists to be "symbols of fertility, diversity and richness." "Manguetown - The City" points to the pernicious effects of Recife's modern growth as metropolis of the Northeast: economic stagnation, destruction of the *manguezais*, the worst unemployment in the country, a population over fifty percent of which live in slum conditions, and the distinction of being classified as the fourth worst city in the world to live in, according to a Washington D.C. institute of population studies. "Mangue - The Scene" suggests that the solution to this condition is to "inject a little energy in the mud and stimulate what fertility still remains in the veins of Recife." Calling themselves a "nucleus of pop ideas," the *mangueboys* aimed to "engender an 'energetic circuit' capable of connecting allegorically the good vibrations of the *mangue* [swamps] with the world network of the circulation of pop concepts." Their symbol is a parabolic antenna sunk in the *lama* (mud) of Recife, picking up signals from around the world, or a *caranguejo* (crab) remixing the album *Ánthena* by the Euro-tech group Kraftwerk on the computer.

The Consolidation of Recife's "New Music Scene"

With the launch of *mangue*, various other pop bands appeared and began to play small shows in venues such as Soparia in the Pina neighborhood and at small parties (Interview: Pires 1998). According to Paulo André Pires, these events "didn't attract more than two hundred people; it was very much an alternative thing" (ibid.). At the end of 1992, the aforementioned Rádio Rock went off the air, leaving "zero space for the Pernambucan bands"; but there was no way to reverse the momentum of Recife's "new music scene," which kept developing and attracting more attention (Interview: Pires 1998). For instance, at the end of 1992, after hearing of the *manifesto mangue*, MTV came to Recife and sought out Chico and Fred; the subsequent footage was broadcast on the Brazilian MTV channel during the Hollywood Rock festival in January 1993 (Interview: Zero Quatro 1998). During the intervals of Nirvana playing in Rio, snippets of this material from Recife were shown, causing a stir in São Paulo (ibid.).

Paulo André Pires traces the consolidation of Recife's "new music scene," culminating with his creation of the Abril Pro Rock (April For Rock) festival, now one of the scene's annual highlights and touted as the largest showcase for young bands in Brazil:

> Around twenty to thirty pop bands had come up in the city, making music and trying to record an album. And as I had this record shop [Rock Xpress], I think that I was one of the few people who, not being from a band, managed to visualize this space that was to come, through the originality of these bands. And I decided to bring together in a festival twelve local bands, all without a record company, and I think only one with a record, which was vinyl at that time. And ironically, the bands that at the time played on Rádio Rock today don't exist anymore, because they were bands with more of a pop sound, less experimental than Chico, Mundo Livre.

Paulo André describes the inclusion in his festival of Nação Pernambuco, a pioneering folkloric troupe in Recife's "new music scene":

> So, parallel to the bands . . . the Maracatu Nação Pernambuco [the Pernambuco Nation Maracatu, a folkloric *maracatu* band] began a project to make a more roots music, which was drums and voices, without keyboards, without guitar, and began to bring together in Olinda every Sunday thousands of young people to hear *maracatu*. And I was impressed with the quantity of people that went to hear *maracatu*, young people. And I think that there, at that time, a recapturing of the valorization of Pernambucan rhythms began to awaken in the young people of the city. People began to open their ears to what was being produced. . . . [So] I called the Maracatu for the first Abril Pro Rock, recognizing that they, too, were responsible for all this valorization of Pernambucan music. I called a VJ [video jockey] from MTV to be the host of the festival [together with] a music critic named Carlos Eduardo Miranda, who at the time wrote for ShowBizz, which at the time was Bizz, which became ShowBizz, which is the

only pop music magazine in Brazil. Today there are others, but at the time it was one of the only ones. Today, you have others.

Paulo André explains how the first Abril Pro Rock was a landmark event in Pernambucan music and a catalyst for the emergence of CSNZ and Mundo Livre S/A:

> So, from that [first] Abril Pro Rock [1993], things began to happen. We managed to unite a public of 1,500 people to see only local bands, which was a public that until then hadn't been brought together. And a music critic from here named José Teles, who had accompanied the whole music scene of the '70s here also, he said that since the 1970s, that nothing so important for Pernambucan music had happened in Recife. He considered Abril Pro Rock one of the most important [things] in recent years. Soon after, Chico Science & Nação Zumbi and Mundo Livre S/A made their first trip to São Paulo and Belo Horizonte [capital of the state of Minas Gerais] to do shows. And consequently, Chico was contracted by Sony Music and Mundo Livre by the Banguela label, which at the time was of the band Titãs ["The Titans," a popular rock band from the '80s]. And Eduardo Miranda, that critic from the magazine, was to be the producer of the label and he produced Mundo Livre S/A's first record because of this connection. Already at the second Abril Pro Rock, Chico was the principal attraction one day and a name act—Gabriel o Pensador ["Gabriel the Thinker," a popular Brazilian rapper] of Rio de Janeiro—the other. The festival went to two days. (Interview: Pires 1998)

Mangue to the World

In 1994, both CSNZ and Mundo Livre S/A had their debut CDs released. The title of Mundo Livre's album, *Samba Esquema Noise* (Noise Samba Scheme), is a play on an album by MPB star Jorge Ben (now known as Jorge Benjor), called *Samba Esquema Novo* (New Samba Scheme). Jorge Benjor is a pioneering Brazilian pop musician who fused samba with North American soul and funk, and he is one of Fred Zero Quatro's foremost influences. Mundo Livre took the samba-soul-funk sounds of Benjor and adapted it to the raucous strains of punk and new wave music, hence "Noise Samba Scheme." CSNZ's debut, *Da Lama Ao Caos* (From Mud To Chaos), on the other hand, is a volatile mixture of regional Pernambucan rhythms and styles—such as *maracatu, ciranda, côco, and embolada*—with heavy rock guitar and funk grooves, among other influences. Paulo André Pires assesses the impact of the band in the beginning:

> Until that time in Brazil there didn't exist a rock band with [Afro-Brazilian] drums [the *bombo* drums of the *maracatu* style] in its formation. And a lot of people thought it was strange in the beginning. (Interview: Pires 1998)

This initial shock that Chico caused is confirmed by current drumset player for NZ, Pupillo, who told me: "[CSNZ] caused a very big scare . . . because no one understood and thought at the same time it was an absurdity, the sound that he was making, something completely different and such" (Interview: Pupillo 1998). But, despite this initial shock on the part of some listeners—including prominent local musicians—the Brazilian press recognized the importance of *mangue* from the beginning (Interview: Pires 1998). The biggest difficulty according to CSNZ's impresario was in booking gigs since "no Recife band even today from the '90s was heavily played on the radio" (ibid.). Pires maintains that of these bands, CSNZ had the most visibility because Sony got two of their songs ("A Praieira" and "A Cidade") onto two *novelas* (Brazilian soap operas) of the Rede Globo, the biggest national television network (ibid.). Even though the *novelas* are watched at night by the great majority of the Brazilian population, and hence have a strong cultural impact (ibid.), radio is still the primary vehicle for gaining entry into a music circuit. Beyond this, several of the most prominent Recife bands, including Nação Zumbi, have had to move to Rio or São Paulo to have a chance at performing outside of their home state.

With the release of their CD, Chico and band embarked on their first international tour in five European countries and in the U.S., where they opened up for Gilberto Gil at the 1995 SummerStage Festival in New York's Central Park. Back home in 1995, CSNZ was the biggest draw for that year's Abril Pro Rock Festival, which had been expanded to four nights with a total of eight thousand ticket buyers (Abramo 1997: 76). Meanwhile, *mangue* and the "new music scene" began to expand. In addition to the aforementioned Soparia bar/restaurant, which had become the "in" spot for local bands, Moritzstadt (named after the colonial Pernambucan Dutch leader Maurice who advocated cultural liberty) became another important locale in Recife's downtown. In its heyday, Moritzstadt featured two to three *mangue* shows per night for twenty to 500 people, as well as DJs who would play jazz, R&B, hip-hop, punk, and *mangue* (Interview: Filho 1998).

Since early 1995, the "Minster of Information" of the movement, Renato L., has led a radio program on Rádio Caetés FM in Recife called "Mangue Beat," which is still heard from 8-9 p.m. every Monday through Friday. Renato explained to me the role of this program on the scene:

> This was the first program in Recife to provide a space for the bands of the so-called "new scene of Recife". . . . Recife had—still has—a very interesting musical scene, but this scene didn't have a space on the radio. And "Mangue Beat" emerged with this objective: to provide space for the music of the bands and also to bring here to the city a type of information that doesn't generally circulate in the mass media. For example, we play African music, we play Arabic music, we can also play some more avant-garde electronic music trend that doesn't have space in the big stations, this type of thing. (Interview: Lins 1998).

In 1995, *mangue* also appeared in cyberspace: the site MangueBit launched the movement's manifesto on the Internet. Since then, various other web sites have emerged based on *mangue* and the Recife scene, including Manguetronic, an Internet radio program by Renato L. (See Discography for a list of Internet addresses.)

The year 1996 saw the release of CSNZ's even more exploratory, critically acclaimed second CD, *Afrociberdelia*, another European tour, and a notable appearance, along with fellow Pernambucans Mundo Livre and the Banda de Pífanos Dois Irmãos de Caruaru (a drum and fife band from the interior of Pernambuco), in Brooklyn's Prospect Park as part of New York City's Brazilian Music Festival. CSNZ was also one of the national attractions that year at the Hollywood Rock festival in Rio. In the area of cinema, the Pernambucan film *Baile Perfumado* by Paulo Caldas and Lírio Ferreira, which was the winner of the Festival de Brasília in 1996, has a soundtrack by Chico Science, Fred Zero Quatro, and Siba of the band Mestre Ambrósio. By 1996, CSNZ had conquered a niche in the fickle Brazilian pop music circuit while gaining critical acclaim and audiences throughout Brazil and the world. Indeed, having participated at some of Europe and the U.S.A.'s most prestigious music festivals (including Central Park SummerStage, Montreux Jazz Festival, and the Sphinx Festival in Belgium), the band had brought *mangue* to the world, or at least the "First World."

The Recife Scene Loses Its "Greatest Exponent"

Early in 1997 CSNZ played their last show for the Recife public at the Clube Portugûes. Then, on February 2, while driving his Fiat Uno from Recife to Olinda, Chico Science hit a pole and died almost instantly, leaving a vacuum not only for friends and family, but also for Brazilian music.[20] In tribute, the next day, the Carnival *bloco* Na Pancada do Ganzá ("In the Stroke of the *Ganzá*," fronted by Pernambucan musician Antônio Nóbrega) marched along Boa Viagem Avenue in silence (Teles n/d: 45).[21] The news of Chico's death quickly reached the national media. According to local DJ and former owner of the club Moritzstadt, José Antônio de Souza Leão Filho, it was news of Chico's death on television that forced the country to recognize what it had lost. Before his death, the band would play for about 1,000-1,500 people, with an audience formed from Recife's poor and middle class. But after the massive media coverage of Chico's passing, José asserts, "the rich people recognized and started to like him" (Interview: Filho 1998). According to Chico's father, whom I also interviewed, his son's popularity tripled after death (Interview: Francisco França 1998).

Indeed, even in death, Chico remains a guiding spirit of Recife's music scene. Many bands on the Recife scene these days either copy Chico's concept or are directly or indirectly indebted to his influence. Youths who attend shows dress in Chico Science t-shirts and some wear the straw fisherman hat and cool sunglasses he made popular. All around Recife, graffiti art pays respect to him. The use of baseball caps, certain expressions (such as *figue antenado*, or "stay connected," borrowed from the antenna symbol), and the formation of one's hands into the shape of crab claws are all part of a fascinating youth subculture in Recife that comes from its swamp movement. Plastic artists and designers have claimed to create *mangue* styles, and "Zambo," the first dance theater piece inspired by the *mangue* movement, was debuted in Recife in early 1998.

Pupillo believes Chico's greatest contribution was the fact that as a humble guy from the periphery of the city he did things that someone with more money could not have done. As both Pupillo and Renato L. told me, Chico assumed his "Brazilianness" and his "Pernambucanness" in the wake of an era, the 1980s, in which local rock or pop bands mostly copied what came from abroad (Interview: Pupillo 1998; Interview: Lins 1998).

Meanwhile, despite the loss of its foremost musician, Recife's current music scene continues to evolve, gaining more and more attention outside of Recife In 1997, for example, the Pernambucans Mestre Ambrósio, Cascabulho, the Banda de Pífanos Dois Irmãos de Caruaru, and Lenine with percussionist Marcos Suzano participated in an expanded five day Brazilian Music Festival in New York City at Central Park's SummerStage; the entire festival, filmed and edited by HBO Brazil into a special program and later rebroadcast on the U.S. Public Broadcasting System television network, was dedicated to Chico Science.

The next chapter assesses *mangue*'s place and importance in the history of Brazilian popular music, touching on some of the similarities and differences it has with the national rock boom of the 1980s, *tropicália*, and prior Pernambucan tendencies that also actively fused local and global influences.

Chapter Three

Mangue in the Context of Brazilian Pop Music History
A Comparison with Other Movements

Introduction

The *mangue* movement manifesto *Caranguejos Com Cérebro* (Crabs With Brains) speaks of an "energetic circuit" linking local and global traits and ideas. Such a circuit has, in one form or another, been extant in Brazilian popular music ever since its inception. Thus, not surprisingly, *mangue* shares much with other Brazilian pop music trends before it, but it is also unique in some respects. This chapter examines three of the most important precedents for *mangue*, beginning with the internationally renowned *tropicália* movement, followed by artists and trends specifically in Pernambuco that predate the emergence of *mangue*, and culminating with the 1980s boom in Brazilian rock. I briefly compare each of these with *mangue*, attempting to arrive at a notion of *mangue*'s place within the history of Brazilian pop music.

Tropicália

The *tropicália* or *tropicalismo* (tropicalism) movement of the late 1960s is particularly germane for a comparison with *mangue* because it represents a pioneering juncture in the history of Brazilian popular music—one which took into account for the first time, and ironically juxtaposed, the range of music that Brazil had "digested" up until that point in its musical bowels. As *tropicália* pioneer Caetano Veloso explains:

> We were using lots of rock 'n' roll type electric guitar with Brazilian melodic styles and quotations from tangos and the Afro-Bahian thing. And a posture of being in the world, not like a Third World country that keeps being towed along behind what happens in the developed countries. (Dunn 1992)[1]

Indeed, *tropicália*, as bossa nova before it, was not destined to be a movement that lagged behind pop music of North America or Europe; instead, it radically reshaped music-making in Brazil and has come to serve as a particularly sophisticated example of cross-cultural syncretism for attuned Western listeners.[2] Ironically, a movement that at the time (1967-68) thrust Brazilian music firmly into the modern world—chiefly by assimilating the new global pop and rock 'n' roll originating in the U.S. and England and fusing this with local styles among other influences—is in the 1990s being rediscovered as hip by U.S. fans, critics, and musicians (see Ratliff 1998, Harvey 2001). The latter have included Beck, the late Kurt Cobain, and other revered underground bands of the moment (see Ratliff 1998). Such interest is being attended to by the re-release of several important *tropicália*-era albums on CD, which reportedly are currently being sold in the thousands in the U.S. (ibid.). As *New York Times* critic Ben Ratliff notes in a 1998 article, "In a recent trip I took to Chicago, it seemed that all the musicians and critics wanted to talk about Tropicália" (ibid.). In assessing the myriad influences of Caetano Veloso's song "Baby," the writer asks,

> Is all this worship of Americanness fake kitsch or the real thing? It's a double score of beauty and irony that even Beck hasn't topped. This is as modern as pop gets. . . . Despite a few dated psychedelic touches, this music sounds current; it can be appreciated with the same ears that understand the collage mentality of 'Pet Sounds,' De La Soul, the Beastie Boys or Beck. We knew something like this must have existed but had no idea it would be so perfect (ibid.).

My point here is not to validate *tropicália* by appealing to its acceptance by North American critics, but rather to underline that as it spreads out to the world, embracing its influence, modern Brazilian pop music has in turn influenced the world. *Mangue* is latest in line of a string of Brazilian tendencies aimed at participating in a global network of music-making in which musicians create new hybrid identities by negotiating a complex array of local and global cultural influences in innovative amalgams. CSNZ, a band that, among other of its accomplishments, has helped recast Brazil irrevocably into modern pop culture, has received similar praise by U.S. critics, serving as an exemplary comment on this global cultural collision for a new era.

Although *tropicália* was a short-lived musical phenomenon (from 1967 to the end of '68, during which time it affected visual art, poetry, architecture, and drama), it established a precedent for the active and experimental assimilation of diverse regional, national, and foreign sources in Brazil's music. As such, *tropicália* functioned as an artistically liberating reference point for all Brazilian pop musicians who followed in its wake. Paulo André Pires maintains that there was no direct influence of *tropicália* on *mangue* (Interview: 1998). Yet the fact that a figure like Chico Science could so naturally locate himself within a hazy nexus of local and global idioms without having to align himself exclusively with any one of them is not simply indicative of a very recent postmodern aesthetic so fashionable in '90s pop; it should also be regarded as the outgrowth of a thirty-year-old tradition that began with *tropicália*.

MPB

Tropicália is subsumed under the broad category of music known as "*Música Popular Brasileira*" (Brazilian Popular Music), or just MPB. The acronym MPB came into common usage in the late 1960s in Brazil to apply to any "original composition rooted in or derived from Brazilian traditions, usually with acoustic instrumentation"; this was contrasted with international pop music and rock 'n' roll in the early '60s style, exemplified by the Beatles, which employed electric instruments (Perrone 1989: x). This original distinction became blurred in the 1970s, however, as composers readily adapted and assimilated international trends (ibid.). Today, MPB is generally applied to an eclectic cohort of popular musicians and composers that made its mark in the late 1960s (Perrone 1989: x); many of these artists have remained remarkably vital. Since then, several new generations of MPB have emerged. Drawing from a wealth of local and global influences, MPB is not tied to any particular genre, and it often defies easy categorization (McGowan and Pessanha 1998: 75). MPB compositions range from "stylizations of simple folk tunes to avant-garde sound collages. . . . Song is used to address social issues, to voice protest of authoritarian control, to make aesthetic statements, and to explore philosophical and spiritual themes." (Perrone 1989: x).

A Brief Synopsis of Tropicália

One of the most controversial developments within MPB of the 1960s (Perrone 1989: xxxii), *tropicália* was launched in São Paulo in 1967 by Bahian musicians Caetano Veloso and Gilberto Gil in the context of the nationally televised, competitive popular music festivals.[3] The festivals had become vehicles for a passionate national debate over politics and aesthetic issues. The country had been under a harsh military dictatorship since 1964, and popular music was subject to strict government censorship. Enamored of Brazil's "quiet revolutionary of the '50s," bossa nova pioneer João Gilberto, the *tropicalistas* found themselves "caught in the contradictory currents in the music of the day" (Dunn 1992). By the mid-'60s, bossa nova had fallen out of favor with young Brazilians, who saw it as failing to speak to the new sociopolitical conditions of the country. Nationalistic left-wing students saw their voice in domestic protest song, while a less politically-minded urban youth enjoyed and cultivated their own version of 1960s rock 'n' roll, known in Brazil as *iê-iê-iê* (from the Beatles' "yeah, yeah, yeah") (ibid.). This imitation of English and North American rock was represented by the *Jovem Guarda* (Young Guard) of Roberto Carlos and Erasmo Carlos and was criticized by the nationalistic left, which regarded it as a symbol of American colonialism (McGowan and Pessanha 1998: 83-84; 187).

Meanwhile, Veloso, Gil, and the *tropicalistas* borrowed from everywhere, both in and outside the country (Dunn 1992). They challenged the views of the urban left by

> [proposing] creative openness and critical revision of Brazilian popular music in general. . . . [Brazilian rock of the *Jovem Guarda* was not rejected but incorporated] into a flexible framework that included pop music, traditional samba and Bossa Nova, protest and sentimentality, kitsch and avant-garde poetry, folklore and modern technology. (Perrone 1989: xxxii)

According to Caetano Veloso, the *tropicalistas* were "aggressively nationalistic" as opposed to the "defensive nationalism" of the protest singers (Dunn 1992).

Two years before the launch of *tropicália*, Veloso and Gil, both from Bahia, moved to São Paulo, where they encountered a thriving artistic community and met up with the brothers Augusto and Haroldo de Campos. The two writers served as intellectual mentors of the movement, introducing the young Bahians to the work of modernist concrete poet Oswald de Andrade. In particular, Veloso and Gil were inspired by Andrade's 1928 *Manifesto Antropófago* ("Cannibalistic Manifesto"), which advocated a kind of cultural cannibalism. According to Haroldo de Campos, this work proposed "critical assimilation of foreign experience and its re-elaboration in national terms and circumstances, allegorizing, in this sense, the cannibalism of our savages" (quoted in Perrone 1989: 54). In other words, this meant "you swallow everything from everywhere and digest it however you like" (Dunn 1992). *Tropicália*'s representative songs embodied this "aggressively nationalistic" imperative in an artistically sophisticated manner, fusing rock, samba, bossa nova, pop kitsch, concrete poetry, Brazilian folk musics, and classical arrangements in striking combinations.

On the musical front, *tropicália* marks the first time in Brazil that rock 'n' roll was mixed with domestic styles of music, among other influences (McGowan and Pessanha 1998: 84), filling a gap and forging a union between supposedly irreconcilable kinds of music. As Recife music producer Zé da Flauta remembers:

> I think *tropicália* was very important because it was a movement that managed to show Brazilians that it was possible for us to mix each influence that we were receiving from American music with Brazilian poetry. When I heard Caetano Veloso sing [mimics opening electric guitar line to Veloso's 1967 song "Alegria, Alegria"], [I thought] "You can!" (Interview: Zé da Flauta 1998)

In a general sense, the movement helped break down ideological barriers while contending with the contradictory juxtaposition in Brazil of the archaic and the modern, the regional and the universal. The movement embodied the shock that the Bahian musicians felt when they encountered the modern metropolis of

São Paulo, and their songs simultaneously celebrated and parodied modern Brazil (Dunn 1992):

> Overhead the airplanes
> Below the trucks
> Against the wide plateau appears
> My nose
> I organize the movement
> I orient the carnival
> I inaugurate the monument
> Upon the central plateau of the country
> Long live the bossa-sa-sa
> Long live thatched huts (palhoça-ça-ça).[4]

Ill-understood by the audiences of the music festivals, and criticized by a culturally nationalistic left, *tropicália* eventually met its demise from political repression of the military regime: In late 1968 both Veloso and Gil were arrested and then compelled to voluntary exile in England for two years. By the early 1970s, however, the ideas espoused in the movement were openly accepted, "greatly accelerating MPB's musical experimentation and hybridization" (McGowan and Pessanha 1998: 86).

Tropicália and Mangue

The idea and practice of "anthropophagy," or cultural cannibalism in MPB, which is applicable to post-'60s Brazilian pop in general, can be traced back to the *tropicalistas*. Indeed, the past thirty years, as well as the future, of pop music history in the country has been irrevocably impacted by *tropicália* for its manner of gobbling up all sorts of influences and spitting them out as something new, different, and—despite resistance by some cultural conservatives—embraced as decidedly Brazilian.

At the same time, *tropicália*, as bossa nova in the late 1950s, embodied both a sense of participation in the modern world on a more equal footing and a desire to tap into a more universal expression (see Béhague 1973). The proposed aim of *tropicália*, excerpted below from various publications, foreshadows the objectives and even some of the terminology of *mangue*:

> The present state of development of our music and the discrimination which the nationalists have proposed would confine us to a role as suppliers of raw material for other countries. It was the bossa nova that ended all this by creating something which, for the first time, Brazil could export. *Tropicalism* is an attempt to unite all possible combinations of elements. It is also called *som universal* [universal sound] because it unites the most recent international accomplishments (Beatles, Jimi Hendrix, the second rock generation). But it also includes choro, Noel Rosa and música caipira (rural music). (Quoted in Schreiner 1993: 166-67)[5]

Like *tropicália* before it, *mangue*, too, sought a "universal" sound that results from a diverse combination of elements—a sound that fuses the most modern genres and influences from abroad with regional and national musical traditions. Compare the preceding with this quote from Nação Zumbi's Pupillo:

> I think that—speaking more directly about Nação Zumbi—I think that this reference that Nação Zumbi has a new sound is precisely this: the union of all the elements. For you to create something new, you have to influence yourself. This prejudice is ending, this thing of metal head is metal head, funk is funk. There came a time when there wasn't anything new anymore. (Interview: 1998)

Indeed, both movements responded to what were perceived as closed-minded attitudes about musical boundaries and identity. *Tropicália* emerged at a time in which there was a sharp division between "domestic" and "foreign" musics; in response, it opened the way for a much freer interaction between these camps and, in the process, made the subsequent boundaries of what could be considered national music more flexible.[6] *Mangue* came almost thirty years later with both "new" domestic (specifically regional) and foreign influences, in effect updating and reinvigorating, in the same anthropophagous manner as *tropicália*, an MPB which some critics saw as stagnated.

Clearly, *mangue* owes a large debt to *tropicália* and subsequent developments in MPB; but *tropicalistas* Caetano Veloso and Gilberto Gil also recognize in *mangue* a sibling musical movement. For his part, Gil has visibly associated himself with the movement, performing several times with CSNZ (including at Central Park's SummerStage) and appearing as a guest vocalist on the song "Macô" (*macô* is short for *maconha*, or marijuana) from the band's second CD, *Afrociberdélia*. Caetano, too, has lauded the work of Chico Science. According to Paulo André Pires:

> One time Caetano Veloso said that what Chico did is what he [Caetano] always wanted to do but didn't think he was competent to do and that he waited for a Pernambucan to do it, which was to use the *maracatu*, which is Pernambucan, and put this inside the universe of pop music. (Interview: Pires 1998)

Both Caetano and Gil include songs on their latest CDs clearly influenced by *mangue* and the renewed interest in the 1990s in Pernambucan themes and rhythms.[7]

What, then, can be regarded as the critical differences between *tropicália* and *mangue*? According to Renato L., the two movements are characterized by contrasting relations to foreign and domestic musics:

> It's funny because while the people of *tropicalismo* went from Brazilian Popular Music [both Veloso and Gil began their careers playing in a bossa nova style] to approach international pop, which for me this is a type of—if you live

> in a country of the South, of the Third World, or whatever label you want to use, it's a relation that's always present. You're always—*you have to dialogue* with what comes from outside because there's a series of [slight pause] even impositions. But the people of *tropicalismo*, they went from Brazilian Popular Music to dialogue with rock of the '60s, for example. But in the case of Nação Zumbi and of Mundo Livre, I think that the contrary occurred. Of course it was part of Chico's day to day life to listen to the *maracatu* in Carnival, but it's like this, for me, in my opinion, the primordial reason that led him in the beginning of the '90s to re-approach the *maracatu* is the passion that he has for the *groove*, the passion that he has for the *groove* as a big fan of rap, as a b-boy [from "break boy," referring to a break dancer], a boy that grew up listening to rap, was a part of rap groups with dancers, graffiti, understand? So, like this, he approached the *maracatu* not with an exclusive preoccupation to preserve a root—a folk culture. But instead, primarily because he was a guy fascinated and impassioned by the *groove*, understand? And the *maracatu* has a fascinating *groove*. . . . (Interview: Lins 1998)

In fact, Chico Science has said that the use of local rhythms within a base of high-tech international pop is a way for these rhythms and this local culture to receive more exposure and to be understood in a global context (Interview by Marty Lipp: Chico Science and Paulo André Pires n/d). Chico may not have wanted to preserve the local folk culture in a rigid way, but he certainly seemed intent on widening its appreciation, precisely through its incorporation into international pop. I would not say that *tropicália* was as explicitly concerned with revitalizing and exposing Brazilian regional culture.

Renato elaborates on this distinction between *mangue* and *tropicália*:

> The *tropicalistas*, they were guys who had a background in Brazilian Popular Music, understand? So they went from Brazilian Popular Music and sought to interact with psychedelic rock of the '60s, that whole thing, while Nação Zumbi and Mundo Livre, I think that they kind of made the opposite path: They went from funk or rap—or in the case of Mundo Livre, because Fred was very much influenced by new wave, that new wave, English punk, '76, Clash or Patty Smith or David Bowie and such—they went from that and came—[says quickly and somewhat dismissively] of course when he was a kid he liked the samba of Jorge Ben and such. But I think that there's that type of passion that you have at fourteen, fifteen, sixteen that really marks you, right? And it was this sound that they listened to—in this case what Fred listened to at the time when he was a teenager—and Chico listened to funk, James Brown, the beginning of rap: Kurtis Blow and such. From there they returned to MPB [i.e., the Brazilian influences], understand? (Interview: Lins 1998)

Other people in Recife's music scene apparently also subscribe to this view: A saying I heard goes, "The *tropicalistas* put the electric guitar in MPB, while *mangue* put MPB into the electric guitar."[8]

But even as Renato argues for the primacy of foreign music in Chico and Fred's musical backgrounds, his quotation does not hide the unavoidable fact that both domestic and foreign influences are key players in the musical formation of the *mangueboys*, as they are, in fact, in that of most Brazilian pop musicians. To be sure, whether an MPB musician comes from a more international background and then rediscovers his or her "Brazilian" heritage (e.g., Chico Science and Fred Zero Quatro), or vice versa (e.g., Caetano Veloso and Gilberto Gil), the point is he or she is exposed to and influenced by both "types" of music, to greater or lesser degrees.[9]

Hence, despite any significant differences in trajectory between the *tropicalistas* and *mangue* musicians, they both arrive at a similar point. Both united Brazilian folk and popular idioms with the most modern international styles for their time; both have aimed for a more universal sound by fusing a diverse array of domestic and foreign musical elements; and both managed at first to shock their peers with their (for the time) unusual musical experiments. Moreover, both movements made exemplary aesthetic statements in their respective times about the contradictory juxtaposition in Brazil of the traditional and the modern. Aside from the contrasting musical and lyrical contents of the two movements, *mangue* differs somewhat from *tropicália* in the musical trajectories of its primary musicians, in the more explicit valorization of the local folk music and culture, in its increasingly global outlook, and in its postmodern identification with a specific locale (Recife, Pernambuco) over and above the nation as a whole. I explore some of these ideas further in Chapter Five.

Pernambucan Precedents to *Mangue*

Unlike *tropicália*, which was led by Bahian musicians in São Paulo and launched through the national mass media, *mangue* is a regional phenomenon from Pernambuco that later gained national and some international attention. There are several important Pernambucan precedents for *mangue* that were informed at least in part by *tropicália*. I begin with a vital movement in Recife in the early 1970s that paved the way for such renowned local MPB composer-performers as Alceu Valença and Lenine Pinto.[10] Then I examine in more detail the case of Alceu Valença, for long a national symbol of northeastern music and a local pop icon in Pernambuco.

The "Confusion" of the 1970s

In *Meteoro Chico*, journalist José Teles reveals a little-known pop music trend in early 1970s Recife that he regards as an antecedent of *mangue*, as well as of related '90s bands such as the Raimundos and Jorge Cabeleira. Represented by artists such as Lula Cortes, Zé Ramalho, Lailson, Zé da Flauta, Flaviola, and the band Ave Sangria, this movement had its roots in *tropicália*, psychedelia of the 1960s, and hard rock of the 1970s, and its recordings, like those of the *mangue* musicians, "were impregnated with Pernambucan rhythms" (Teles n/d:

12). As Teles observes, "It was felt in all these artists the longing to link Recife up culturally with whatever was most modern in the country and in the world" (Teles n/d: 13). But just as with the *tropicalistas*, this group of Pernambucan musicians ran into problems with the government. Ave Sangria, for instance, launched a promising career but had its only LP censored. Furthermore, according to Teles, "The band also had its sound polished, they [the authorities] wanted it to sound like the Quinteto Violado [a quintet from Pernambuco that popularized northeastern folk music in the 1970s], when in truth it was more like Led Zeppelin" (ibid.).

A former member of the Quinteto Violado and of Alceu Valença's band and today one of Recife's foremost music producers, Zé da Flauta (whose name means "José of the Flute") remembers this era well:

> In '71 this band that I had, Efeitos [Effects], we mixed *banda de pífanos* [a typical fife and drum band from the interior of Pernambuco] with Jethro Tull. We mixed *viola* [a guitar-like instrument of the region] songs with the guitar of Jimmy Page of Led Zeppelin, do you get me? We did this *without even knowing what we were doing, it was such a natural thing* that we did that one time Zé Rodrigues, a musician from down in São Paulo, came to play here in a festival in which we also played and said, "You guys have a very interesting fusion project," and we didn't even know it was fusion. For us it was a *confusion*, right? [laughs]. But Alceu Valença saw in us a very cool aspect of knowing how to make this mixture and called me and Paulo Rafael [player of the acoustic guitar, or *violão*] to play with him. To this day Paulo plays with him, twenty-six years of Alceu Valença. (Interview: Zé da Flauta 1998)

Zé compares *mangue* with the work he was doing in the 1970s vis-à-vis the mixing of domestic and foreign influences:

> [*Mangue*] is certainly also a different form of mixing. In that era [the 1970s] when we began to mix things, we began to mix *baião* [one of the most popular of the northeastern dance rhythms, divulged nationally by Luiz Gonzaga beginning in the '40s with rock. These days the globalization, we live in a universe much better informed where information is rapid [snaps fingers], understand? We didn't have information. For example, Led Zeppelin would release a record in London; we would only have this record here one hundred months later. [Sarcastically]: What speed, one hundred months later we would have the record here! It would arrive in Brazil pressed with a horrible sound, understand? If you bought an import, it was a stupid [i.e., great] difference in sound! So things were difficult. We didn't have easy access to information. These days with the Internet, with cable TV, with fax, with these things, the whole world has become an internal city, everyone knows about the life of everyone else.... So with this swiftness of information, with this globalization of information that we have, for example, for Chico [Science] to mix a *côco* with hip-hop ... to mix an *embolada* with rap, these things, but it was like this [snaps fingers]. But everything was there.... Chico didn't only invent the

rhythmic mixture, or this fusion. He invented a way of expressing poetry through music that no one had done. Who sang like Chico Science before him? *No one!* And now everyone wants to sing like him. And there are the fakes, because you see they're [merely] imitating Chico, and there are the true ones who know that it's through [a real] influence. (Interview: Zé da Flauta 1998)

To understand better the role of Chico Science in the history of MPB, and specifically of Pernambucan music, one needs to examine the work of Alceu Valença, who came out of the same rich musical environment as Zé da Flauta and subsequently became a kind of de facto musical symbol of his state. As Nação Zumbi drumset player Pupillo told me, "Ten years ago, Recife only had Alceu Valença to show the world" (Interview: Pupillo 1998). Indeed, Alceu Valença occupied a singular, coveted position in his state prior to the *mangue* movement, making inevitable a comparison between Alceu on the one hand and Chico Science and Fred Zero Quatro on the other—respectively, the old and new wings of Pernambucan music (Teles n/d: 33). The perceived predominance of Valença led Chico Science to remark: "First came the sugar cane cycle, then the cycle of Alceu. Now its *mangue*" (Interview by Luis Antonio Giron, *Estadão*, December 7, 1995, quoted in Teles n/d: 20).[11]

Alceu Valença

Before the arrival of the *mangueboys*, Alceu Valença was virtually the only Pernambucan musician in more than thirty years to have become nationally recognized and to have entered the pantheon of MPB's greatest stars (Teles n/d: 33). Leader of a northeastern music wave that descended on Rio in the early 1970s—which also included Pernambucan Geraldo Azevedo and the *paraibanos* [from Paraíba state, which borders Pernambuco to the north] Zé Ramalho and Elba Ramalho—this group of post-*tropicália* musicians popularized northeastern musical styles on a national level. Such a distinction places this cohort precisely in the middle of a lineage represented by forefathers Luiz Gonzaga and Jackson do Pandeiro on one end (1940s and '50s) and such Recife artists as CSNZ, Mestre Ambrósio, Cascabulho, and Dona Selma do Côco on the other (1990s and beyond). But this northeastern group was also a part of the first generation to assimilate the globally popular rock and pop music of the '60s, which they blended with their regional roots. Taking their cues from bossa nova, *tropicália*, and rock, these musicians added pop arrangements and an electric instrumentation to such regional idioms as *baião*, *xote*, *côco*, *frevo*, *embolada*, and *maracatu* (McGowan and Pessanha 1998: 147-148).[12]

Born in 1946 to a middle-class family in São Bento do Una in the interior of Pernambuco, Alceu Valença's early musical influences were Luiz Gonzaga and Jackson do Pandeiro as well as the folk music of the local troubadours, passed on to Valença by his grandfather who played guitar. Valença moved to Recife at age nine, and he began to play the guitar at fourteen. In the capital, the young musician witnessed countless folk performances on the streets while on the radio he heard imported pop music from Rio and abroad; of the foreign artists, Valença was particularly impressed with Ray Charles and early Elvis Presley. He started his career in Recife playing northeastern music, which his middle-class colleagues disdained. After obtaining a law degree but deciding against a legal profession, Valença headed to Rio in 1970, where he launched an enduring career (McGowan and Pessanha 1998: 148-149).

Musically, Valença represents a meeting ground between early rock 'n' roll and blues and various northeastern styles. One of his signature rhythms is "*forrock*," a concoction that unites *forró* (a generic term for northeastern dance musics) with electric guitar and drumset. With these and other exciting stylistic fusions, Valença achieved critical acclaim and commercial success in the 1970s and '80s.

It is precisely this success, coupled with the perception voiced by some of my consultants that Valença has had little concern for helping other musicians, that has caused some *mangue* adherents to view Alceu through an antagonistic lens. As Chico Science claims in an interview, "Some people already worked [with Pernambucan rhythms] like Alceu Valença, but not as a collective thing, understand? To take the regional rhythms and work with them like Jamaica did with reggae" (Interview by Marty Lipp: Chico Science and Paulo André Pires n/d). The implication here is that in contrast to the work of Alceu Valença—which for years has stood alone as the primary extant representation of Pernambucan popular music—*mangue* was born out of a more cooperative, communal desire to rework the region's musical legacy in a pop context. Indeed, *mangue* has spawned a vital music scene where practically none had existed, creating opportunities for local musicians who aspire to national and global impact.

Aside from any discrepancies in personality or approach, there are certainly some important musical differences between Alceu and CSNZ. In an interview, Chico Science was asked to comment on these differences:

> It's even uncomfortable to speak about what differs. But it's different! I think that we worked things one way and he another. If you were to analyze the two works, you would see, it's easy . . . What we do is more modern. There exists a hunger for information. It's not only music, but about everything that happens in the world, in society, in technology, in the science of today. We take the rhythm the way that it is . . . I play with *tambores* [drums, referring to the *bombos*], *caixas* [snare drums] and not with drumsets. I can use the drumset, but according to necessity. What is different is that the idea that we had we're going to put in the songs. We're not going to be afraid of doing anything, we're not going to stop having a hunger for information. We don't want to keep doing the same thing the whole time. There is the difference! Did I answer your question? (Interview with Luis Claudio Garrido, *A Tarde*, Bahia, April, 30 1994, quoted in Teles n/d: 31)

Despite the antagonistic overtones, this comment alludes to the fact that the music of CSNZ is part of a general tendency in Recife in the '90s, embodied in the *mangue* movement, to link the region up to much more information (whether scientific, musical, cultural) than was ever available in past decades. More than a simple modernizing effort, Chico's music forms part of a broad postmodernist immersion in the information society in post-dictatorship Brazil. Accordingly, the specific foreign influences in the music of Nação Zumbi—from heavy metal to funk to rap and *raggamuffin* to electronic genres and samplers—are more varied and, in some instances, more contemporary than the kinds of foreign references in Valença's music (e.g., '60s and '70s-style international rock, pop, and blues). Moreover, there is a particular kind of youthful aggressiveness present in CSNZ characteristic of hip-hop or heavy metal (exemplified, for instance, by an exceedingly gruff voice, heavily distorted guitar, rap-like vocals) which is a recent aspect of MPB, stemming from the appropriation of such genres by Brazilians only after the return to democracy in the middle to ate 1980s.

The two artists' association with the region's local musical heritage is another, more complex matter. Chico says, "We take the rhythm the way that it is," begging the question, "Does Valença not take the rhythm the way it is?" Although Valença has relied more on drumset than has CSNZ, both artists have made extensive use of regional Pernambucan rhythms and percussion instruments in their respective musics.[13] The one conspicuous difference in this regard is that Chico has revitalized such regional rhythms and instruments in the 1990s, contributing immensely to their wide popularity today among Pernambucan youth. Foremost in this popularization has been the pervasive use of the *bombo* drum (characteristic of the Afro-Brazilian *maracatu*) in contemporary Brazilian rock and pop bands, an influence directly attributable to CSNZ.

Fundamentally, however, despite any artistic differences between them, he two musicians form part of the same basic musical lineage; and as such, *mangue* is, in fact, historically as indebted to the work of Alceu Valença as it is to that of the *tropicalistas*, if not more so. As José Teles reminds us,

> In effect, the mangueboys, above all Chico Science & Nação Zumbi, and Alceu Valença created a music that at bottom is very similar, forged from the same mortar. Alceu took traditional elements and mixed them with information from rock of his generation—Elvis, the Beatles—while the mangueboys used equally the local elements, but mounted on a parabolic antenna, bits and chips, not limiting themselves to that which was successful abroad, but absorbing more information than was thought possible in such a backward region [i.e., Pernambuco]. (Teles n/d: 33-34)

This comment supports Zé da Flauta's earlier assertion that one of the defining characteristics of the *mangue* era versus the 1970s (the time when Alceu Valença came to the fore) is the globalization of information.

Mangue as a Response to the 1980s

According to some of my primary consultants, Pernambucan music suffered in the 1980s. Indeed, the overall situation of Recife in the '80s—socioeconomic crisis and cultural stagnation—supplied the need for something to "recharge the batteries" of the city (to use an expression from the *mangue* manifesto), making *mangue*'s impact on the region (and nation) that much more profound the next decade. Paulo André Pires contends that since the resurgence of northeastern music in the 1970s and early '80s, nothing new occurred in Pernambucan music, and that *mangue* was a response to this situation:

> So *mangue* was this: It was a "nucleus of pop ideas," as they called it, to try to do something in the city to revert the situation that was. Why? Since the '70s, when Pernambucan and Paraiban [*paraibanos*, from Paraíba state to the north of Pernambuco] artists established themselves on the national scene, as is the case of Zé Ramalho, Elba Ramalho, and the Pernambucans Alceu Valença and Geraldo Azevedo, who were revealed to Brazil at the end of the '70s, beginning of the '80s, since this era nothing happened in Pernambucan music—nothing new. And so came *mangue*. So a lot of time passed with everything stopped, nothing happened in Recife. A lot of shows happened, but of bands from other states and not local people. So it was kind of like a kick at the door as the first Abril Pro Rock was done to open the space, to show that there were good people producing good music in Recife. (Interview: Pires 1998)

But the perceived impoverished state of pop music was not limited to Pernambuco in the '80s. If in the 1970s the experimental fusing of local and global styles was an important trend, the 1980s were a decade in which this practice was believed to have died down, not only in Recife, but also nationally. When I asked Pupillo if the fusion of rock and *maracatu*, for example, which is a marked feature of *mangue*, was a new thing, he replied with the following statement:

> In the 1970s, [people] already did this. Alceu Valença did this in the '70s. The Quinteto Violado was a very cool band of the '70s. There are people who did this here, except that it stopped. Since the '80s it stopped. People consumed foreign things a lot. I think that there was a bit of a complex on the part of the people from Recife. In that era [the 1980s], it was considered the fourth worst city in the world; misery reigned here. . . . In terms of culture [*mangue*] is precisely this: the recovery [of] a thing that was totally forgotten here. We [Brazilians] had a very big mania of copying what came from abroad. In São Paulo, in Rio de Janeiro, in the biggest cultural centers, it was difficult for you to do cool work with a Brazilian face. Because it didn't exist in the '80s. If you were to do research about Brazilian music in the '80s, there wasn't anything new . . . there were only some bands that wanted to copy bands from abroad [at least in the area of rock music]. So for the time it seemed crazy for you to want to make your own sound—and it was in our own hands, only no one perceived

this. It took a while to perceive. But it was still good that the one who perceived this was an illuminated person like Chico [Science], who perceived it in the best way possible and worked with it in the best way possible. So it was even easier. He provided a foundation. [*Mangue*] wasn't a predetermined movement. It was born from very intelligent people that from a simple thing emerged all this that's happening today in the city. (Interview: Pupillo 1998)

According to Pupillo, interesting fusion music that incorporated local styles flourished in the 1970s, died out in the 1980s, and then reemerged in the 1990s with Chico Science and the *mangue* movement.[14]

Renato L. takes this kind of argument a step further, characterizing the period after *tropicália*—that is, both the 1970s and 1980s—as a stagnant period for MPB, a situation which *mangue* musicians Chico Science and Fred Zero Quatro attempted to rectify in the 1990s:

I think that Chico, together with Fred Zero Quatro of Mundo Livre . . . created the pop music, the *Música Popular Brasileira* [MPB] of the year 2000. I think that Brazilian music after the renovation that happened with *tropicália* and with Jorge Ben, who for me was a precursor of all this, was sort of stopped in the '70s and '80s. Stopped as much in terms of the production concept. I don't ike the sound of the majority of Brazilian records in the 1970s and '80s. I think hat African artists, Jamaican artists, for example, resolved this question of production better, they managed to create alternatives to produce a pop music of quality, as interesting aesthetically as in terms of sales. And Brazilian music was sort of stagnated I think, and Chico and Fred, they managed to resolve or tried to resolve this question of production. And they organically incorporated into Brazilian music things like punk, new wave, and in the case of Nação Zumbi, funk, rap—very important things in international pop music, they incorporated organically into our tradition: to the samba, to the *maracatu*, as such creating a really very interesting hybrid. (Interview: Lins 1998)

Whether one wants to assert that *mangue* filled a gap in Pernambucan music inherited from the previous decade, or that it corrected misguided national imitations of foreign groups in the 1980s, or even that it put MPB back on track after twenty years of stagnation, there is a tremendous temptation to regard any new movement as an "answer" to the deficiencies of a previous era.

There are certain facts that are more easily accepted: that *mangue* was the next major movement in Pernambucan music after the northeastern wave headed by Alceu Valença, and that in the 1980s a slew of rock bands (mostly from the wealthier South) did model their sound to a large degree on foreign examples. However, further assertions require closer inspection. For instance, the active fusion of local and global elements—perhaps the one constant in MPB—certainly never *stopped* in Brazil at any period, even if it may have lessened or acquired a different character. Even the rock music of the period (generally considered, for its largely foreign makeup, to be outside the realm of MPB) at its most adventurous creatively molded styles such as reggae, ska, bossa nova, samba, and even northeastern idioms into a rock and pop base. The Paralamas do Sucesso were probably the best example of this, but other artists such as Cazuza, Lulu Santos, and Lobão also performed music that mixed genres. Hence, whereas many insiders may understandably see the singular qualities that separate *mangue* from other previous trends, one could just as easily see the connections among these trends; indeed, connections provide continuity and enable us even to talk of an entity called "Brazilian popular music" in the first place. The next trend to be discussed, the aforementioned boom in Brazilian rock in the 1980s, was significant for *mangue*, because, if nothing else, it made rock 'n' roll for the first time a highly commercially viable activity for Brazilians. As such it laid the groundwork for and made feasible the rock-influenced (or rock-based) music of CSNZ and other 1990s groups.

Rock Brasil: The 1980s Boom in Brazilian Rock

While in Rio—and nationally—Brazilians experienced a renaissance in "rootsy" samba music made by a new generation of composers in the 1980s (known under the rubric of *pagode*), bands in southern cities such as São Paulo, Brasília, and Rio sparked a boom in domestic-made rock music that decade. By the mid-'80s, rock music had not only *become* a veritable tradition in Brazil, passed on now to four generations of musicians, but it had also earned its place as one of the most popular of these musical traditions, alongside domestic mainstays such as the samba. In the words of Luiz Carlos Mansur, "Brazil now possesses its rock tradition—and in the confluence of so many modes of expression and so much experimentation, rock is part of the nation's cultural landscape" (quoted in Cáurio 1988: 251).

A Brief Synopsis of Rock Music in Brazil

Although it dates back to 1957, rock music in Brazil did not come into its own until the 1980s.[15] There were several reasons for this. Two more objective factors were the availability of quality instruments and equipment by this decade, and the increase in industry support for the music (McGowan & Pessanha 1998: 135). Furthermore, Brazil's devastating socioeconomic crisis coupled with the government's lift on censorship in the '80s gave the young people much to criticize and allowed them the free reign to express their dismay with the state of their country, lending much rock music of the period a vital, aggressive quality (ibid.).

After a series of covers of U.S. and European rock tunes in the late 1950s and early '60s came the so-called "Young Guard" (*Jovem Guarda*). Led by Roberto Carlos (now a global megastar who sings in a romantic ballad style, à la Julio Iglesias) and his colleague Erasmo Carlos, this movement emerged in 1965, garnering massive success via TV until the end of the decade with a straight-ahead '60s rock sound. *Tropicália* absorbed rock into its musical melting pot at the end of that decade, and under the auspices of this movement, the acclaimed

Os Mutantes (The Mutants), which included singer and flautist Rita Lee, became the first major rock band in Brazil.[16]

After going underground in the '70s during the toughest period of government repression, rock entered a new phase in its Brazilian history beginning in 1979 in São Paulo with punk groups such as Inocentes. The new wave trend hit the charts in 1981 with the Rio group Gang 90 e Absurdetes, while the rocker Lulu Santos, who got his start in the previous decade, had his music featured on TV and in the cinema that year. *Rock Brasil* became mainstream with the commercial breakthrough in 1982 of the band Blitz, leading the way for the notable success (measured in gold and platinum recordings) of other acts such as Lulu Santos, Ritchie, Barão Vermelho, Marina, and Kid Abelha in 1983 and 1984. Meanwhile, the inventive groups Os Paralamas do Sucesso (The Mudguards of Success) and Ultraje a Rigor (Formal Outrage) were emerging on the scene at this time.

Perhaps the peak of *Rock Brasil* occurred in 1985—the year the military abdicated its authority in the path to democratic rule—in the form of the largest multi-day rock festival ever: Rock in Rio, which brought together some of the leading lights of Brazilian and international rock on one stage. In 1986, he nation's Cruzado Plan and price freeze meant high sales for rock bands (as well as *pagode* samba acts), the signing of hundreds of new record contracts, and the crowning success of the São Paulo techno-pop band RPM, which sold more than two million units of its LP, a record-breaking figure in Brazil. The economic crisis of 1987, however, made the path to success more difficult for bands. Some of the most important rock acts of the 1980s include, in addition to those already mentioned, Lobão, Cazuza, Titãs, Legião Urbana, and the Engenheiros do Hawaii (Hawaiian Engineers).

Rock Brasil and Mangue

When I asked Renato L. if there was one factor that led Chico Science and Fred Zero Quatro to return to MPB from their earlier more exclusive interest and background in international musical styles, he replied that it was the purported lack of Brazilian ingredients in the previous generation's brand of rock music:

> I think that, first, during the '80s there was a boom of Brazilian rock, rock bands like Titãs [The Titans] and such. But these bands were bands that were very much influenced—they had little Brazilian in their sound. And I think that they contributed little to the history of Brazilian pop music, *Música Popular Brasileira*. And people perceived this. Of course this wasn't a thing that happened only here in Recife because in other places in Brazil also, in the '90s, people began to perceive that it was necessary—damn, we have a musical heritage, I think, I don't know if in the twentieth century perhaps Brazil is among five countries, who knows, the United States, let's put the United States, Jamaica, that whole area of the Caribbean which is Cuba and such—but Brazil also has a very strong popular music: bossa nova, samba, and from there it goes on. And it's stupid for you to dispense with all this. There are so many

interesting things, why not also work with this and search for, not to conserve this in a, you know, *vidro de formol* [formaldehyde jar] but to bring this into the twenty-first century and such, to play this into the future, not to leave it tied to the past, understand? I think that they had this *insight*. (Interview: Lins 1998)

Although as a whole, *mangue* utilized more Brazilian elements in its sound than *Rock Brasil* (and moreover *mangue* was emblematic of a vital new Pernambucan identity), the '80s rock boom was not devoid of local color. As I mentioned previously, certain of the *Rock Brasil* acts did compose fusions in the 1980s; reggae and ska were dominant influences on many bands, but a few groups also made use of Brazilian styles.[17] However, these were mostly nationally-identified sounds from Rio such as samba and bossa nova as opposed to the regional rhythms utilized by many new Pernambucan and other bands.

The Paralamas do Sucesso and other groups sometimes offered exceptions to what was largely an imitative trend. Such '80s examples, together with *tropicália* and the northeastern wave of the '70s epitomized by Alceu Valença, show that *mangue*'s local-global fusions had precedents of some kind in every decade since the 1960s.[18] This historical connection confirms that for all its significant innovations, *mangue* did not emerge out of nowhere, but rather comes out of a strong national tradition of active musical fusion and experimentation in which the local and global are both critical components. *Mangue*'s most significant contributions to this legacy are that it has updated MPB with some of the most important international sounds and technology that youth around the world have embraced in the last several decades since *tropicália* and the related work of Jorge Ben (e.g., punk, new wave, heavy metal, hard-core, rap, styles of Jamaican popular music, electronic dance genres, and samplers); and secondly, it has played a major role in bringing out of obscurity, revalorizing, and rejuvenating the rich panoply of Pernambucan folk musics, which, even if present in previous generations of Brazilian pop, now are proud symbols of local identity, critically among young Pernambucans.[19] Indeed, *mangue* has reinvested Pernambuco—a state rich in expressive diversity but long disparaged as a poor backwater—with a strong sense of cultural value in the 1990s, not only for itself but also in the rest of Brazil and internationally. In this sense, *mangue* is one of the most important of a series of new trends this decade that have refocused listeners on the varied richness—and global potential—of Brazil's regional musical cultures.[20]

Chapter Four

"*É do Caralho Ser Pernambucano, Pôrra!*" ("It's Damn Cool to Be Pernambucan!")
An Ethnography of the Recife Music Scene

Introduction

While attending the 1998 edition of the city of Recife's now nationally famous Abril Pro Rock (April For Rock) festival, I attempted to assess the musical influences of the featured bands, especially the varied use of regional folkloric elements in a rock band format (one of the principal ideas behind *mangue*). Having served as a launching pad for *mangue* and other acts from Recife's *nova cena*, the now three-day festival has become possibly the most important showcase for young bands in Brazil, who play side by side with established national rock or pop attractions as well as performers of northeastern folk music and sometimes international guest bands. As such, the festival serves as an exciting crossroads for the spectrum of trends on the Recife scene and other current Brazilian and foreign sounds.

A large percentage of groups in the festival presented music that was overtly foreign-derived. For example, the Rio-based Funk Fuckers delivered a cross of straight-ahead heavy rock with rap-like vocals (a trend from the U.S. that has resonated in Brazil), while the Ratos do Porão (Cellar Rats) reminded me of Metallica with Jimi Hendrix-inspired lead guitar. Another group, Sheik Tosado, one of the newest bands from Recife, also had a heavy rock basis. However, their rhythmic underpinnings (at one point it was a samba, at another point a northeastern *forró*) and *embolada*-inflected vocals carried a slight but unmistakable Brazilian flavor. Although their fusions did not sound to me as worked out as those of CSNZ, Sheik Tosado is one of the more notable of the many current *mangue*-identified bands that follow in the footsteps of Nação Zumbi. The lead singer of the group admitted Chico's influence and dedicated a song to the *mangue* pioneer. At the end of their set, the vocalist triumphantly stated into the microphone: "*É do caralho ser pernambucano, pôrra!*" which translates roughly as "It's damn cool to be Pernambucan!"

Upon hearing this, I was struck with the following question: How is it that a music with such a dominating rock, and hence foreign-derived, sound with only minute domestic (both regional and national) references could serve as the vehicle for the articulation of Pernambucan pride? In other words, what does rock have to do with a regional Brazilian identity? And why are elements of the local "traditional" culture placed here *within* the broader context of an international music?

Another band in Abril Pro Rock '98, the Devotos do Ódio (The Devotees of Hate), provoked my curiosity a step further. A hard-core band from the poor neighborhood of Alto José do Pinho, one of Recife's strongholds of both folkloric arts and the *mangue*/rock/rap wave as well as samba, they have no overt "Brazilian" musical characteristics. But crucially, the band's lyrics are concerned with the social context of Recife, and particularly, their neighborhood of origin. In their Abril Pro Rock performance, the lead singer—Cannibal, a black bassist with dreads who has become a role model for youth in his neighborhood and throughout the city—introduced one of their songs thusly: "*Afoxé, maracatu,* punk rock, samba and *pagode*. This is Alto José do Pinho."[1] Here, hard-core music is the vehicle through which this band articulates neighborhood pride, which itself celebrates the diversity of regional, national, and international components of the local culture. The day after this performance, the front page of the cultural section of one of Recife's two main newspapers showed Cannibal holding up a Pernambucan flag on the Abril Pro Rock stage. Hence, in the case of Devotos, one of the most popular Recife bands, neighborhood and regional pride—official state pride, no less—are associated with a music that in its content is purely international.[2]

Many Recife bands and artists have reinvigorated the folk culture of the region, which is now popular in certain circles both in more "unadulterated" manifestations as well as in various projects, epitomized by *mangue*, that fuse these elements with global pop styles. To be sure, the current music scene of Recife displays a remarkable range of musical expressions, from once obscure folk styles to rock, pop, and rap and much in between. All of this music, whether "local" or "global" in origin, or an intended hybrid of the two, has become intertwined with a newfound pride in things Pernambucan and in the culture and social situation of Recife and the Northeast in general.[3] Indeed, *mangue* and the "new music scene" of Recife have yielded a new regional Pernambucan identity that has been embraced not only by segments of the city's youth but also by the local media. *Mangue* has also strongly impacted the official culture.

In light of these observations, this chapter is an attempt to sort out questions such as: What is the relation of the various kinds of bands and artists on the Recife scene with the folk culture of the region and how have aspects of this culture been adapted by these diverse groups? Why and in what ways have international musical forms been used as a vehicle for a regional Brazilian identity and how are these forms to be interpreted in their Pernambucan context? What is the relation between local folk styles, global pop idioms, and *mangue* fusion on Recife's scene? How do musicians theorize about the fusing of local and global elements? What is the connection among the various sectors of the music scene (e.g., rockers, rappers, *mangue* artists and others who fuse local and global traits, and folkloric groups and artists), and how do such factors as social class, race, and gender figure into these interrelationships?

Ultimately, this dissertation is concerned with investigating the interaction of the traditional, modern, and postmodern, the local and global, and the domestic and foreign in the *mangue* movement. Here, I widen my scope to the entire music scene of Recife, providing a highly selective ethnographic account of that scene in light of these interactions. The purpose of this is to situate *mangue* within its wider sociocultural context and to compare *mangue* with how other artists and groups on the scene have contended with diverse sources in their music, in their aesthetic approaches, and in their cultural identities.

The headings of this Chapter comprise a broad taxonomy of the various groups and artists that participate on Recife's alternative music scene. I call this scene "alternative" because the music it represents is not nearly as popular as the nationally dominant contemporary styles *pagode* samba and Bahian *axé-music*. Indeed, from what I could tell, the vast majority of youth in Recife prefer these styles (along with electric pop *forró* during the *Festas Juninas* [June festivals]) to the local pop and folk music of their region. Nevertheless, certain festivals such as Carnival, Abril Pro Rock, and *São João*, as well as various other events during the year, attract large followings for the local pop and folkloric music and culture.

Folklore and Recife's Middle Class: New Folkloric Associations

On my first night in Recife I boarded a bus on Domingos Ferreira, the third avenue parallel to the beach, where buses go from Boa Viagem into the downtown area and beyond. I was on my way to *Maracatudo* (a play on the words *maracatu*, a kind of local folk music and dance, and *tudo*, meaning "everything"), an event which was to take place that evening in Recife Antigo (Old Recife). This recently restored colonial section of town, and now one of Recife's most pleasant nightspots, was featuring a series of free, outdoor cultural events every week sponsored by the local government during the Carnival season. One among many similar festivals that occurred during my stay, this program was symptomatic of the cultural renaissance, now coming into full bloom, that *mangue* and a series of other local bands and artists had sparked in the city beginning in the early 1990s. One of these bands scheduled to perform that evening was a *maracatu* ensemble known as Nação Pernambuco (Pernambuco Nation), who had participated in the debut Abril Pro Rock festival in 1993 and whose CD I had bought in New York.

The driver let me off in a dark, deserted part of town, which I passed through to reach a bridge leading to the old city. After traversing the bridge, I followed the dispersed crowds through the cobblestone streets and beautiful colonial buildings, while tracking the booming bass drums of Nação Pernambuco from a distance. Turning a corner, I found a small group of young, racially diverse drummers dressed in light, colorful clothing, rehearsing on the street for an imminent procession. The drummers were mostly male but notably a few women were playing the *bombo*—a cylindrical, double-headed wooden bass drum with goatskin heads and ropes for tensioning. While a lone *caixa* (snare drum) player hammered out an incessant rhythmic underpinning, these bright red *bombos* of various sizes, each with a different rhythmic function, iterated rolling syncopated grooves that cleverly skirted over the downbeats. A *onguê* and *agogô* (single and double bell, respectively) grounded the other rhythms with characteristic high-pitched patterns, while one musician shook an instrument known as either *mineiro* or *ganzá* (a metal tube filled with pellets), swaying his arms in dramatic gestures. Together these various parts formed a moderately slow, hypnotic groove that is certainly as fascinating as any of the multitude of rhythms that Brazil has produced. Performed traditionally by poor, mostly black urban *maracatus nação* ("nations") who parade as a syncretic royal court during Recife's Carnival, this rhythm is technically referred to as the *maracatu de baque virado* ("*maracatu* of the turned, or turned-around beat"). Baque virado has become one of the preeminent sonic emblems for the new Pernambuco. (For an example of this rhythm as played by the traditional Maracatu Nação Estrela Brilhante, refer to Appendix 2, Figure 1: *Maracatu de Baque Virado: Baque de Marcação*.)

Nação Pernambuco cannot accurately be called a *maracatu* "nation" in the strict usage of the term.[4] Of a higher social status than the style's original low class "nations," this middle class group is often criticized on the scene as inauthentic. Founded less than ten years ago, it has neither a direct connection to the *orixás* (deities) of the *Candomblé* religion nor any historical lineage; an obligation to the *orixás* and an established history are both defining aspects of the city's few remaining traditional *maracatus nação*. Moreover, it has informed its choreography with outside influences such as classical ballet and recently added instruments such as electric bass, electronic keyboards, and horns to some of its performances.[5] Hence, despite its name (the group is informally known as the Nação or "Nation"), Nação Pernambuco is best classified as a folkloric troupe or band as opposed to a "nation." Nonetheless, it deserves credit as purportedly the first group to begin revalorizing the region's folk culture, especially among young Pernambucans, even before the launch of *mangue* (Interview: Mestre Bernardo 1998). Perhaps the greatest evidence of Nação Pernambuco's influence, aside from its prodigious following and official sanction, is the recent proliferation and popularity of other similar middle class *maracatu* bands in Greater Recife.[6]

After some time, Nação Pernambuco began its informal procession down the street with several small lines of mostly female teenage fans trailing faithfully behind them. Bearing their Nação t-shirts, the girls smiled joyfully while executing a unison step that involved raising the forearms and turning from side to side. I assumed at the time that this was the basic *maracatu* dance step; I later learned, however, that it was part of a stylized dance vocabulary that expands on the simpler, non-choreographed moves of the *nações*. Meanwhile, Mestre Bernardo, a slight bearded man, artfully conducted the drummers with hand signals and a whistle, occasionally cutting the *bombos* out and bringing them back in again.

I found a space for myself between the musicians and the curb where I could best hear and see the drummers as they marched. Transfixed with a rhythm and tradition that was foreign not only to most of the world, but also to most Brazilians, I noticed that even some of the locals seemed to be in a process of rediscovery. We passed several cafés filled with people who lined the curb and stood from their seats to watch. Winding their way through the renovated colonial streets, the Nação culminated their parade in a large populated square, where they performed for a while before mounting a stage in the back.

The group's stage performance was markedly different from their procession. Beginning as a didactic presentation of the *baque virado* rhythm and its various instrumental parts, followed by Nação Pernambuco's own modified version of this rhythm, the performance turned into more of a folklore show. An electric bass and two horns were added to the ensemble, which displayed a whole series of styles, not all of them pertaining directly to *maracatu*. Each style featured its own dance, which audience members in the square, many of them young people, performed extemporaneously; small groups of friends showed off impressive unison dance steps. One of these pieces was an example of the *maracatu de baque solto* ("*maracatu* of the free rhythm"), which, featuring a ricochet of snare drum and bell, was much quicker, more frenetic, and less syncopated than the *baque virado*.[7] Some other pieces were drawn from the Afro-Brazilian liturgical realm of *Candomblé* (known in the region as Xangô, for the importance of this deity in local temples). Here, dance members of the troupe performed on stage, dressed in the garb of specific *orixás*. What had started on the street as a procession that musically approximates what the *maracatu* "nations" do during Carnival turned on stage into what some Pernambucans would term a "stylized" presentation of various facets of Pernambucan folk music.[8]

Maintaining certain elements of the tradition, while dispensing with or changing others, Nação Pernambuco has served to popularize the *maracatu*. The group has represented the *maracatu* to more and more Pernambucans, as well as other Brazilians and foreigners (the Nação has done several tours in Europe), not only during the Carnival season, but year-round. According to local journalist Pedro Rampazzo,

> In December of '89 a different kind of group from anything that already existed in the city emerged in Olinda, Pernambuco. A group of young men and women of the middle class were getting together to play and dance maracatu. A rhythm until then performed only by traditional groups or by artists such as Alceu Valença, Geraldo Azevedo, Elba Ramalho, and Quinteto Violado. Even though they were not a traditional group, they called themselves Maracatu Nação

Pernambuco. The first shows or open rehearsals, as they were known, happened outside in the historic section of Olinda and attracted a large quantity of people, young people of the middle class, who in the large majority were friends of members of the group. Among these young people was Francisco de Assis França or Chico Science, as he would come to be called in the near future. Nação Pernambuco innovated in bringing to the public a rhythm that until that time was performed exclusively in the Carnival period. (Rampazzo n/d)

I interviewed founder and percussion director Mestre Bernardo (Master Bernardo) about Nação Pernambuco. Here, Bernardo addresses the intentions of the group and the role he believes it has played on the Recife scene:

PG: Clearly, Nação Pernambuco carries a special importance on the cultural scene of the city. Could you talk about the history of the Nação and how it began?

MB: The Pernambuco Nation Maracatu, the Cultural Guild and Pernambuco Nation Maracatu was born on the 15th of December of 1989. And it was born with the proposal of . . . the universe of *maracatu* in Pernambuco. During his period, we felt the need to start a project with *maracatu* that would again come to give Pernambuco the musical potential that it always had but that it had lost for a long time with the invasion of other rhythms which didn't have this weight, this cultural characteristic that the *maracatu* possesses. . . . So today [as of March 31, 1998] we have been in existence for eight years and the main proposal was this: It was to emerge with a contemporary proposal of doing *maracatu*, rethinking the historical musical universe of the *maracatu* and at the same time being able to . . . contemporary works with this universe—with *maracatu de baque virado, maracatu baque solto, to create* new [rhythmic] cells of *maracatu* with a basis in this richness that we have, the rhythm here in Pernambuco. And it was very important because *after* Nação Pernambuco, with its appearance many other bands emerged. Because we had the courage to create a project in the street that brought together a lot of people to watch, to dance, to play, to sing. And this was very important for Pernambuco because really . . . it was the origin of this scene that resulted afterwards, with the appearance of Chico Science & Nação Zumbi, of Mestre Ambrósio, of Cascabulho, of Mundo Livre, and a series of other musical projects. . . . [Nação Pernambuco] put on big shows in the street that brought together a lot of people, and these people began to awaken their interest *even more* for the music from here, from Pernambuco, be it, as they say, "roots music" . . . as is the case of the traditional groups, in the case of Maracatu Elefante, Maracatu Porto Rico [two venerable *maracatu* "nations"], Maracatu Piaba de Ouro [a *maracatu de baque solto* group led by folk musician Mestre Salustiano], and also the traditional *bumba-meu-boi* groups [a processional dance of northern-northeastern Brazil that involves the death and resurrection of a bull]. In short, this whole scene, this musical richness of Pernambuco came to have a great importance after the emergence of the Maracatu Nação Pernambuco here in Olinda. (Interview: Mestre Bernardo 1998)

In these comments, Bernardo suggests that Nação Pernambuco was the pioneering band in the *nova cena musical do Recife*, predating the launch of *mangue* and sparking a renewed interest in the traditional "roots music" of the region. According to Bernardo, "this whole scene, this musical richness of Pernambuco" was highly valued after the emergence of his group. Yet despite the foundational role that the band can claim in the rediscovery and revalorization of Pernambucan culture in the 1990s, Nação Pernambuco is still criticized by some in the *maracatu* and *mangue* worlds for attempting to perform folk traditions for which they, as middle-class interpreters of these traditions, purportedly have no authority to represent.[9]

What constitutes legitimate folklore, or an acceptable use or adaptation of folklore, and all of the ethical issues surrounding this question are important concerns for many on the Recife scene—including both for "traditional" folk musicians and for performers who, whatever their relation to the folk culture, borrow from these traditions. Understandably, folk artists and groups of the lower classes might resent a University-level ensemble such as the Nação assuming the authority to represent and reinterpret traditions of the *povo* (the "people," or lower classes) not only for Brazilians but also for the outside world and then achieving a higher visibility and favorable professional status as a result. But a musician's higher status alone, whether socioeconomic or professional, is not sufficient to cause lower-class musicians to resent him or her. Recife's lower-class folk or popular musicians will probably perceive a middle-class or trained performer differently depending on what this musician chooses to adapt of the folklore and how he or she does this.[10] For all its popularity with the Recife public at large, Nação Pernambuco not only bears a confusingly close resemblance to its predecessors (including the name "Nation"). But as a troupe that remains functional year-round, it also overshadows the *nações* as representers of the *maracatu*; for at least some, the group may even represent an "improvement" over the lower class "nations" it is modeled after. Given this reality, it is easy to understand why Nação Pernambuco has become a target for criticism, even though they were among the earliest pioneers of Recife's *nova cena musical*. All disputes aside, however, the group has helped to generate a renewed interest in *maracatu* over the last nine years, which more than likely has positively affected the image, visibility, and performance opportunities of the previously unsung "nations," even if indirectly.[11]

"Regional Rhythm Bands": Bands That Work Predominantly With Regional Folk Styles

Nação Pernambuco and other similar folkloric troupes affirm a middle-class participation and interest in, as well as reinterpretation of, traditions previously relegated almost exclusively to sectors of the *classes populares* (lower classes). Another trend on Recife's "new music scene" struck me as having a less overtly conflicted but still complex relation to the folk culture. This was the presence of young bands comprising diverse class, race, and gender profiles that have created sounds molded largely after regional folk styles with varying degrees of international elements in the mix. Such groups are distinguished from Nação Pernambuco and other similar associations precisely because they are not set up like Carnival clubs. And they differ from *mangue* fusion bands precisely by having more of a focus on the folkloric end with the overt foreign traits, when present, serving as careful additions. Several of the most notable current Recife bands that have reinterpreted regional folk and popular traditions as the foundation of their work are Mestre Ambrósio, Cascabulho, Comadre Florzinha, and Chão e Chinelo. Each of these bands is distinct and would offer its own illuminating contribution to this ethnographic account. As one example, I will discuss the case of Mestre Ambrósio, which presents an interesting point of contrast to *mangue*.

Mestre Ambrósio
With the death of Chico Science and subsequent short-term hiatus of Nação Zumbi, Mestre Ambrósio (formed in 1992), followed closely by the emerging Cascabulho, has become the most prominent band from the Recife scene, although they currently reside in São Paulo.[12] Drawing from musical influences that range from a panoply of regional folk styles to rock and other foreign-derived sounds, Mestre Ambrósio was spawned from various musical projects developed by Éder Rocha (known as Éder "O" Rocha), Sérgio Veloso (known by his nickname Siba), and Hélder Vasconcelos that fused thrash metal and *maracatu* (Murphy 2001a: 248).[13]

In 1990, Siba was studying at the Federal University of Pernambuco in Recife and playing guitar when he met the U.S. American ethnomusicologist John Murphy.[14] The two began to travel regularly to the interior (*zona da mata norte*, or north woods zone) to study the *cavalo-marinho*, a regional folk play depicting life on the sugar plantations. Siba since conducted research on the *rabeca*, a folk fiddle of Portuguese origin that serves as the main melodic instrument in the *cavalo-marinho*, becoming an accomplished player. Siba has also studied and participated actively in the *maracatu rural* (i.e., *maracatu de baque solto*), a style that pertains to the *zona da mata norte*. Meanwhile, percussionist Éder Rocha, who grew up listening to rock and disco in the 1970s and later performed in a wide variety of musical styles (e.g. rock, blues, thrash metal, *xote*, *forró*, samba, and classical music) began to involve himself in the coastal drumming of the *maracatu nação* (i.e., *maracatu de baque virado*). Hélder Vasconcelos, who moved to Recife at age eleven from the interior of Pernambuco, met Siba at around age sixteen when both began to play guitar. While finishing his engineering degree, Hélder became interested in percussion, and he and Siba played rock together.

Éder describes how the band was formed:

And in time, Siba and I formed the band Mestre Ambrósio [the name comes from one of the characters in the *cavalo-marinho*] together with Hélder, who also through Siba began to participate in *cavalo-marinhos* and *maracatu rural*. And the three of us began to condense our sound exclusively toward Pernambucan music. And in the beginning we still had some touches of Caribbean music and these things, initially playing a lot of electric things. (Interview: Rocha 1998)[15]

In fact, in its early stage the band created parallel projects called Mestre Ambrósio *acústico* (acoustic) and Mestre Ambrósio *elétrico* (electric). The electric side of the band featured Hélder on keyboards, Mazinho Lima on bass, Siba on *rabeca* and electric guitar, Éder on drum set, and Maurício Alves on percussion. The acoustic side of the band (featuring Éder on *zabumba*, Siba on *rabeca*, Maurício Alves on *pandeiro*, Mazinho on triangle, and Hélder on *ganzá*) presented a style known as *forró de rabeca* (two years after the band was formed, Sérgio Cassiano entered the band as a percussionist). The *zabumba* is a shallow bass drum played with a mallet on the upper head and a thin stick on the lower one. The *pandeiro* is a typical Brazilian frame drum flanked with a series of inverted jingles. The *ganzá* (also known in Pernambuco as *mineiro*) is a shaker consisting of a tube filled with pellets. Aside from these instruments, the *forró de rabeca* may include maracas, *agogô* (double bell), and *baje* (a type of wooden scraper).

The umbrella term *"forró"* encompasses a host of northeastern music and dance forms; the original usage of the word is for a party where these styles may be played and danced. There are two related varieties of *forró* music: one, known simply as *forró*, associated with the innermost region of the northeastern interior, the desert-like *sertão*; and the other, known as *forró de rabeca*, pertaining to the *zona da mata*, the region of the interior adjacent to the *litoral*, or coast. Although the two styles of *forró* share similar percussive accompaniments, the *sertão* style—first made nationally famous as a commercial genre by Luiz Gonzaga in the 1940s—features the accordion while the lesser-known *zona da mata* style features the *rabeca*. Although *forró* in both regions may encompass a variety of different performance genres, in both cases it is closely associated with a genre known as *baião* (or *baiano*) (see Appendix 2, Figure 14 for a transcriptions of a *baião* rhythm in the accordion-dominated style). John Murphy elaborates on this point:

> The *rabeca* is the principal melodic voice of the northeastern Brazilian dance genre known as *baiano*. Adaptations of this and other regional genres for accordion by Luiz Gonzaga became known as baião in the 1940s, and later as forró. (Murphy 2001a: 247)

Indeed, the term *"forró"* (the accordion variety) is also used by some people to refer to a *baião* with different rhythmic variations (see Appendix 2, Figure 15 for a basic *zabumba* drum part in the accordion *forró*). Featuring call and response vocals and a light, buoyant rhythm, *forró de rabeca* reveals a strong Arabic influence in the *rabeca* (an instrument originally brought to Portuga by the Moors) and vocal style as well as a notable African imprint on the rhythm (Interview: Rodrigo Costa 1998). (Refer to Appendix 3, Tracks 4 and 5 for examples of *forró de rabeca* and *forró*, respectively.)

According to Éder, Siba heard people speak about the *forró de rabeca* in his travels to the interior but had never heard it performed. Siba began to learn some *forró* tunes from musicians who played in the *cavalo-marinho* and would bring these compositions to the band, which made its own arrangements of them and performed the songs in bars and at parties.

The band's acoustic project was much more practical since the instruments were all easily portable. As a result, the band members began to develop their acoustic repertoire over the electric one and in the process garnered a significant local following. At a certain point, however, Mestre Ambrósio decided to merge its acoustic and electric sides. Éder describes this process:

> And we began to work with a way of bringing together the two things, as much the acoustic *forró* as the electric part. . . . The first thing that we began to do was add the bass with the percussion. And then [Maurício] . . . who had a strong connection with *Candomblé* and *Umbanda* [local syncretic religions] . . . brought an instrument to . . . the band, which was the *ilú*, a traditional instrument of *Umbanda*. And he brought this instrument together with the bass, with the button accordion, which Hélder played. . . . And Siba with the *rabeca* and such, we began to bring these two things together, understand? We began to bring together and mix everything, and another language resulted that was much stronger than just the acoustic and much stronger than just the electric because it was the union of these two things. (Interview: Rocha 1998)

The results of these experiments, documented on Mestre Ambrósio's 1996 self-titled debut recording on an independent label, emphasize the band's local northeastern "roots" over global influences, which are manifest in smaller doses mostly as embellishments. The band arrived at this point through processes they identify as *autodescobrimento* (self-discovery) and *limpeza* (cleaning) (Murphy 2001a: 250-253). Siba associates the process of self-discovery that Mestre Ambrósio experienced with the recent self-discovery of Brazil itself:

> Brazil in the 1990s is still waking slowly from 20 years of military dictatorship (1964-1985), and as it seeks its self-image in the mirror it has begun to value music more highly. This process, which began by increasing drastically the percentage of Brazilian music heard on the radio (most of which is excessively commercial), has also served to bring greater prominence to the music of Carlinhos Brown, Chico Cesar, Marlui Miranda, Antonio Carlos Nóbrega, and Mestre Ambrósio, among others.[16]
>
> Finally, we are beginning to view traditional cultural performances of each region with more respect, and to understand more readily that there, in rural

performance venues, in the diverse street performances, in religious events, dances, instruments, poetic forms and special ways of playing and feeling music, dance, theater, visual arts and even human relations, the essence of Brazilianness is revealed as alive and dynamic. (Quoted in Murphy 2001a: 250-251)

The peculiar notion of *limpeza*, or "cleaning," is how the band describes their attempt at redefining their musical identities. For Mestre Ambrósio, *limpeza* entails removing foreign stylistic elements in order to discover the true value of their local heritage (see Murphy 2001a: 252). In this process, the foreign references are not completely absent but are put into perspective. Again, Siba explains:

> To be truthful, for the music that we play today to be possible, we've been through a long process of self-cleansing. Cleaning ourselves of rock, of jazz, of art music. Cleaning not in the sense that these things are good or bad, but in the sense that as we grow up with these other styles, living with them on a daily basis, we completely lose our meaning, our specific references, as musicians, as persons, and even as Northeasterners and Brazilians. (Quoted in Murphy 2001a: 252)

The music of Mestre Ambrósio can thus be regarded as a return to the traditional: in a process of "self-discovery" and "cleaning," the band has sorted through and put into perspective their diverse musical influences with the result that the local "roots" have assumed a primary importance in both their sound and cultural identity. The other international elements are still present to a small degree but are in service of this more "traditional" identity.

While *mangue*, too, can be viewed as a kind of return to "roots" and local tradition, CSNZ, Mundo Livre, and other *mangue* bands situate these local traditions within the context of global pop. The music of Mestre Ambrósio, by contrast, situates global elements within a context of local, traditional music. Moreover, the proportions or roles of "local" and "global"—or "traditional" and "universal" as Éder Rocha prefers—are different in each case:

> So when we began to do this [refine our sound], at the same time the *mangue bit* movement was starting . . . which was something that came in a parallel fashion with the work of Mestre Ambrósio and other projects that had nothing to do with *mangue bit*. But *mangue bit* began to develop a thing that we also developed, only that we took opposite paths, let's say it like that. We took off from the pure tradition, something as traditional as possible and sought something universal, while CSNZ and Mundo Livre and such came from the universal to the traditional. It was the opposite path, using elements, little things only to add to rock 'n' roll, to funk, to rap. And we, no—we were using the traditional and using small elements, little doses of rock 'n' roll, of jazz, and other things. Where we have something in common [with *mangue*] is exactly

the elements that are used, only in different quantities of the traditional and the universal. (Interview: Rocha 1998)

There is even a terminology for these divergent approaches to the fusing of local and global traits. According to the members of Mestre Ambrósio, when they or other like groups build on a grounding of local (in this case regional) music and add global influences, this is called *de dentro para fora* ("from the inside out"); whereas when *mangue* groups such as CSNZ add regional elements to global styles such as rap, funk or rock, this is referred to as *de fora para dentro* ("from the outside in") (Murphy 2001a: 252).[17] (Refer to Appendix 3, Tracks 2 and 3 for a musical demonstration of these distinctions using the *maracatu de baque solto*.)

The implication here is that the former ("from the inside out") is based on the local tradition with the global elements serving a secondary role, while the latter ("from the outside in") is based on global traditions with the local elements functioning as added flavor. Although in general this is a useful distinction, it is only partially true. First, some *mangue* songs could be said to represent a more even blend of local and global elements such that the regional references function musically as much more than flavor. Moreover, even where local traits in *mangue* are more minute, regarding them simply as "little things" diminishes what I believe to be their actual symbolic significance and potential. Indeed, the local elements in *mangue*, whether in large or small doses, culturally do not function as flavorings at all, but they assume a heightened importance, serving as sonic emblems of a renewed Pernambucan identity. In short, both CSNZ and Mestre Ambrósio have contributed to a revalorization and revitalization of their region's traditional culture, albeit in different ways.

The meeting of diverse racial, class, gender, and cultural backgrounds among bands and within bands is one of the most remarkable features of the *nova cena*. Like Nação Zumbi and other bands, Mestre Ambrósio's members come from diverse musical and socioeconomic backgrounds. Hélder Vasconcelos, percussionist and accordionist for the band, comments on this attribute:

> I think that there's a confluence of very special things [in Mestre Ambrósio]. For example, we have people with an academic training in the band and there are—this has nothing to do with the quality, I'm only talking about degree of [academic] training —people with the purest musicality that one can have, since birth. In the band there's Siba, Cassiano trained in music. I'm a mechanical engineer. Éder is trained in music, in the Centro de Criatividade Musical [Center of Musical Creativity]. Maurício studied there also. We have this connection with the *agreste*, the *sertão* [the two regions in the northeastern interior following the *zona da mata*], whereas Maurício has [a connection with] the hills [slums] of Casa Amarela [a Recife neighborhood]. He was raised in this environment . . . I mean . . . we have a very diversified confluence of information [which is affected by social class and geographical background] at

the same time that we have diverse educations within music itself. (Interview by Tânia Lima: Veloso and Vasconcelos 1997)

Given these diverse backgrounds, what is the relation of Mestre Ambrósio's members to the folk culture of their state? As indicated previously, the band's members have worked in a variety of both local and global styles, and they have since reoriented themselves back toward what they feel are their roots in a process of "self-discovery" and "cleaning." As John Murphy concludes:

> Although the traditional Brazilian source musics the members of Mestre Ambrósio draw on can be legitimately considered a part of their own musical heritage, the status differences that separate them from traditional practitioners and the way band members conceptualize their use of roots styles are worthy of closer examination. . . . The authenticity of their music rests not on its having been uncorrupted by outside musical influences, but on the effort they have expended to return to musics they feel are essentially their own after having played others extensively. (Murphy 1998: 2)

This return has entailed a sustained relationship with both musics that the band members began hearing in their childhood and with the traditional performers they have learned from (ibid.: 4). Dedication to the folk music and respect paid to its traditional performers, in addition to a high level of performance ability, have given Mestre Ambrósio credibility on the scene. This scenario is evidence that musicians of both middle and lower class background, when separated by status differences from the "tradition" (by being in a nationally or internationally visible band, for example), must work to maintain their connections with that tradition and its primary practitioners. Status and generational differences as well as extensive experience in international styles have made Mestre Ambrósio's relation to the local folk culture and artists a complex one, in which they are simultaneously insiders and outsiders.[18]

Class, though important, is only one parameter in this complex equation. Based on my fieldwork experience, it appears that members of the lower class who inhabit the *zona da mata* region or *favelas* of the city, for example, are typically accorded more authority on the scene with regard to folk traditions. They are believed to be the natural heirs of the folk styles of their grandparents.[19] Nevertheless, as the case of Mestre Ambrósio, and that of other bands, indicates, middle class musicians may also have or gain a certain authority in folk traditions. But notably, young musicians of *both* the lower and middle class, given the factors that distance both of them from older performers, must fortify connections with this folk heritage through participation and study. Indeed, a self-conscious study of and interaction with one's local heritage is one of the pervasive activities on the scene that cuts across class, race, and gender. It is as relevant for musicians who participate in the folk forms (such as *maracatu* and *côco*) as well as for musicians who play in bands that adapt and fuse these styles. In a word, young Pernambucan men and women of various social classes and races are rediscovering and researching their own traditions and using this knowledge for a variety of performance and educational applications.[20]

Regional Folk Artists and Associations

Certain traditional folk artists and associations in Pernambuco serve as popular sources for young musicians on the scene who want to research their traditions, either to perform and teach within these traditions or as a foundation and inspiration for the reworking of these styles in the context of a band, or both.[21] I want to focus now on one of these institutions that I worked with during my field research: the Maracatu Nação Estrela Brilhante, currently located in the aforementioned Alto José do Pinho neighborhood (which is also home to the hard-core band Devotos do Ódio mentioned at the outset of this chapter). The value placed on this association and others like it by musicians, other participants on the scene, and the local media underlines the revalorization and newfound popularity of the region's folk culture among various social classes in Recife in the 1990s. In particular, the joining of male and female musicians of different social classes and races in Estrela Brilhante sheds some light on the interrelationships among race, class, and gender on the Recife scene.

The Maracatu "Nations": A Historical Overview

The associations known as *maracatus nação* (*maracatu* "nations") have been one of the most studied and cherished aspects of Pernambucan folklore and of the Recife Carnival in particular. The *maracatu* rhythm has earned its place along with the *frevo*, an up-beat festive Carnival music and dance, as one of the defining markers of Pernambucan cultural identity; this fact is evidenced by the popular saying that Pernambuco is "the land of the *frevo* and the *maracatu*' (*a terra do frevo e do maracatu*). More specifically, the *maracatus* are a vital component of Afro-Brazilian culture in the region. As such they are considered to be one of the most "African" of the folk traditions in the state (Benjamin 1989: 81).

The origins of the *maracatu* "nations" are widely believed by scholars to be in the *Instituição do Rei do Congo* (Institution of the King of the Congo). The peoples brought to Brazil as slaves since 1538 came from diverse regions of the African continent. In Brazil, the authorities assigned Africans to different "nations." These were based in part on ethnicity and in part on the various ports of origin from which the human cargo was shipped, thus functioning as trade names (see Kubik 1979, Browning 1995: 2, and Silva 1988: 1). Following the example of France and Spain in the fifteenth century and Portugal in the sixteenth, the Portuguese colonizers of Brazil enabled certain blacks to be designated "kings" and "queens" of their various "nations." Serving under the protection of the religious brotherhoods (*irmandades*) Nossa Senhora do Rosário dos Pretos and São Benedito, these legitimate political figures were invested with the power to "reign over" the black subjects in their district to maintain order and subordination among them (Silva 1988: 1-2). The Congo "nation"

"É do Caralho Ser Pernambucano, Pôrra!" 81

especially stood out within these religious brotherhoods (ibid.: 2), hence the predominance of the "kings and queens of the Congo."

If not before, certainly with the abolition of slavery in Brazil on May 13, 1888, the Institution of the King of the Congo ceased to exist since there was no more need for the ruling classes to grant authority to certain blacks to maintain order and subordination within their communities (Silva 1988: 4). However, the *cortejo*, or procession, of the *Rei do Congo* persisted; in Recife this practice ostensibly evolved into the *maracatu* (ibid.).[22]

In a classic study of the *maracatu* from the 1950s, musicologist César Guerra-Peixe points out that the *maracatu* groups were formerly designated "*nações*" where their administrative function within the Institution of the King of the Congo was concerned, and "*afoxés*" where they exhibited themselves in the coronation parties of the black kings (1980: 29).[23] Anthropologist Katarina Real confirms this claim in her 1960s study on the Recife Carnival. One of Real's eldest informants, who was one hundred six years old at the time, "Seu Veludinho," recalls: "Maracatu didn't even have the name maracatu. The name was Nação [nation]. In the African word it's 'Afoxé of Africa'" (Quoted in Real 1990: 58). However, although they share similar origins, for some time the groups known as *afoxés* and *maracatus* have been distinct entities with different geographical associations. Folklorist Édison Carneiro asserts that the procession of the King of the Congo turned into the *maracatu* in Pernambuco and *afoxé* in Bahia (1953: 35).[24] Among other important differences, the *maracatu* "nations" still retain the figures of the king and queen while the *afoxés* no longer do (Carneiro: ibid.).[25]

The etymology of the word "*maracatu*" is not clear. Several hypotheses have been proposed, including that the term comes from *maracá* (a native shaker) and *catú* (meaning "beautiful"), both of indigenous origin; as such "*maracatu*" purportedly would mean "beautiful dance" (Mário de Andrade, cited in Alvarenga 1982: 112). Guerra-Peixe dismisses this possibility since the *maracá* is not an instrument found in the *maracatu*; rather, he suggests, as other authors have, that the word is of African origin and that it designates the rhythmic aspects of a particular form of *batuque* (generic name for Afro-Brazilian dance) (1980: 26-31). Guerra-Peixe proposes the idea that the sense of the word was enlarged to mean the regal procession itself (or rather the group performing the procession), which is accompanied by this rhythm (ibid.).

The word may have other connotations. Further supporting the above suggestion that "*maracatu*" is a recent name for the practice, Seu Veludinho told Katarina Real in January of 1966:

> Maracatu didn't have the name maracatu. The name was nação [nation]. . . . This word [*maracatu*] emerged from the big men [presumably the authorities or members of the ruling classes] . . . when they heard the baques [refers to specific rhythmic patterns] of the bombos [bass drums] they called it *"that maracatu"!* (Quoted in Real 1990: 184)

Lending credence to the idea that the term has had a negative connotation, Neide Alves, one of the members of Estrela Brilhante, revealed to me that in the popular language, "*maracatu*" is used to refer to a crazy combination of things, such as, for example, a strange combination of clothes or colors (e.g., "*Que maracatu é esse?*" "What kind of craziness is that?") (personal communication, 1998).

Currently both "*maracatu*" and "*nação*" are employed to designate the groups that perform the regal procession. The words appear together in their official titles (e.g., Maracatu Nação Estrela Brilhante) and in the popular language of the participants and others on the scene either "*maracatu nação*" or simply "*maracatu*" are used. The word "*afoxé*," as stated previously, is no longer a synonym for the *maracatu*, but rather refers to another, related kind of Afro-Brazilian group present in Salvador da Bahia, Recife, and other cities.

The *maracatu* "nations" initially performed on the patios of churches in Recife and Olinda and on the island of Itamaracá, promoted by the Nossa Senhora do Rosário dos Pretos and São Benedito religious brotherhoods (Soares et. al 1996: 29). The *maracatus* were initially condemned by the dominating classes in Recife, some of whom vehemently requested police intervention via the newspapers (Silva 1988: 4). Eventually, however, they became incorporated into the city's annual Carnival festivities. Although the exact date in which the *maracatu* "nations" began to participate the Carnival is not clear, they were already apparently a feature of the pre-Lenten fest in 1872, according to a notice in the *Diário de Pernambuco* (ibid.).[26]

Though originally promoted by brotherhoods whose mission was to Christianize blacks in Brazil, the *maracatus* have retained strong links with the Afro-Brazilian religious heritage. The inclusion of the name "*nação*" (nation) in their title points to this connection. The African "nations" in Brazil, aside from serving as a means for the authorities to control their slaves, were subsequently reclaimed by Afro-Brazilians as a way to identify cultural affinities among themselves (Browning 1995: 23). The use of the concept of "nation" has persisted to this day in various manifestations of Afro-Brazilian culture, most notably in the realm of religion. As such, the *casas* ("houses" or places of worship) of *Candomblé*, the most "traditional" of the Afro-Brazilian religions, are each typically associated with one or more "nations," a practice that reveals the cultural characteristics and orientation of a house, rather than the specific ethnic backgrounds of its members which may be diverse (ibid.: 23-24). The *maracatus nação*, like their cousin *afoxé* groups, are intimately connected to the *Candomblé* religion, which is sometimes referred to in Pernambuco as *Xangô*. According to Leonardo Dantas Silva, "The maracatus nação have among their followers the devotees of the African sect of the nagô lineage [linked to the Yoruba people of West Africa], hence the inevitable syncretism of the entertainment with the values of that cult" (Silva 1988: 6).[27]

The *maracatu* performance constitutes a regal procession in which mostly Afro-Brazilians (but more recently also members of other racial groups) parade as a syncretic court to the accompaniment of a percussion ensemble. The latter comprises the bass drums called *bombos* (previously designated *zabumbas*), *gonguê* (single bell), and *caixa* and *tarol* (snare drums). Some *maracatus* such as Estrela Brilhante also utilize *ganzá* (a shaker referred to in Pernambuco as *mineiro*) and *xequerê* (the Yoruba-derived beaded gourd used in *Candomblé*, known in Pernambuco as *abê*). The characters in the procession include the *rei e rainha* (king and queen), who are protected by a canopy and attended to by *damas de honra* (ladies of honor); the *damas de paço* (ladies of the palace), who carry *calungas*, a type of doll associated with *Candomblé* that is essential to the procession; the *baianas* (females dressed as women from Bahia state); and various other members of the court.[28] The most important figure in a *maracatu* "nation"—the one who is said to command—is the *rainha* (queen); this is possibly linked to the matriarchal influence of *Candomblé*.[29]

The songs of the *maracatu nação*, called *toadas*, point to the diverse origins of the practice, containing references to the coronation of the black kings as well as to the local divinities of the *Candomblé* religion. African words can be found interspersed in the mostly Portuguese lyrics. The songs themselves are directed by a main singer (in the case of Estrela Brilhante, it is Mestre Valter, the director of the percussion), and responded to or repeated by the *baianas* and other members of the *nação*. A whistle often signals the beginning and end of a *toada* or succession of *toadas*. The specific rhythms of the percussion section are referred to as *baques* or *toques* (See Appendix 2, Figures 1 and 2 for transcriptions of various *baques*.).

It remains to mention in this overview the distinction between two different kinds of *maracatu* in Pernambuco—the just described *nação*-affiliated urban, Afro-Brazilian *maracatu* and another separate type of group from the sugar-cane region of the interior (*zona da mata*) also called *maracatu*. This latter group, referred to as *maracatu de baque solto* (*maracatu* of the "loose," "free" or "alone" rhythm), is considered to be of Afro-indigenous cultural origin. Its members, typically poor sugar-cane cutters, are, according to Guerra-Peixe, practitioners of the native-influenced *Catimbó* religion as opposed to *Xangô* (Guerra-Peixe 1980: 22). (Refer to Appendix 3, Track 3 for Mestre Ambrósio's interpretation of the *baque solto*.)[30] The *baque solto* groups are believed to have emerged later than the *maracatus nação* of the coast—some authors posit the 1930s (Real 1990: 72)—as a fusion of various cultural traditions from the coast (including the *maracatu nação*) and the interior (ibid.: 73). In contrast to the more recent *maracatu de baque solto*, the *maracatu nação* is known as the "*maracatu de baque virado*" (*maracatu* of the turned or turned-around rhythm); both designations purportedly refer to the rhythmic quality of the drums in their respective styles.[31]

The oldest surviving *maracatu* "nation" is widely recognized to be the venerable Maracatu Nação Elefante (Elephant), whose date of foundation is cited as 1800. Other important traditional *maracatu* "nations" still in existence include Leão Coroado (Crowned Lion, founded in 1863), Estrela Brilhante (Brilliant Star, founded in 1910), Porto Rico do Oriente (founded in 1916), Cambinda Estrela (founded in 1935), Almirante do Forte (Admiral of the Fort, founded in 1935), and Indiano (Indian, founded in 1949) (Soares et al. 1996: 35).

The Maracatu Nação Estrela Brilhante on the Recife Scene
Based in the Alto José do Pinho neighborhood, Estrela Brilhante has been, for the last six years, under the leadership of President Queen Marivalda, whose courtyard there serves as the group's headquarters, and Secretary-Percussion Director Mestre Valter, who lives in nearby Água Fria (Interview: Ferreira de França 1998). Of the existing "nations," Estrela Brilhante is probably the most visible on the *nova cena musical*. In 1998 it performed in city events such as *Maracatu Atômico* (Atomic Maracatu), was featured on the local TV Jornal (the main television source for Recife's cultural scene), and recorded for the CD *Pernambuco em concerto* (Pernambuco in Concert). In addition, it performs for many parades and events in Carnival every year. Moreover, the *maracatu* "nation" from the Alto José do Pinho—itself a main source of current bands on the scene and an "in" spot for the culturally hip middle class to visit[32]—has served an important role for musicians studying and immersing themselves in the local folk culture. Aside from its core membership, which comes predominantly from the Alto, the percussion section of Estrela Brilhante contains several male members of popular Recife-born bands (i.e., Éder Rocha of Mestre Ambrósio and Jorge Martins da Silva of Cascabulho) as well as a group of female musicians and researchers from the Federal University of Pernambuco (among others). As such, the organization proved to be an interesting field in which to examine the interrelationships among various sub-groups in the city and their connections to the regional folk culture.

Perhaps part of Estrela Brilhante's appeal and impact on the scene has been its openness to "new blood." During my stay I learned that at the inception of its new incarnation under Dona Marivalda and Mestre Valter's leadership, the group was in need of new members and that some new recruits filled this need. Among these were three female percussionists from the Federal University of Pernambuco—Neide Alves and the sisters Virginia and Cristina Barbosa—who have since earned their respect as women players within a domain of the *maracatu* (drumming) that is male-dominated. In an interview with Neide Alves and me, Mestre Valter speaks about the incorporation of these new drummers into Estrela Brilhante:

> There's a story of when these girls arrived—in this case, we have to say really that it was Neide, Cristina, Virgínia. . . . So this trio in my sector gives me a lot of strength, you know? Because several years ago when I was part of Leão

> Coroado, a girl came to play *alfaia* [another name for the *bombo* drum used in the *maracatu de baque virado*]. As in the realm of *Umbanda* and of *Candomblé* it isn't permitted for a woman to play *ilú* [Afro-Brazilian religious drum], they had this same divergence in the *maracatu*. So Leão Coroado had a girl who came to play *alfaia*. But when these girls arrived to drum for Estrela Brilhante they were discriminated against. You couldn't play. *But I felt that they had something good* for Estrela that could reformulate the rhythm of the *baque virado*, that it was going to excite the public of Recife, that it was going to appear in the media, the televised and written press. And [people were going to] look much more [at Estrela Brilhante], as it *is* looked upon now. They are these important figures in the Maracatu Estrela Brilhante and in the *baque* [rhythm of the *maracatu*]. (Interview: Ferreira de França 1998)

In the beginning, the inclusion of women drummers in a traditional *maracatu* was looked down upon (although Mestre Valter does not indicate by whom). However, this later became a feature that for Valter could differentiate Estrela Brilhante from other *maracatu* "nations," granting them a special space in the media and in the eyes of the public. Mestre Valter does play up this aspect of the group. In performances during Carnival 1998 he announced that Estrela Brilhante is the only *maracatu* "nation" to have six female drummers (three more women joined the group since Neide, Cristina, and Virgínia). And he was right about the media interest: Estrela Brilhante was featured on a program for the local TV Jornal called *Som da Nota*, in which several of the women players were interviewed about their participation in the group. Cristina talked about how the women had to work even harder to prove to Valter and the group that they could play.

Gender is one of the factors that differentiate this sub-group from the rest of the percussion section of Estrela Brilhante, which consists mostly of adolescent boys from the Alto; another is formal education. Neide, Cristina, and Virgínia were all studying in the undergraduate music program of the Federal University of Pernambuco in 1998, and the latter two were using a school grant to conduct a research project on Estrela Brilhante. The tricky boundaries between participant and observer—often discussed with respect to the foreign scholar—were notable here as well. Even though they had proven themselves as players and were accepted into the tradition, Cristina, Virgínia, and Neide are also scholars who have an interest in researching and documenting the tradition. Along with their status as women, and the fact that they are not from the Alto José do Pinho, this factor inevitably sets them somewhat apart. As such, their roles within the group seemed to be fluid, flexible, and at times ambiguous.

This situation revealed to me how there may be different levels of insiders and outsiders of a given scene or tradition. In other words, being from Recife and having prior grounding in its folk culture does not grant one immediate access to the world of the *maracatu nação*, for example. However, one's participation and acceptance within this tradition can be earned. Moreover, in spite of any tensions it may or may not cause, this mutual collaboration is exemplary of a citywide trend on Recife's scene for people of various backgrounds (social, racial, gender, musical, etc.) to come together for a common good, even as each party may have its own agendas and reasons behind such a collaboration. Indeed, the music scene of Recife would probably not thrive—or even exist—in such an economically-oppressed environment without the benefits accrued from such links across established gender, socioeconomic, racial, musical, and other boundaries.

Rock, Rap, and *Mangue*

The Relation between Folklore and Pop on the Recife Scene
As I discussed earlier, *mangue* was a musical and cultural path pioneered by Chico Science, Fred Zero Quatro, Renato L., and others that arose more or less amidst other related projects in Recife that sought to revitalize regional traditions while exploring international influences to various degrees (e.g., Nação Pernambuco, Mestre Ambrósio, etc.). Identified most closely with CSNZ, *"mangue beat"* gave much impetus to other bands and artists, subsequently becoming a label used by the media for practically all of the new music associated with Recife's scene in the 1990s. For instance, both Devotos do Ódio (a hard-core band) and Mestre Ambrósio (a band that has a strong connection to the "tradition") are considered to be *mangue beat* (Interview: Éder Rocha 1998). I have already pointed out some of the distinctions that the members of Mestre Ambrósio make between their music and *mangue*. For their part, Devotos do Ódio have said they are not *mangue* for their sound but for their friendship with *mangue* musicians (Interview: Pupillo 1998).

It is friendships, in fact, that provide ties all across Recife's music scene, enabling it to cohere as one scene as opposed to a smattering of smaller, independent scenes. These friendships and working relationships not only cross lines of race, class, and gender but also embody a remarkable openness to musical diversity. As such, rockers in Recife "hang out" with and enjoy regional rhythm bands or *mangue* fusion groups, who in turn support rock and rap; and some of all of these musicians have established links with "traditional" folk performers. This is not to say that everyone on the Recife scene is open to everything or that there are no rivalries or points of conflict. Rather, as a general trend, there is a mutual interaction among diverse musical groups and artists and seemingly a widespread acceptance of different kinds of musical expression, from the popular to the folkloric. In a similar way, although there are many different types of listeners on this heterogeneous scene, the audiences for many styles and trends are at least partially overlapping.

Explanations for this situation may vary. One factor is certainly that without links across lines of class, race, gender, and musical style in Recife's disadvantaged socioeconomic environment there might not be a scene at all to speak of. It is also important to consider that the dynamic of these interactions in Recife is peculiar. Since its population is overwhelmingly poor, middle class residents may have found it easier to work with the lower classes toward a joint cultural movement, rather than assert their own. This presents a contrast to a city like Rio, where a formidable bourgeois population generally operates within a very different social sphere.[33]

A specific explanation for the remarkable interactions among diverse musics in Recife may derive from a local cultural characteristic: Many people told me that Pernambuco's folk culture is already marked by diversity and fusion, hence positioning *mangue* as a "natural" outgrowth of the culture. This was the gist of the explanation that acclaimed folk musician Mestre Salustiano gave to me when I asked him what he thought about the fusion of regional folk with international pop sounds in Recife (Interview: Salu 1998).

On the other hand, as we learned in Chapter Three, a lack of experimentation in the realm of pop music and a marginalization of the region's folk music had created a situation in which these local cultural traits of diversity and fusion were perceived as not being used to their full potential. As confirmed by Nação Zumbi drum-set player, Pupillo, *mangue* was in part a reaction to the limitations imposed by this situation and by the existence of genre categories in the first place:

> This prejudice is ending: Metal head is metal head, funk is funk. There came a time when there wasn't anything new; there wasn't anything to be created. There was samba, there was dance music, there was jazz. From the union of various rhythms you create a new thing, like *mangue beat*, maybe. I think that to break this type of barrier is already a very great evolution for the world. It's time—I think that globalization will be fundamental for the Third Millennium now. Because it doesn't work to remain bound to a determined style because people want new things, each day people are in search of new things. So, for this, a union is needed. . . . (Interview: Pupillo 1998)

Mangue was a reaction to a more rigid conception of musical boundaries and as such it promoted musical experimentation. However, the fact that this fusion was not only accepted but also identified with Recife and Pernambuco, even on official levels, is a testament to a readiness for fusion on the part of the local culture.

The broad diversity and mixing of styles on the scene may also have been affected by the particular situation of audiences in Recife. According to DJ José Antônio de Souza Leão Filho, Recife simply does not have much of a public for each separate style (Interview: Filho 1998), creating the need to mix styles to attract more people to events. As such, José Antônio asserts that Recife was the first city to mix techno and punk, for example, while in the much larger cosmopolitan city of São Paulo there is a large audience for black music (e.g., hip-hop), but that this could not be mixed with techno (ibid.).

Beyond this, I would argue that *mangue* fulfilled a need for a strong social and cultural identity for the 1990s that could set Pernambuco apart and give it prominence nationally and internationally. Indeed, for this—barring the imposition of one style—"a union was needed" among the diverse genres, influences, and musical camps in the state. The need for socioeconomic changes, which the *mangue* movement however modestly helped to initiate, was surely also a factor in the local embrace of *mangue*, as was the perceived high quality of many of the most prominent bands of Recife. The lack of full-fledged commercial avenues for either the local folk or popular musics, and the lack of massification of this scene in the media, might also have helped to bridge gaps among different groups, avoiding a rigid separation of the "traditional" and "modern"/"commercial"/"international" elements in the scene.[34]

Finally, it must be acknowledged that the peculiar affinity between folk forms and pop/fusion sounds in Recife owes to the perceived need for the folk culture of the region to be rediscovered, revalorized, and revitalized. *Mangue* and the "new music scene" in general fulfilled these needs. Through the work of CSNZ, Nação Pernambuco, Mestre Ambrósio, Cascabulho, and many others—and the wider exposure these groups have achieved nationally and internationally—the regional folk culture has been imbued with a high value in the eyes of the public of Recife. In turn, folk artists such as Dona Selma do Côco and Zé Neguinho do Côco (practitioners of the *côco*), Mestre Salustiano (an expert performer of various folk traditions), and Lia de Itamaracá (a singer of the *ciranda*) have all seen their careers grow and public increase as a result, in large measure, of the recent explosion in popularity of young fusion bands.[35] As one person told me, "*Côco* used to be something you read about in a book." Now, *côco*, along with the *maracatu de baque virado*, has become a hip genre as opposed to a nearly extinct remnant of folklore; and its representatives have achieved this while thus far maintaining the music's traditional, "rootsy" quality.[36]

I am suggesting here that the relation between *mangue* (and international pop influences) and the folk culture of the region is one of symbiosis: As *mangue* gained much from its use of regional rhythms, these regional styles in turn received a boost from *mangue*. Chico Science himself recognized this symbiosis when he said that he did a lot for the *maracatu* but that the *maracatu* also did a lot for *mangue* (Interview: Renato Lins 1998). Likewise, musicians in these various styles have in many cases benefited from each other's work, at least indirectly. As DJ José Antônio told me, the mixing of the folkloric with the "modern" is one way to preserve the folkloric music (rather than to dilute it) since the "roots" will always need to be present to give influence to the mixtures that musicians continually create (Interview: Filho 1998).

More than representative of a mutual affinity among these elements, *mangue* suggests a kind of radical overlapping of boundaries. In 1994, Chico Science was quoted in the press as saying: "Music is a thing that you recycle. You take the old and make the new. You take the new and make the old. It's a little like the theory of chaos" (Interview in the *Jornal de Brasília*, quoted in Teles n/d: 26). It is precisely this interpenetration of old and new, traditional and modern, local and global, domestic and foreign—and the concurrent separation of a rigid line between these categories—that characterizes the music of CSNZ. Pupillo, current drum-set player for Nação Zumbi, sees the whole spectrum of bands, artists, and figures on the Recife scene as completely modern. As he told me in an interview:

> An industry of information was created that includes everything. From [the band] Mestre Ambrósio that does the more traditional to Nação Zumbi that mixes the traditional with modern things, let's say it like that. I think all of this is really modern, because it's a novelty for everyone. As much the *caboclo-de-lança* [a figure from the *maracatu de baque solto*] of the interior as . . . [the hardcore band] Devotos do Ódio [the Devotees of Hate]. They are extremely new things because they were discovered now. (Interview: Pupillo 1998)

Mangue's fusion of traits, instruments, and even costumes from regional folk traditions with contemporary foreign pop unequivocally recharacterizes these folk traditions as modern—critically, without letting them lose their identities. And at the same time, using modern, foreign musical elements in Brazilian pop, *mangue* groups also reaffirm these elements as ever more traditional—that is, a part of the Brazilian tradition. This process of interperetration, in which the discreteness of established categories is questioned, is one of the main aspects of *mangue* and Recife's scene.

Mangue could be thought of as a paradoxical return to the traditional through modernization. Indeed, what was most remarkable to me was the general acceptance of Chico's fusion music by proponents of local folk traditions. For instance, on a bus from one gig to another during Carnival 1998 in Recife, I witnessed young members of the Maracatu Estrela Brilhante launch into a percussion and voice rendition of an ironic CSNZ cover of a song by Roberto Carlos, who himself was a pioneer of Brazilian rock in the '60s. I asked Mestre Valter, percussion director of Estrela Brilhante, about this:

> [The boys in Estrela] like him! Chico gave the greatest support to us." And he himself. He made it reemerge. Because he *brought* the people to us—he brought adults, he brought young people, he brought children. He made our rhythm, our culture, our color reemerge. (Interview: Ferreira de França 1998)

And when I asked him about the tendency to mix foreign and regional influences in Pernambucan music, Mestre Valter had this to say:

> I think [this tendency] is cool . . . because at least, when they made this mixture, they didn't leave out the *maracatu*. By the way, I am giving the most support I can to a band that's coming out now. . . . Geração Mangue [*Mangue*

Generation] is their name. I have the greatest human warmth for these kids. . . . They adore me, have the greatest respect for me, they love Estrela Brilhante; not only Estrela Brilhante itself, but the *maracatu* rhythm. I mean when they made this mixture . . . they weren't only thinking of themselves.[38] They thought about the culture, the music, the rhythm—that caldron of rhythms, which is very cool. The human being has to be respected, and you have to give support to the culture. [This band] was discriminated against—it's from the *mangue*. So it's in the *mangue* where our culture is. (Interview: Ferreira de França 1998)

Mestre Valter is not alone in his assessment of *mangue* or of Chico Science. Other folk artists have made similarly laudatory or accepting comments about Chico, *mangue*, and local rock musicians. Indeed, the music of CSNZ has been accepted into the Pernambucan tradition, being played at Carnival and used also as a symbol of a proud Pernambucan identity, even by the local government.

Traditionalists in Brazil tend not to accept musics that purport to be samba or *forró* or any local tradition in which elements of these styles are so thoroughly blended into international pop sounds, that they are perceived at times to lose their essential character. So why have they accepted and even praised Chico Science for revitalizing Pernambucan traditions? As Chico himself has said, "Our basis are the Brazilian rhythms reworked in an experimental way. I didn't want to take the *maracatu* and change the way of playing it, but to take the pulp of that which is done in Recife and mix this with a pop vision" (Interview in the *Folha de São Paulo*, quoted in Teles, n/d: 25). *Mangue* does not pretend to be the tradition or to replace it. Chico Science did not purport to play *maracatu* but reinterpreted and highlighted essences of this and other rhythms in a way that has directed a focus on the most traditional proponents of Pernambucan folk music, helping them share in the current renaissance of Pernambucan culture. Chico's personal relationships with local folk figures such as Mestre Salustiano and Dona Selma do Côco probably also helped foster this acceptance and praise.

CSNZ, *mangue*, and the *nova cena musical* have allowed the interested observer to rethink what is old and new, what is traditional and modern, what is local and global, and what is regional and foreign. A general open-mindedness and willingness to experiment on the part of musicians, the use of more "alternative" global genres rather than the typical foreign pop present in the Brazilian music industry,[39] the scene's as-of-yet lack of massification in the Brazilian media, and a perceived need for the folk culture of the region to be brought out of obscurity and valorized, all enabled a less rigid separation between the "modern" and "traditional" to develop in Recife.[40] This less rigid separation is embodied in the interaction and mutual acceptance among a variety of bands and artists on the Recife scene, from rockers and rappers to traditional folk artists, from "regional rhythm bands" to *mangue* musicians. To reiterate, the ways in which regional folk influences are perceived to be highlighted in experimental fusion music, rather than "diluted" into international commercial pop, is essential to the embrace of *mangue* by traditional musicians. In short, the case of Recife reveals how even the symbolic use of music and culture perceived to be local and traditional, integrated experimentally into the most "modern" and updated sounds from abroad, can have striking ramifications, especially in the hands of a highly charismatic leader. The work of Chico Science and his band has had a reinvigorating effect on local cultural identity, has contributed to a renewed interest in and revitalization of the "tradition" itself, and has even helped to blur the socially constructed lines drawn between the traditional and the modern, the local and the global, the regional and the foreign.

Aside from the use of folkloric elements in *mangue*, which is critical, *mangue*'s adoption of international pop genres—and the cultivation of these musics in general in Recife—embodies an imperative to "modernize" the local culture and make it relevant for the late 1990s and beyond. As I explore further in the next chapter, *mangue* positions Recife's population, and particularly its youth constituency, as citizens of the world. It is for this reason that the music of CSNZ and related *mangue*, rock, and rap groups in Recife are intimately associated with a host of national and international bands. My initial question—What does rock have to do with a regional Brazilian identity?—can be answered by appealing to the ideological power of rock and other globalized youth sounds in investing what could be relegated to a national or regional nexus with a more "universal" identity.[41] It is as if to say that the young people of Recife are part of the same global youth diaspora that New York or London kids are, but that Recife has its own contribution to this international culture with its peculiar mixing of local and global ingredients.[42]

Are we to understand the use of regional rhythms within a base of international music, then, as a strategic move designed to give local music more prestige, making a music that's also more palatable to more people in Pernambuco, Brazil, and the world? This is very likely one possible motivation. Chico Science has suggested that a high-tech pop sound can even serve as a vehicle for the exposure of local *cultura popular* (folk culture) to a wider audience:

> *Cultura popular* is very restricted. Because if it stops being of that simple people and comes to be mass culture, it's no longer *cultura popular*. . . . But I think this is a very retrograde thing. I think that *cultura popular* has to be a thing that expands. You have to combine it with technology for it to be understood in the entire world, I think. (Interview by Marty Lipp: Chico Science and Paulo André Pires n/d)

One could just as easily see the injection of "vital" local roots into global genres, however, as revitalizing to *these* genres. To be sure, rock itself (not to mention jazz) has long benefited and evolved from its interaction with a variety of outside genres and influences, from Afro-Cuban to Indian to Pernambucan. In other words, the question of which side of the equation has supported the other "weaker" side is moot; as I asserted above, the process here is one of mutual benefit (symbiosis).

The assertion that *mangue* represents an "Americanization" of Pernambucan music is an interesting one. This is the kind of argument made by Ariano Suassuna, Secretary of Culture for the State of Pernambuco, one of the most outspoken, die-hard opponents of the *mangue* movement:

> I always protest when people say that the music that the *mangue* movement added to the *maracatu*, for example, was international music. No, it added American music, moreover American music of a low quality, right? Bad American music. . . . I think Elvis Presley is a perfect idiot [laughs], understand? A complete imbecile! [laughs]. I don't have anything against— people think that I'm hostile to American culture. But in truth, I'm not hostile to American culture, as I'm not hostile to the culture of *any* country. As I told you, I like Melville a lot, the great American writer, I have *nothing* against him. . . . Look, for example, the Beatles are of a better quality, but this is because the Beatles added to Elvis Presley the influence of a *great* Indian composer, Ravi Shankar, understand? Ravi Shankar was the one who provided the Beatles with a better path enabling them to go beyond Elvis Presley. . . . Look, in my opinion . . . a movement like the *mangue* movement has no need to latch onto the land of bad American music to add to the *maracatu rural*, which is a very good thing. (Interview: Suassuna 1998)

For Suassuna, Brazil already has the equivalent of a Beatles's Ravi Shankar—its folk culture, which, in his mind, is better than rock. Thus, as Suassuna maintains, Pernambucan folk music does not need to be valorized by mixing with anything—especially "bad quality" music; if anything, rock, which is in a dying state, has been valorized by being injected with *maracatu* (ibid.). According to this position, it is the local folk culture that has benefited the "weaker" and "poorer quality" rock music.

Suassuna's highly conservative position stands out in Recife's music scene, where, as I mentioned previously, I encountered a highly tolerant regard if not predilection, for various kinds of music and the fusions between them. Much more common among the members of the *nova cena* was a kind of dual appreciation for both foreign (primarily U.S. American and English, but also other Latin American, African and Arab musics, etc.) and domestic Brazilian musics and a recognition of their dual local influence. Of course, the "new music scene" was predicated on fusion, and the folk artists who are a part of the scene, even if they do not like rock or fusions of their music with other styles, might have at least to pay lip service to this to keep their space in the scene and to appeal to the younger audiences. Indeed, "purists" in today's Brazil are a minority and face an uphill battle in commercial contexts.

It should be acknowledged that—regardless of whether its influence is good or bad or whether it is "American" or "international"—rock, though foreign in origin, is more of a pervasive music in Brazil than are the regional styles used in *mangue*. In a very real sense, rock, rap, and other foreign-derived styles are now not only Brazilian but also *Pernambucan* musics. They have been "indigenized," that is adapted to pertain to peculiar local social situations; this is manifested in the lyrics and in local musical flavors added to these styles. As such, international musics in Brazil, as anywhere, are not adopted wholesale as monolithic impositions with fixed ideologies or social functions (whatever these may be). Rather, these global musics are used to fulfill any number of local functions even in cases where their contents remain completely "foreign." One could also argue that in all cases the way a Brazilian interprets hard-core or rap, for example, will be slightly different from the way a North American does, even if these differences are not overtly manifest.[43]

The accusation of "Americanization" on Recife's music scene is further countered by the fact that certain bands have, in the last several years especially, extended their influences beyond the U.S. When I asked if Maureliano and Hamílton of the *mangue*-type band Via Sat agreed with the assertion that the majority of foreign influences on the scene were from the U.S., Hamílton responded:

> No. Maybe it was one or two years ago, but today no. Today, even as we speak normally with others, we seek out information of the whole world, like this record of Greek flute, but they play Arabic music on the record [because of the Middle Eastern influence in Greece]. (Interview: Tenório and Ribiero 1998)

Maureliano explains how this record of Greek flute was utilized in one of the band's songs: "So we use a thrash metal guitar, and drum-set, too, and there's this flute sound [from the record] and there's this Muslim phrase [There is no God but God]" (ibid.).

If this appears to be a more random combination of elements (which on closer inspection it may not be at all), other groups and artists on the scene have articulated the historically-grounded connections between northeastern Brazilian music, which has a strong Arabic imprint via the Moorish influence in Portugal, and musics of Asia, the Middle East, and Africa. As Éder Rocha of the band Mestre Ambrósio told me:

> It's a mixture. It's as if you brought together one element x with one element y and it yields an element z, which is that thing itself. You can't say anymore that the element z is either x or y. . . . It's a new thing. Which logically, you took from here, you took from there, you took from there, you took from there, but you created another thing. This is the origin of Brazil, isn't it? And this [mixing] is going to happen more and more, this relation. When Mestre Ambrósio, for example, does its music, it has an open mind to everybody. For example, in this CD [their debut recording] there is a song called "A Roseira" that works the *viola* [double-coursed lute typical of the Northeast] with the *zabumba* drum and such, very traditional, in the structure of a *repente* [northeastern musical style with *viola* played by troubadours involving

improvised verses] . . . enlivened by a *baião* rhythm, a *baião de repente*. We see the relation of this music with Oriental music. The relation of the *viola*, the tuning of the *viola*, the strings that are used which are double-coursed. It gives an Oriental sound to the thing. . . . from India and such, and much more from East Africa . . . the ud, this type of sonority. *There is this similarity!* The *rabeca* [folk fiddle of Brazil used in the aforementioned *forró de rabeca, cavalo-marinho*, etc.], for example, *is* an Arabic instrument. It was the Arabs [Moors] who brought it to Portugal and Spain and it was through them that this came here to the Northeast. And more and more we see the relation between these things and start to work with them. (Interview: Rocha 1998)

Éder maintains that this process is a natural one because the band listens to a lot of North African, Indian, and Middle Eastern musics, and so when they play, these connections come out naturally, without being forced. In a similar way, Chico Science revealed the connections between rap and *raggamuffin* and the northeastern *embolada*—which itself can sound very reminiscent of Arabic music. Proportionally, U.S. or European genres may be much more represented on the scene than genres from other parts of the globe (which itself makes sense given the powerful influence of and predilection for these musics in Brazil and worldwide). Nevertheless, there persists a strong desire on the part of young local musicians to tap into the music and culture of the entire planet.

Defined by José Antônio de Souza Leão Filho as the fusion of folkloric music with any kind of "new music" (Interview: Filho 1998), *mangue* concretely encodes myriad strains of regional, national, and international influences in Recife, standing squarely in the middle of the spectrum of musics on the scene. In its sound and identity (dress, speech, etc.) *mangue* epitomizes the fusing of the local with the global in Pernambuco. And all arguments of domestic versus foreign music aside, I see *mangue* more as a balance between the diverse trends that inform it, embodying their mutual importance, relevance, and interaction.

Music on the Morro (Hillside Slum)

An overlapping counterpart to the *mangue* movement has developed in slum communities throughout Recife. Two neighborhoods have emerged as important musical/cultural centers: Peixinhos and the Alto José do Pinho. As mentioned in Chapter Two, Peixinhos is home to Lamento Negro, which has supplied Nação Zumbi and other bands on the scene with their drummers. The Alto Zé do Pinho (as it is popularly known) boasts the city's best known hard-core and rap groups (Devotos and Faces do Subúrbio, respectively), and it is a stronghold of regional folk culture (e.g., *caboclinhos*, *afoxés*, and the Estrela Brilhante Maracatu Nation). Producer Zé da Flauta claims that the Alto Zé do Pinho contains forty-two bands, while there are more than forty in Peixinhos (1998). As he explains:

[The Alto Zé do Pinho and Peixinhos] only appeared in the newspaper, or the radio, and on television when there was news of criminals. . . . Today, the people [of these neighborhoods] stand out in the social columns of the newspapers, in the cultural sections. . . . According to the data of the military police of the state, the occurrence of criminality in [the two neighborhoods] has diminished by fifty-five percent. And so I ask, "What other kind of social work could the government do in a place like this to obtain such a result?" No other, no other. It's the power of the music. So the power of music is doing very important social work in these places. (Zé da Flauta 1998)

The Alto Zé do Pinho is now seen as safer and better off than it used to be. As one of the designated hip spots for aficionados of Recife's new cultural scene, including among the middle class, the neighborhood is emblematic of the positive changes in the city that *mangue* and the "new music scene" have helped produce.[44]

Todos Com A Nota (All With The Note)
In late February 1998, I had my first dose of what could be termed the social context of the "new music scene" of Recife—specifically that side of the scene that is represented by the poorer youth sectors of the city. Part of a recent government campaign to help subsidize activities such as films, concerts, and theater for Recife's poor population, this event was one manifestation of the formidable governmental support of the local culture since the explosion of the *nova cena*. The campaign is called *Todos Com A Nota* (All With A Note) and it works like this: One accumulates receipts from purchases until one has the equivalent of $50 *reais* (just under fifty dollars U.S.); then one trades in these receipts for a special ticket that can grant one free access to different events. The musical component of this program was taking place at the Animal Exhibition Park of Cordeiro in the neighborhood of Caxangá. It was a concert series produced by Paulo André Pires, one of the scene's foremost producer-impresarios. Paulo André assured me that the night of February the 28th would be particularly relevant for my research.

I took the long bus ride to Caxangá from Boa Viagem. The bus was filled with many young guys on their way to the show; many were dressed in Iron Maiden, Metallica, or Faces do Subúrbio (a local rap act) t-shirts. The space for the event was packed with people. The demographics were overwhelmingly young males in their teens or twenties; the large majority were poor and non-white. I saw guys wearing shirts of Planet Hemp (a Rio-based punk-rap band), the Ramones, the internationally famous Brazilian metal band Sepultura, and Chico Science. I met Paulo André who escorted me to a booth that looked out over the huge, excited outdoor crowd. The people around me, many from the local media, looked more middle class. Evidently this booth was for VIPs.

The four bands that played (each for thirty minutes or so) were particularly representative of the current *mangue*, rock, and rap trends on the Recife scene. The first two were prominent *mangue*-style bands. Although musically competent, R.D.A. have been criticized for copying CSNZ down to the exact instrumentation—three *bombo* drums, drum-set, electric guitar, electric bass, lead vocals. Fusing heavy rock rhythms, harmonies, and distorted vocals with the *maracatu de baque virado* in various ways, the band had a presence that reminded me of a heavy metal or hard-core band, while the singer's antics revealed a detectable rap influence. Especially in front of the stage an aggregation of people was jumping up and down enthusiastically or running around in a circle with unbridled energy.

The racial make-up of the group—the drummers and the lead singer are black—defies the traditional notion in Brazil of rock (at least mainstream rock) as a "white" middle-class genre. In fact, in Recife, heavy rock and rap are both now closely associated with poor, largely black or non-white youth from neighborhoods in the *periferia* (the periphery, or outskirts of the city) and the *favelas* (slums) where the lower class residents of Recife live. This situation also goes against at least the conventional media images of these genres as they pertain to the U.S., where rock and rap have been presented as separate: the former as a "white" music and the latter a "black" one.[45] The merging of these styles in the Pernambucan context reflects what appears to be an openness to various influences, while reinforcing the idea that the local context can determine which influences are borrowed and how they are used.

R.D.A. is from Peixinhos. Like the Alto José do Pinho, Peixinhos is a prime source of local bands on the scene. The aforementioned Via Sat (from "Via Satellite") from Peixinhos is one of the most interesting *mangue* groups. Their specialty is "code-switching" (Slobin 1992), that is, moving from one set of sounds and associations to another between pieces or within the same piece. Comprising electric guitar, electric bass, drum-set, two percussionists, turntables and lead vocals, the band began with a psychedelic Jimi Hendrix-style distorted guitar and other electronic sounds. From there, they moved into a funky groove with a shaker and *pandeiro* (Brazilian frame drum) accompaniment. There was scratching on the turntable, a practice borrowed from hip-hop. At one point, Pácua, the lead singer, a thin, light-skinned black man who wears an afro, suddenly began to scream and jump frantically up and down for several seconds, exciting the previously mellow crowd. At another psychedelic interlude, the singer said "cool jazz" and a trumpet entered the sonic picture. Then this suddenly changed to a rapid-fire sub-genre of heavy metal (refer to Appendix 3, Track 18).

At another point the band launched into a *maracatu* groove and the vocals paid homage to the "Daruê Malungo" (the association that helps youth in poor communities; see Chapter Two). Another song was introduced by the words, "This is *frevo*"; the piece melded the typical Pernambucan Carnival march rhythm to heavy rock. Yet another piece carried the unmistakable mark of the syncopated *côco* rhythm. Via Sat also made use of samples. The intro to the song "Make It Funky" by James Brown was the prelude to a live song.

Some members of the crowd took certain sonic cues in Via Sat's performance—particularly the heavy rock moments—to sway their arms and jump frantically as if in a fight. For the last song, the singer did a "mosh" (i.e., a dive off the stage into the arms of the crowd).

What can made of Via Sat's highly dense musical explorations that draw on a range of sources from both in and outside of Brazil? In light of my earlier discussion of *mangue* as an assertion of the Recife resident's global citizenship, the connections among the band's various influences—from James Brown and Hendrix to *maracatu, côco,* and *frevo* to hip-hop, heavy rock, and jazz, etc.—can be taken as attempts to articulate cultural links from Recife to world. In an informal conversation I had with Pácua, he told me that "*Frevo* is the jungle [English-based electronic dance music genre] of Brazil." Indeed, there is a similarity in the rhythms of the two styles, as there are, for example, among the *embolada,* rap, and *raggamuffin* influences, or the *maracatu* and funk, in Nação Zumbi's music. (See Appendix 2 for a demonstration of some of the similarities among these styles in the music of CSNZ.) Rather than simply representing an appeal to international styles in an effort to bolster the image of local music (a one-way influence), these articulations of cross-cultural connections as well as differences assert the participation of Brazilians in a transnational musical-cultural network. In this participation, foreign styles such as rock, rap, and funk are incorporated as local ones, and conversely, local Brazilian styles (in this case, regional Pernambucan ones) take on a more global identity.

But for all the importance I have been placing on the local musical ingredients in *mangue*, perhaps equally important—if not more so—is simply the fact that Pernambucans, particularly poor Pernambucans, are creating viable careers in music at all and serving as an example for their communities. Many people on the scene see Chico Science's greatest contribution to Pernambuco and Brazil as forging a path that other musicians could follow and take off from. In fact, since his death, Chico has become a martyr on the scene for people of all classes: His image has been painted all around the city and many diverse bands on the scene take his work as a point of reference. Paulo André Pires takes his impressions of the February 28th Todos Com A Nota show as a point of departure to assess Chico's role in the *nova cena*:

> So I was impressed because that public that was there, one part of it is from the middle class and can pay for Abril Pro Rock and for music shows in the city, but the *great majority* of that public *doesn't* have money to pay for shows that happen in the day-to-day life of the city. . . . So there it showed that if given an opportunity, there is a public. And I think that Chico really helped this question of the *periphery*. He is very much respected by the youth of the periphery because, like them, he was a young, lower middle class guy from the periphery who managed to make his international career viable. So it's as if he were a symbol for a guy who overcame his situation in life, who managed to go from nothing, from zero money to a very successful artistic career in the little time that it existed. (Interview: Pires 1998)

The use of local influences was crucial for CSNZ and other groups, but rock and rap acts that draw very little or not at all from traditional Pernambucan sources are also significantly popular with youth from the periphery of the city. Even so, the lyrics and images of such bands affirm a strong localized identity, often one of resistance. The third act on the Todos Com A Nota program the nationally visible black and mulatto rap band Faces do Subúrbio (Faces of the Suburbs) from the Alto José do Pinho, is one such group. A favorite among many poor youth in Recife, the band performs assertive protest rap overtly borrowed from a U.S. model. It was formed in 1991 as a conventional rap group with two MCs and a DJ but later incorporated electric guitar, electric bass, and drum-set (Interview: Oni 1998). Returning to the question of what this kind of music has to do with *mangue* or with the local folk culture of Recife, I could reiterate that all these musics are linked precisely because of the friendships and multiple connections of various people on the scene, because of the fact that the public of Recife is more limited for separate styles, because diversity is a hallmark of the culture, and so on. But this only addresses part of the issue. The electric guitarist for the band Faces do Subúrbio, twenty-one year-old Oni, makes another interesting observation about Recife's current scene that, in fact, shows the hidden presumptions behind such a question:

> What I think is the coolest of all this is that the youngest people, the people who these days are adolescents, feel free to use the sound that's in their head. I'm not talking about your homeland, because sometimes you're in a place that isn't your place. Your homeland is your head, understand? The sound that's happening in your head is the sound of your homeland. It's [that] you use that sound to speak about the things that you feel. And the people of thirteen, fourteen years old these days feel really free, they feel supported, by the people who started this, they feel supported . . . it's a kind of a *healthy* musical anarchy. This happens in Pernambuco. . . . The coolest of all is to see the people, boys of fourteen listening to Selma do Côco [the traditional singer of the *côco*]. Selma do Côco burst onto the scene two years ago, but I already heard Selma do Côco ten years ago, understand? But as such, they feel a lot of freedom to do what they want. . . . The young people today feel as free to listen to Selma do Côco as to Raimundos [a Brazilian punk band with some northeastern flavors], as Racionais [Brazilian rap band], or Metallica, you know?. . . . The people listen with the same desire to understand Selma do Côco and Rage Against the Machine, for example, you know? (Interview: Oni 1998)

The idea that "your homeland is your head" recalls the Bahian Timbalada's 1995 CD, *Cada Cabeça É Um Mundo* (Each Head Is A World). One of the principles of *mangue* is precisely the union of the various "worlds of influence" of each component of a band to create a new sound. Oni said he considers Faces do Subúrbio part of the *mangue* movement only in the widest sense: "Faces do Subúrbio . . . is considered to be a rap band, which, among its elements, are six

"É do Caralho Ser Pernambucano, Pôrra!"

people and each one brings an influence. And *this* is the principle of the *mangue* movement, this thing of miscegenation, mixing" (ibid.).

An assumption that certain musics should not be, or are not "naturally" associated, contributed to the construction of the very boundaries that the members of the *mangue* movement sought to deconstruct. This "musical anarchy" of which Oni speaks could just as easily be considered the "natural" state for Recife, Brazil, or any other locale in the 1990s. When I asked him how such diverse music could be a part of the same musical scene, Oni replied:

> To respond to you I will cite a personal example, my example. I live in Imbiribeira, which is a neighborhood that has two *escolas de samba* ["samba schools," social clubs that parade and play samba for Carnival]. One is in front of my house, Império do Samba [Empire of the Samba]. . . . I was sixteen years old, I would listen to Black Sabbath on a Saturday until around eleven o'clock, full of vodka, a boy, right? Full of vodka. At eleven o'clock, the samba started. Until the samba started I would listen to Black Sabbath, Led Zeppelin, Deep Purple. But eleven o'clock was samba and I would leave for the samba, understand? And I would go there and glue myself to a girl, I don't know what, bring her to the house. I would get to the house and put on that more *relax* sound. I would put on Jorge Ben [classic MPB], something like this. It's a lot like this. As Recife is a port city, there is a lot of this thing of information. Sometimes something arrives here that hasn't even arrived in São Paulo [Brazil's biggest and most industrialized city]. . . . You listen to the Raimundos, Slayer, Metallica, these things, but at the same time you find that by your house there's a sound that pleases you, understand? There's a *macumba* [Brazilian syncretic religious ceremony] that makes you want to go there and dance. People feel very free. . . . As a person of Recife, of Pernambuco, I'm from this environment. I can give you this example to respond to this question, because I'm from this, I'm a product of this. (Interview: Oni 1998)

As of late, the band has come to embody this kind of "freedom" in their sound. Apparently Chico Science used to criticize Faces do Subúrbio in a friendly sense, urging them to draw on their own local heritage (Interview: Pires 1998). The 1998 Todos Com A Nota show of the band featured a segment in which the two MCs each took a *pandeiro* (Brazilian frame drum) and began to trade verses in the regional *embolada* style. Whether explicit musical miscegenation results from encouragement or whether it derives from a band's already extant musical proclivities, in Brazil in the late 1990s, as in practically any other part of the world, "your homeland is your head"—in other words, your identity is what you make it.

The last group to perform—the one-hundred percent hard-core band Devotos do Ódio—is possibly the most popular of the four bands that graced the Todos Com A Nota stage. At the time of the performance, this fact frustrated and fascinated me. What did this music have to do with the music of Chico Science not to mention the local folklore, I wondered? In the wee hours of the morning, as the strains of an electric guitar and thousands of singing fans echoed in my ears on the bus ride home, I spent another four months or so pondering and investigating exactly this question. But by now, it makes perfect sense to me how hard-core music as well as the sound of a *côco*, samba, or *maracatu*, or any other sound, could fit into the musical identity of a young person from Recife. And, as I came to believe, in many ways *mangue* was the glue for these diverse strains to come together under one roof. Indeed, "It's damn cool to be Pernambucan!"

Chapter Five

Mangue, Postmodernity, and the Global Culture Debate

Introduction

The recent Carlos Diegues film adaptation of Jorge Amado's novel, *Tieta do Agreste* (1996), offers a particular vision about the interplay of tradition and modernity in present day Brazil. The film centers on Tieta, a rich São Paulo widow (played by Sonia Braga) who returns to her hometown in the interior of Bahia, from which her father exiled her for losing her virginity many years earlier. On this return trip, Tieta deceives her Bahian family and the townspeople into thinking she and her stepdaughter Nora lead glamorous lives in the big city. Using her wealth and influence, Tieta challenges and flagrantly disrupts the value system of the community, which is in awe of her; Tieta's family lust after, and bend their morals to get closer to, her money and lifestyle. Serving as a symbol for the untouchable, wealthier industrialized South, Tieta also brings modernity to Santana do Agreste by succeeding in getting the state government to install electric light in the quaint northeastern town.

At the end of the film, we learn that, in fact, Tieta and Nora were involved in prostitution and that they came to the *agreste* to escape their lives in São Paulo. At first, this amounts to a devastating deception. Ascânio, a local political figure, looked up to and wanted to marry Nora; after discovering her true identity, he is angry and disillusioned. Yet, in one of the film's final scenes we find Ascânio running desperately toward the "Road Express," the modest van that has broken down on its way to take Tieta and Nora to catch a plane in Salvador. Ascânio decides that even though she was a prostitute, Nora deserves his love, and the two return to Santana do Agreste to marry. The van's driver, Jaro, fixes the van and takes Tieta to the airport. The ensuing dialogue takes place in the van on the way to the airport:

101

Jairo: [Referring to the fixed van]: "Thank you beautiful. I knew she wouldn't let me down. . . . See. A few kind words and she gets better. Deep down she just wants to be loved."
Tieta: "And who doesn't?"
Jairo: "The people from Agreste are actually good people."
Tieta: "I know."
Jairo: "A bit ignorant but then who isn't. They like you very much. They'll never forget you."
Tieta: "With all the mess I've made, of course they won't."
Jairo: "That's life, Mrs. Antonietta. Some people were born just to make a mess."
Tieta: "Tieta, Jairo. Call me Tieta."

After this, we are shown the inauguration of electricity in the town square with the Brazilian national anthem playing. The final scene, narrated by Jorge Amado himself, shows the old plaque in the town square, a blue metal sign that reads "Coronel Artur da Tapitanga Square," being changed to a wooden one in honor of Tieta, "The Light of Tieta Square." As Jorge Amado declares: "[The old blue sign] didn't last long. It was replaced by a wooden one made by someone's anonymous hands . . . the people's hands." The film ends with the *samba-reggae* theme song by singer-composer Caetano Veloso.

On a more explicit level, the film makes a scathing commentary about a Brazilian lust for money and "sophistication" at the expense of moral values. But, particularly based on the final scenes, one could read this film on another level as a kind of sociocultural imperative: that as Brazil modernizes (symbolized by the coming of electric light), it needs to have respect and love for its heartland and traditions. In other words, it needs to appreciate what it already has. Jairo's statement, "She just wants to be loved" can apply to the van, to Nora, to the Bahian town, and, by extension, to Brazil itself.

At the end of the film, the changed plaque signals a decided leap into modernity, as opposed to the outmoded, feudal-like world represented by the older plaque honoring a local political figure. But at the same time, the plaque that symbolizes modernity is a work of the people made by the people, wooden and rustic in contrast to the older official, metal sign. In this way, the film seems to say, "Enter the modern world, yes, but not without acknowledging the value of the traditions of Brazil." The *samba-reggae* theme music—a perfect example of a hybridized, contemporary tradition from Bahia—which caps the film sonically embodies both of these imperatives simultaneously. In the beginning, Tieta represents a glamorous First World existence that her family only wishes it could have. By the end, by forcing the townspeople to go through a self-deception, Tieta compels some of them at least (such as Ascânio and Tieta's younger sister) to accept if not appreciate who they already are. In other words, they do not have to aspire to be what they are not; they can participate in the modern world and still be from rural Bahia.

Mangue, *Postmodernity*, and the Global Culture Debate 103

More than this, the film suggests that the local can embrace the global on its own terms.[1] In such a reading, prostitution is posited as "commerce" with the outside world, representing a kind of rejection of the authentic and local. Accordingly, although Tieta presents her decision as glamorous, Tieta's and Nora's lives are devoid of the solidarity and ontological security provided by the home, roots, locality and tradition, and so Tieta returns to find these things (to rectify her relation with her family and roots). The film's conclusion offers a resolution of this conflict in the marriage between a symbol of local tradition (Ascânio) and Nora, a woman, like Tieta, who lacks grounding in locality and roots. Brought from the outside by a local returning to her roots, the "light" of Tieta is symbolically embraced by the people (in the form of their new sign), but crucially on their own terms.

In that way, the film offers a relation between local and global and a vision of Brazil in the modern world similar to that offered by *mangue*. Like Tieta, Chico Science (along with many other Brazilian popular musicians of the last several decades) teaches that Brazil should seek to revalorize its traditions while it strives to continue modernizing and globalizing. As such, both *Tieta do Agreste* and the work of Chico Science advocate the use of foreign culture and/or technology while they simultaneously refocus attention on an area within Brazil that for long has been considered backward (the Northeast), investing this region with a strong cultural value.[2] And they advocate critically embracing these influences precisely as tools in the recovery of locality, roots, and tradition.

The ways in which *mangue* musicians engage with global culture make use of ideas often attributed to postmodernism. As the heirs to a national tradition of digesting foreign, First World culture, mixing this with local traditions, and refashioning the result for world consumption (e.g., bossa nova, *tropicália*, etc.), *mangue* musicians do not reject modern, foreign influences, nor do they slavishly aspire to them or accept them as a given. Instead, as members of a subaltern region and communities, they operate at the forefront of cross-cultural fusion and hybridization, creating products that could be—and often are—viewed as even more "up-to-date" than much First World popular music.[3] This emphasis on the so-called "margins" of the world system and on subaltern groups, and particularly their cutting-edge appeal and universal cultural role, is an important aspect of postmodernity. The relative decline of the state (Brazil) as the primary conduit for cultural representation, the opportunities afforded to peripheral groups and communities in general by new economies and technologies (such as the Internet and computers), and the recent importance placed on the local and locality are also key postmodernist traits embodied by Recife's *mangue* movement.

This chapter uses a reading of *mangue* style and ideology as a springboard into an analysis of some of the modernist and postmodernist aspects of the movement (which in the Brazilian situation are often fluid and overlapping). It reveals how *mangue* artists make use of Brazilian modernist practices such as *antropofagia* (cannibalism) to refashion tradition, locality, and a sense of history in a particularly postmodern manner as they engage with global (youth) culture. Suggesting a newly configured, postmodern mapping of culture, my findings show how in *mangue* (along with other contemporary popular trends) the local and global have both assumed heightened importance, becoming articulated within each other in a new way. This new articulation has much to do with challenges to nationalism and national identity in the postmodern picture of culture; here I argue that *mangue* reflects and contributes to a growing challenge to the nation-state in its role as the principal vessel of musical and cultural identity. In the final section I contextualize my findings in Recife within recent debates on world music, politics, and aesthetics. In such a way, I hope to contribute to a clarification of how local musicians (particularly those in the so-called Third World) fit into and relate to an increasingly global network of culture, information, and industry.

Mangue Style and Ideology

The work of Nação Zumbi, Mundo Livre, Via Sat, and other *mangue* bands draws on a variety of traits, discourses, and symbolic resources from within and outside of Brazil. The influences of these bands are by no means uniform—part of the strength of Pernambucan music and culture is precisely its diversity—but there are some binding elements. Although my aim here is not to provide a comprehensive stylistic analysis of the movement, I will point out what I regard as a few of its salient musical and extra-musical features, focusing primarily on Chico Science & Nação Zumbi. Throughout, I will correlate certain aspects of the movement to modernity and postmodernity in the Brazilian context.

First, *mangue* is a decidedly urban phenomenon, linked to the wide range of social and cultural influences that co-exist in 1990s Recife. These span from makeshift houses built on stilts in the mud to computer technology; from mammoth shopping malls and mansions to dirt poor *favelas*; from the "folkloric" *côco, ciranda, maracatu*, and *caboclinho* to rock 'n' roll and the latest electronic dance music trends (e.g., jungle, drum 'n' bass).[4] This postmodern juxtaposition of information technology and global culture with "traditional" folklore and virtually pre-industrial conditions has been reworked in *mangue* in a fluid manner.[5] Paulo André Pires describes what he sees as the successful meeting of "tribal" and "tech" in *mangue*:

> So I think Chico managed, in his science—in the nickname, the scientist of rhythms—to use the traditional with the pop influences and to put this together very well, with the technology, as he talked about so much. Chico talked a lot about technology. This technology that he used was precisely the samplers, it was the instruments that he would be able to use to develop even more this type of music. So he always defended the use of technology. But he never forgot about the tribal side, which were the instruments, *maracatu* drums, in the same way that they were used in the time of slavery, when the slaves brought them from Africa to here.[6] The instrument that he used was exactly the same: a rustic wooden drum with strings and skin from an animal, generally goat, goatskin. So

> I think that his contribution to Brazilian music was very big. I think that he continues to be the most original thing that emerged in *Música Popular Brasileira* [MPB] in the '90s, and with this ascension that we had in the world . . . I think that he managed to take the music and he helped put Pernambuco on the map of world pop music. (Interview: Pires 1998)

The same aesthetic was applied to the band's visual presentation, which mixed the hip and modern with the folkloric and traditional. As Renato L. explains it:

> Also I think that there was a strong influence of the *maracatu* in Chico's gestures on stage. Chico took a lot of gestures of the *maracatu* spear-throwers [*caboclos de lança*] and such. And sometimes even the clothing itself. . . . Because in the guys' visual, it's funny, this mixture [that's present in the music] is already there. The guys use Rayban sunglasses, they already anticipate this mixture in their visual like this. . . . They use Rayban sunglasses with [the clothes] of the [*caboclos de lança*].[7] (Interview: Lins 1998)

In addition to the *caboclo de lança* costume, Chico and band mates sometimes wore the *chapeu de palha*, or straw hat, typical of local fishermen. These traditional folk items—just as the elements of regional folk music—serve as symbols of pride in the local culture for Pernambucans. This postmodern emphasis on locality is a feature I will return to shortly.

Commenting directly on the recent growth of the capital that primarily affected the region's "haves," much *mangue* and the music of other related Recife bands could be taken as an urban sociopolitical commentary from a lower-class perspective.[8] As the DJ and former owner of the club Moritzstadt, José Antônio, told me in English, "Most of the *mangue* people are poor and what they say is fucking true! They sing a reality that they live" (Interview: Filho 1998).

One of CSNZ's most popular songs, "A Cidade" (The City), written by Chico Science, illustrates these points well. The song also represents an assimilated fusion of diverse local and global musical influences. The piece begins with a sample from a song by Velho Faceta, a regional folk musician. This rustic, "rootsy" piece with accordion fades into the assertive sound of *bombo* drums culled from the *maracatu de baque virado*, beating out a composite funk-*maracatu* pattern; this is coupled with a synthesized chordal riff that recalls electronic dance music. Suddenly the other instruments enter: a raunchy distorted guitar, a funky guitar groove, a snaking bass line, and a funky snare drum hammering out a backbeat (refer to Appendix 2, Figure 4 and Appendix 3, Track 8). Chico's inimitable vocal style here recalls, to my ears, new wave and rap mannerisms, as well as inflections of the *embolada*, a northeastern Brazilian musical-poetic form (refer to Appendix 2, Figure 5). The song's lyrics comment on the unstoppable growth of Chico's native Recife, critiquing its ever-widening social gap:

The sun rises and illuminates the evolved stones
That grew with the strength of suicidal stonemasons
Horsemen circulate keeping watch on the people
It doesn't matter if they're bad, nor does it matter if they're good
And the city presents itself as a center of ambition
For beggars or the rich and other elegance
Transport vans, cars, motorcycles and buses
Workers, bosses, police, street peddlers
The city doesn't stop, the city only grows
What's on top goes up and what's below goes down
The city finds itself prostituted
For those who use it as a search for a way out
Illusory for people from other places
The city and its fame go beyond the sea
In the realm of international *esperteza* [cleverness or malice]
The city isn't even so bad
And the situation always more or less [so-so]
Always some with more and others with less
The city doesn't stop, the city only grows
What's on top goes up and what's below goes down
I'm going to make an *embolada*, a samba, a *maracatu*
Everything real clever, good for me and good for you
For us to get out of the mud and face the vultures
On a sunny day Recife woke up
With the same stench as the previous day.[9]

Beginning and ending with a reference to the sunlight of the day, "A Cidade" poetically and vividly reveals the socioeconomic contradictions of a day in the life of modern-day Recife. It highlights the fact that as the city "grows" or modernizes, the rich get richer and the poor get poorer. "Going up" s symbolized by the constructing of buildings, while "going down," although not explicitly so here, may allude to a descent into the swamps or *mangue*, where large communities of poor live. Indeed, Recife grows upward—referenced by the "evolved stones" or high rises—but at the expense of the horribly paid, exploited construction workers whom Chico calls "suicidal stonemasons."

"A Cidade" presents a panorama of the city's evils—beginning with "horsemen who circulate," probably a reference to the Brazilian military police, who, the song suggests, can act with impunity ("It doesn't matter if they're bad, nor does it matter if they're good"). Prostitution is mentioned; indeed, Recife has a notorious sex market, including child prostitution, known by internal and international tourists. International tourism and tourists are implicated here. since, as Chico suggests, for those who come to exploit, "the city isn't even so bad." The lyrics also point to the illusory image of Recife that gets sent to the international community: "Illusory for people from other places/the city and its fame go beyond the sea." In short, the song is a critique of the widening

Mangue, *Postmodernity*, and the Global Culture Debate 107

socioeconomic chasm in Recife and a commentary on urban social ills. Both foreign interests and local corruption are implicated in this situation. Many other *mangue* songs can be seen as portraits of life in the city and as social critique. But notably, here, it is the use of regional and national music styles, such as *embolada*, samba, and *maracatu*, that will enable the *mangue* dwellers—and by extension, Recife generally—to "get out of the mud and face the vultures," that is, to confront their grave social problems.

One of the foremost concepts of *mangue* is the association of the social/cultural environment with the natural one.[10] Specifically, as Renato L. told me, the name *"mangue"* was useful for the movement because Recife's swamps are one of the most diverse ecosystems on the planet, and this biodiversity could be taken as a metaphor for the cultural diversity of the city (Interview: Lins 1998). Indeed, the *mangue* itself is very mixed, with all kinds of imput, just like the music associated with the movement of the same name. The various connections between nature and culture in *mangue* are complex, even suggesting such scientific discourses as Chaos Theory. The use of technology (itself a product of culture) is also associated with—in fact, a part of—the local natural environment in one of the movement's earlier names: *mangue bit*, the latter a reference to the computer bit. The symbol of the movement, a satellite dish sunk in the mud, further reinforces this tech-nature connection, while also suggesting a specific relation of the local and global (which I will explore below).

The band's concept of *afrociberdelia* (taken from the linear notes of their second CD of the same name) makes more explicit the connections among nature, genetics, culture, and technology:

> (Taken from the Galactic Encyclopedia, volume LXII, 2102 edition)
> AFROCIBERDELIA (from Africa + Cibernética + Psychedelicism) - s.f. - The art of mapping the primal genetic memory (which in the 20th century was called "the collective unconscious") through electrochemical stimulation, verbal automation and intense bodily movement to the sound of binary music.
> Practiced informally by tribes of urban youths during the second half of the 20th century; only after 2030 was it officially accepted as a scientific discipline, together with telepathy, pataphysics, and psychoanalysis. For *afrociberdelic* theory, humanity is a benign virus in the software of nature, and can be compared to a Tree whose roots are the codes of human DNA (which originated in Africa), whose branches are the digital-information-electronic ramifications (Cybernetics) and whose fruits provoke altered states of consciousness (Psychedelicism).
> (Written by Bráulio Tauares; translation in Moehn 2001: 262-263 with my own slight modification)

For this theory, cultural expression ("intense bodily movement to the sound of binary music")—and, it is implied, drugs—are means of "mapping the primal genetic memory," accessing the "collective unconscious," or getting in touch with one's "roots." In the Afrociberdelic vision, technology is not only an essential means of achieving this objective but also a *part* of the Tree of humanity and of Nature itself. And it is modern "tribes" of youths, imagined in an urban diaspora (Moehn 2001: 263), who are at the forefront of this movement to recover roots through technology. *Mangue* positions itself within such a diaspora. Moreover, this vision claims for Africa the deepest genetic, and by extension cultural, primacy.

The satellite image of the movement suggests a specific kind of relation between the local and global whereby one is like an antenna that is firmly grounded in local traditions (literally in the mud of the locale) while picking up influences from everywhere. The very short introduction "Mateus Enter (intro)" of the *Afrociberdelia* CD, with lyrics by Chico Science and music by CSNZ, succinctly and dramatically illustrates this vision (refer to Appendix 3, Track 13):

> I came with Nação Zumbi to your ear to speak
> I want to see the dust rise
> And a lot of smoke in the air
> I arrived with my universe
> And I land in your thoughts
> I bring the lights of the posts in my eyes
> Rivers and bridges[11] in my heart
> Pernambuco beneath my feet
> And my mind in the infinity.[12]

The following song on the album, "O Cidadão do Mundo" (The Citizen of the World), with lyrics by Chico Science and music by CSNZ and Eduarco BIDlovski, provides a more detailed picture of the mixing of influences (refer to Appendix 3, Track 14). In referencing both the popular roots of *mangue* (here represented by the *Candomblé* doll [*calunga*] used in the *maracatu nação* and venerable folk figures) as well as the new nation of Zumbi and Daruê Malungo, "his nation," Chico makes a link between the old traditions and *mangue*:

> I'm going to gather together my nation
> In the land of the *maracatu*
> Dona Ginga, Zumbi, Veludinho
> Listen to the rhythm of Mestre Salu[13]
> I saw, I saw
> My voodoo doll
> Go up and down in the space
> At the time of the coronation
> Forgive me, sir, forgive me
> But this here is my nation
> Daruê Malungo, Nação Zumbi [Zumbi Nation]
> It's the zoom zoom zoom [buzz] of the capital
> There's only a clever crab
> Coming out of this *mangue* swamp
> I jumped, I jumped

Mangue, Postmodernity, and the Global Culture Debate 109

I ran in the soft kick
I met the citizen of the world
In the *mangue* swamp at the river's edge
Josué!

This text reveals Chico's respect for and assumption of the tradition: He cites some important folk figures, says he will gather his nation in the land of the *maracatu*, and he refers to the *calunga* as "my voodoo doll." Although he makes a distinction between the older figures and the new movement, Chico asks the tradition, in effect, for the permission to innovate ("forgive me, sir, forgive me/but this here is my nation").[14]

Indeed, for Chico, it is this new turn on tradition that serves to captivate the whole city and enable it to negotiate with a complex social reality, symbolized by the biodiverse *mangue*. I have emphasized the connection made between the social and natural worlds in *mangue*.[15] The crab—particularly the crab with a brain—is likened to the self-aware Recife citizen dealing intelligently with his or her social surroundings. It is the human in touch with and able to transform his or her environment. The cry "Josué!" is a reference to Josué de Castro, an important local nutritionist and writer (see Castro 1970) who described the life cycle of crabs and fisherman. This influence highlights the *mangue* movement's connections to the region's scientific history. Chico grounds a *mangue* identity, then, not only in regional cultural practices but also in the mud itself, with its wealth of organic life, symbolizing the cultural diversity, and thus great potential, of the regional culture. Again, music is fundamental to this imperative of the Recife citizen to contend with his or her condition and environment. At the same time, it is a connection to the past and an understanding of one's relation to the environment (social or natural) that serve as Recife's passport to a global existence. The song suggests that the self-aware Recife resident, symbolized by the crab, is clever (*esperto*) and "a citizen of the world."

This appeal to global citizenship is embodied in the musical objectives of the movement. As Chico once said, "We don't think the fact that we use regional rhythms from Pernambuco can make things difficult because the sound that we make is universal. We have a vision of the music of the world without trying to make world music" (Interview with Antônio Carlos Miguel for *O Globo*, quoted in Teles n/d: 23). Being members of the world provides artists in Recife an opportunity not only to speak to the world, but also to have a kind of universal relevance. Buell has argued that with its basis in syncretism and hybridity, postmodernism offers opportunities to "peripheral" communities not afforded by the Western version of modernity.[16] These opportunities enable both a heightened importance to be placed on the locale (e.g., Recife) and a more active engagement on the part of locales with global culture. As I allude to earlier in this chapter, it is the subaltern (and his or her culture) now who comes to take on a more cutting-edge appeal in a postmodern view of the world. Citing George Lipsitz (1990), Robert Walser notes that "in a world where more and more people feel dislocated and disenfranchised, the culture of people who have historically lived with the contradictions of being outsiders becomes increasingly relevant to everyone" (Walser 1995: 210).[17] This applies as much to black U.S. hip-hop as it does to the *mangue* of Recife.

"O Cidadão do Mundo" musically embodies this objective of appealing to global citizenship and universality through fusing the local into the global At both its structural level and in its combination of elements within these sections, the piece could be described as a juxtaposition and hybrid of hip-hop (specifically funk), *maracatu*, *embolada*, *raggamuffin*, and heavy metal influences (refer to Appendix 2, Figures 6-10 for a more complete analysis of the song's form and stylistic components). The form is divided into several distinct sections, which juxtapose in a fluid fashion these various elements. A diagram of this form is shown below:

(A) Hip-hop/(B) *Maracatu de baque virado*/(A') Hip-hop/(B') *Maracatu de baque virado*/(C) Hip-hop with *raggamuffin-embolada* section in vocal/ (end of C) Heavy metal

Chico's vocal style underlines the interconnectedness among various musical traditions. The distorted, processed sound of his voice recalls the Jamaican *raggamuffin* tradition, styles of heavy rock, or even the *embolada*. The manner in which it is chanted suggests an affinity with rap in a broad sense. But the melody of sections A/A' and B/B' is firmly in line with local folk practices and could even be a *toada* in the *maracatu de baque virado* tradition (refer to Appendix 2, Figures 10 and 11). In the third "hip-hop" section (C), over a funk drumset groove and in counterpoint with a *berimbau* (musical bow from the *capoeira* tradition), Chico breaks into an *embolada*, a musical-poetic form from Northeast Brazil in which words are recited quickly in syncopation over a duple meter.[18] This melody (and delivery) also bears similarities to the practice of Jamaican dancehall reggae (*raggamuffin*), specifically for its alternation back and forth between several repeated notes, which contrasts with the formulaic descending phrases of the *embolada* as seen in Appendix 2, Figure 12. (Refer to Appendix 2, Figures 10, 12, and 13 for a comparison of Chico's vocal melody in section C of "O Cidadão do Mundo" and examples of *embolada* and *raggamuffin*.) In the final "heavy metal" section, in which the *bombo* drums launch into a rock groove and distorted guitars enter, Chico delivers a spoken phrase in the harsh, screaming style of a hard-core or heavy metal singer. Science's vocal style, as the band's overall style, is based on a fluid assimilation of various elements borrowed from diverse regional and international idioms; the band helps make the sometimes-surprising connections among these idioms tangible.

The use of collage, juxtaposition, or pastiche is a feature in *mangue* that recalls both hip-hop and the aforementioned *tropicália* movement of the late 1960s. A strong case could be made for *tropicália* being a postmodern movement—for example, its use of musical collage, the juxtaposition of folkloric and modern in both the lyrics and music, and its ironic sense of self-representation. But *tropicália* is informed by a fundamental concept in Brazilian modernist thought known as *antropofagia* (cannibalism).[19] A product of the Brazilian modernist thinker Oswald de Andrade (*Manifesto Antropófago*, 1928), *antropofagia*, or "cannibalism" proposed a particular perspective on foreign influence. As opposed to the racial mixing of *mestiçagem* (another cornerstone of Brazilian modernism discussed below), this discourse urges *cultural* mixing in Brazil, specifically on a global level. According to this imperative, Brazilians "devour" or "digest" diverse foreign cultural traits, reinterpret them within a national framework and "spit out" the results as something new and Brazilian; this process was likened to the practice of cannibalism by some indigenous Brazilian tribes.[20]

The sonic texture of "O Cidadão do Mundo" exemplifies *mangue*'s relation to *antropofagia*. The piece is complemented with the use of digital samples of classic MPB songs by Jorge Ben ("Cuidado com o Bulldog"), Gilberto Gil and Torquato Neto ("Louvação"), and Caetano Veloso and Gilberto Gil ("Batmacumba"). On one level this is an acknowledgement of national popular music pioneers: the *tropicalistas* and other early MPB figures such as Jorge Ben. But the application of "cannibalistic" discourse and practice originally employed by the *tropicalistas* here is ironic and clear: Chico Science and his band have "gobbled up" pieces, which themselves had "gobbled up" various domestic and foreign references, and "spit them out" into a new context as one more element in an ever increasing pool of influences.[21]

The *mangue* musicians' use of *antropofagia* differs from that of the *tropicalistas* principally in how the results are projected. In the late 1960s, the work of Caetano Veloso and Gilberto Gil was filtered through a *national* lens, revolutionizing how all subsequent popular music of the nation could be made. Artists in Recife in the 1990s, by contrast, make use of one nationalist, modernist discourse among many possible ones and interact with a history of Brazilian pop in the course of forging a more locally defined identity. This identity does not reject the idea of nation at all. Rather, it bypasses the confines of nationality to interact with the world in a more particular, more localized way. As such, *mangue* is simultaneously representative of a subculture within a region and a kind of global interculture (see Slobin 1992).

If "O Cidadão do Mundo" presents a culturally anthropophagous cycle, the idea of a literal, environmental "cannibalistic cycle" is evident in Josué de Castro's work, which, as mentioned above, is one of the intellectual influences on *mangue*. As Chico Science describes it:

> We have a hunger for information. In the image of Josué, we are crabs with brains, like the fishermen whom he described in his book *Homem e Caranguejos* [Of Men and Crabs; see Castro 1970]. They fish and eat crabs after which they excrete them in a chaotic cycle. We make a chaotic music

(Interview with Luis Antônio Giron for *Folha de São Paulo*, quoted in Teles n/d: 25).

Mangue takes the literal local hunger described in Josué de Castro's work and transforms it creatively into a global hunger for information as a way of contending with the social predicament of Recife. As I pointed out above the association with the *caranguejo*, or crab, is an enduring metaphor; *mangue* movement adherents are imagined as part of the swamp and its organic life. Chico correlates the natural world, with its chaotic cycles and multitude of influences, to the "chaotic," hybridized music of his band.

This connection between the social and natural environments and the discourse on chaos are elucidated further in the song "Da Lama Ao Caos" (From Mud to Chaos), the title track of CSNZ's debut album (1995) with words and music by Chico Science. The lyrics of the song link the chaos of the region's natural environment—*lama*, or mud—with the chaos of the sprawling urban metropolis, revealing the deep-seated poverty and social differences of Brazil as manifest in Recife. Chico describes the song:

> "Da Lama Ao Caos" [From Mud to Chaos] is a song that reminds me of Josué de Castro. It's a song that talks about chaos, in the mud [of Recife] or in big urban sectors. It's as if a crab-man came out of the *mangue* swamps to an urban center to . . . look for another way of life. And from one side or the other he's always robbed, he's always castrated . . . he's always impoverished. And "Da Lama Ao Caos" is exactly this: It's the face of Recife, the poverty that . . . Brazil experiences, the social differences. And I think of Josué de Castro exactly in this part that says: "Oh Josué, I never saw so great a disgrace, the more misery there is, the more the vulture threatens." ("Chico Science Mangue Star" video, TV Viva/TV Jornal, Recife)

Alluding to Chaos Theory, in which order is found in apparent disorder, the lyrics of the song talk about ordering and disordering oneself: "I can get out of here to organize myself/I can get out of here to disorganize myself/From the mud to chaos/From chaos to the mud/A robbed man never deceives himself." This recalls the idea that modernity is an attempt to order the environment (Bauman 1992: xi-xvii), while postmodernity subverts this order to achieve chaos.[22] In this sense, the song could be regarded as an attempt to understand whom the Recife citizen is in an increasingly complex, modernizing world; to do this, Chico goes back to the natural environment. Another possible association here is the linking of racial/cultural miscegenation—a hallmark both of Brazilian genetics and national identity—with disorder, leading to an unpredictable, "chaotic" result.[23]

Whereas on a structural level the last example represents a juxtaposition of musical elements in which the move from one set of musical codes to the next is noticeable, if fluid, "Da Lama Ao Caos" features an instructive example of a rhythmic fusion or hybrid (refer to Appendix 3, Track 9). In this case, informed listeners may be able to discern what the component influences are, but the whole could be regarded as something new. Created by Maureliano (former member of the band and currently a percussionist for Via Sat), the song's rhythm is an economical fusion of soul and *maracatu de baque virado* (refer to Appendix 2, Figure 3).[24] The *caixa* or snare drum part is a condensation of a soul drum-set groove, while the *bombo* part is constructed as follows: The first and third rhythmic cells are adapted from the bass drum part of a drum-set in a soul or funk rhythm. The second cell consists of two offbeats, which are defining beats of the *maracatu nação* rhythm known as the *baque de marcação* (marking rhythm) (Refer to Appendix 2, Figure 1). The fourth and final cell mimics the rhythm of a typical riff played by a soul horn section (Interview: Ribeiro 1998).[25] Added to this rhythmic base is a heavy metal guitar and Chico's vocals, which here highlight the aforementioned *embolada*, while also suggesting rap, metal, and Jamaican *raggamuffin* influences.[26]

In *mangue* style and ideology, technology is a part of Nature and an indispensable tool for the rediscovery of cultural roots. By the same token, through technology, global influences are captured (metaphorically via satellite) and, in a sense, reconstituted into these cultural roots. The use of technology and of foreign cultural elements is not only *not* antithetical to a reassertion of roots and local identity, but they are also integral to this process. As such, *mangue* positions foreign and domestic sources as integrated, symbiotic, and overlapping, as I demonstrated in the last chapter. At the same time, *mangue*'s local identity—already a complex crossroads of local and global cultural influences— has become a more global one by adopting global sounds and ideas and by participating in a global network of information. Next, I explore the relation between local and global in *mangue*. I submit that Pernambuco has come to interact with the world in a way that, in postmodern fashion, foregrounds the regional locale and poses a challenge to the primacy of the nation in determining cultural identity. But this relation does not represent a rejection of the nation at all. Instead, *mangue* artists retain the liberty to make use of national discourse and nationally associated cultural forms among its pool of diverse influences.

The Local Within the Global and the Global Within the Local:
A Postmodern Challenge to National Identity

Since the 1930s, Brazilian national identity has been shaped and guided by the thought of the Recife sociologist Gilberto Freyre, whose notion of *mestiçagem* (racial miscegenation) has served, like *antropofagia*, as a cornerstone of Brazilian modernist thought. As historian Thomas E. Skidmore points out, the race issue has been intimately tied up in questions of national identity since the nineteenth century in Brazil (Skidmore 1974). Of critical concern to the Eurocentric Brazilian elites has been rectifying the country's largely non-white population with Brazil's national identity and its image abroad (ibid.). Articulated most famously by Freyre in the 1930s, *mestiçagem* is basically a celebration of Brazil's tri-partite racial and ethnic heritage, highlighting the contributions of Africans and indigenous Brazilians to the country's national culture, as well as a celebration of racial mixing (see Skidmore 1974: 190-192).[27] A response to previous racist ideologies such as *branqueamento* (whitening), *mestiçagem* has become a dominant discourse in Brazilian national identity, manifest in both official and popular realms.[28] Indeed, any subsequent racial theory or ideology (such as the articulation of a specifically *Afro*-Brazilian consciousness and identity) has had to contend with the normative idea put forth in Freyre's work that racial mixing has been highly positive for Brazil. It is this Freyrian image of Brazil as a mixed-race country that has been intimately associated with, and reproduced countless times in, the samba, a quintessentially "national" Brazilian music.[29]

The idea of a Brazilian national consciousness in the first place must be understood in relation to a diagnostic of Brazil's perceived "backwardness" compared with the "civilized" countries (Vianna 1995: 156). In contrast to many proposals that have aimed to "develop" the country so that it would approximate the First World—a basic imperative of Western-derived modernity—*mestiçagem* emphasized what was different about Brazil. Notably, this Freyrian discourse posits "indefinition" as fundamental to Brazilian culture. As the Brazilian anthropologist Hermano Vianna observes,

> This regime of "indefinition" (between white and black, between man and woman, between the masters house and slave quarters) would continue to be thought of as our principal characteristic, our great particularity, and also as that which gives us "grace." (Vianna 1995: 147)

As such, *mestiçagem* represents one, albeit important, aspect of—and response to—modernity in the Brazilian scenario:

> Gilberto Freyre and all those who made possible the transformation of the samba into a Brazilian national symbol wanted for Brazil a "different" modernity, a modernity that incorporated the cultural elements until then considered symptoms or causes of our "backwardness" (among them *mestiçagem* and the samba itself). (Vianna 1995: 156)

Vianna claims that "This project and this praxis have had better days" (ibid.). As some have argued, *mestiçagem* and its accompanying idea of a "racial democracy" have contributed to "the mythic projection of Brazil as a nonconflictual society" (Yúdice 1994: 197).[30] But in countering this myth, where can Brazilians turn? Vianna questions whether for Brazilians to combat racism, for example, it is necessary to do away with the traditional fluidity ("indefinition") of racial boundaries in the country in favor of the more rigid racial system of the U.S. (ibid.: 157).[31] "Or is [the adherence to the U.S. racial system] the easiest way for us to try again to adjust ourselves to the modernity of (fragmentary) international capitalism?" he asks (ibid.).

Mangue, *Postmodernity, and the Global Culture Debate* 115

At the same time that he questions the alternatives, Vianna concedes that the Freyrian project is paradoxical: "That which was praised for being open to difference, for including the diverse, came to exclude diversity in the name of its orthodoxy" (Vianna 1995: 158). In other words, apart from what Freyre or others might have wanted, the samba has become an "internal 'colonizing' agent . . . the only [or at least most characteristic] way to be Brazilian" (ibid.). "The undefined became the rule of the definition"—that is, the indefinition of the *mestiço* samba itself became codified paradoxically as a rigid definition of Brazilianness (ibid.).[32]

Some critics have regarded the samba and the *mestiçagem* project in general as part of a national "consensus culture" that masks deep differences and inequities in Brazilian society. George Yúdice wholeheartedly subscribes to this view:

> I would like to suggest, however, that the circumstances have changed, and that not everything will "sooner or later end up in samba" or any other celebration of Brazilian identity that "keeps all social classes and races together in harmony" [McGowan and Pessanha 1998: 53]. The transition to an ever distant democracy in the eighties and nineties has brought to the surface the unworkability of social and political enfranchisement through cultural practices that formed part of a "consensus" that dealt material wealth to elites and ever greater hardship to subalterns. Today the cultural scene is rapidly changing, reflecting the growing dissatisfaction with the nation. . . . The breakdown in Brazilian national identity has taken place politically as well as racially and culturally. As Howard Winant argues: "Today, blacks are beginning to challenge the racial 'common sense,' both mainstream and radical, that race and racism are of limited political significance in the Brazilian context." (Yúdice 1994: 195-196)[33]

Yúdice elaborates on what that national identity has been and what it is being transformed into:

> Brazil, which has a land mass larger than that of the continental U.S., has never been a homogenous country, although samba, carnival, bossa nova, MPB (Música Popular Brasileira) did represent it as more or less coherent. Today, however, a *new politics of representation* has emerged that places the emphasis on difference. The media, the new social movements, and the asymmetrical but pervasive consumer culture all engage in this politics of representation, making it impossible for any one group to maintain control of how it is imaged. (ibid.: 210)

This situation could be seen as a postmodern one in which totalizing narratives (e.g., the so-called "consensus culture") are refused and in which cultural authority is divested, at least somewhat, from the nation-state and shifted to communities. I am reminded here of Bauman's characterization of postmodernity: "[It] is marked by a view of the human world as irreducibly and irrevocably pluralistic, split into a multitude of sovereign units and sites of authority, with no horizontal or vertical order, either in actuality or in potency" (Bauman 1992: 35). At this point such a characterization is too optimistic for Brazil or anywhere—nation-states still wield hegemonic power and not all "sites" are sovereign. Nevertheless, it does point to some important changes: the relative deemphasis on the nation-state as the primary shaper of identity, the growing possibility for the assertion of localized identities within nations, and an expanding relation between these localized identities and a global cultural system. *Mangue* exemplifies these postmodern transformations.

A focus on subaltern groups and expressions of racial and class difference, also postmodern traits, have begun to be articulated more clearly in post-dictatorship Brazilian popular music generally (e.g., in Brazilian rap, in the more political music of the *blocos afro* of Bahia and in some of the songs of Rio's *escolas de samba*.) Concurrent with this recent focus on race and class has been a rising effort to link up Brazilian musical traditions to global popular genres of the African diaspora such as rap and reggae.[34] *Mangue* shows its affinities with these recent trends in its strong social criticism, its emphasis on class difference, and its valorization of black or *mestiço* and lower-class cultural forms within the nation and globally. In a general sense, then, *mangue* offers a challenge to the nation in its participation in a more open, widespread social critique in popular culture (which has been feasible in the country only with the ease of censorship, the fall of the dictatorship, and finally the return to civilian rule in 1985). However, *mangue* does not represent an assertion of racial politics the way some Brazilian rap and *bloco afro* material do. Rather, *mangue*'s postmodern challenge to the authority of the nation has more to do with a new emphasis on, and relation between, the local and the global than with racial, ethnic, or class politics or even to an explicit challenge to a "consensus culture."

According to Frederick Buell,

> The emergent communicational model of globalization theory suggests that one of the chief symptoms and causes of these developments has been the rapid alteration in the circulation of knowledge. . . . In these transformations, old notions about bounded, territorially rooted civilizations and national cultures are utterly broken down. (Buell 1994: 337)

The globalized nature of the so-called postmodern world is part of what Yúdice calls a "breakdown in Brazilian national identity." According to Yúdice it is mostly youth who are making transnational leaps into new territory:

> Perhaps more than any other sector, including the black and other social movements, which continue to invest their cultural-political capital in Brazil *as a nation*, youth, especially subaltern youth, are leading the way to new experiences, often crisscrossed by transnational cultural forms that confound the "consensus culture," and often seem to instill fear in the elite and middle

classes, and suspicion among the leadership of the social movements. (Yúdice 1994: 196)

Yúdice posits Rio funk culture as one such youth phenomenon that has "opted out" of the national "consensus culture."[35] But the reality of this situation may be more complex than this; Yúdice's article problematically opposes domestic and foreign musics in a way that ignores the often symbiotic, mutually relevant, and, indeed, overlapping of such boundaries in the Brazilian arena.[36]

The lack of clear boundaries—manifest in *mestiçagem* and a decidedly syncretic cultural heritage (highlighted in *antropofagia*) that repeatedly dislodges any notion of the purely "domestic" or purely "foreign"—already characteristic of Brazilian modernism, might now also be considered a postmodern phenomenon. As Vianna observes, if Brazilians continued to believe in the Freyrian national project, "We would even be precursors of a deceased postmodernism that believed that the hybrid was chic, or of a North American militancy that today wants the creation of a multiracial category in the U.S. census" (Vianna 1995: 158). Countering the typical arrangement of modernity in which the Third World nations have had to "catch up" to the West, here the West may be trying to "catch up" to the Third World. The current fad for *tropicália* in the U.S. pop world, part of a more widespread turn toward subaltern peoples and "traditional" cultures for solutions in our "confused" time of globalization and cross-cultural syncretism, is indicative of this "catch up" trend in reverse.[37]

The work of CSNZ is sonic and visual evidence of the role of Recife citizens as global cultural navigators. As Frederick Moehn points out,

> to be Brazilian is not in contradiction with being of the world, it is precisely to be of the world. . . . Rather than viewing local musical traditions and values as unchanging, or as losing ground to some kind of homogenized global mass culture, [MPB artists such as Fernanda Abreu and Chico Science] assert that the way Brazilian 'mix' will always be unique (Moehn 2001: 268).

Indeed, since the 1990s, Brazilian pop musicians have increasingly asserted the local identity of their music (in whatever way they conceptualize this identity) as they raid the global soundscape and reach international ears. As Moehn argues:

> MPB artists embrace the possibilities offered by the media and technology for exploration of new musical pathways. Yet this optimistic techno-cosmopolitanism enters into a tension with a construction of identity that asserts a greater role for Brazilian musicality in a world of cultural hypermiscegenation. . . . I suggest that the music makers I discuss here [i.e., Chico Science, Fernanda Abreu, and Carlinhos Brown] are asking to have Brazilian musical values and styles "brought up" in the "global mix." By reinterpreting local musics into transnationally hybrid styles, they are literally increasing the presence of local Brazilian genres in the international popular music scene. (Moehn 2001: 260; 268)

In stark contrast, then, to the typical framing of a Brazilian cultural identity debate as a dichotomization of "national" versus "international" music, or even the portrayal of foreign styles as a means of "opting out" of a rigid national "consensus culture" (see Yúdice 1994), the case of *mangue* and other cutting-edge MPB rather presents much more of a mutual affinity and overlap among local and global musics. Of course this has been a model for avant-garde pop in the country at least since bossa nova. But in the case of CSNZ, Carlinhos Brown, and some other contemporary MPB artists this process is taken to extremes. The music of Chico Science, for example, is arguably both even more "local" and more "global" than much MPB—that is, at once more firmly situated in a specific regional context and more open to the culture of the world, particularly that of a global youth diaspora.

But where does this leave the question of "Brazil" in this debate? In some sense, *mangue*, and particularly the bands that utilize specifically regional elements in their music, are bypassing the role of the nation in determining the identity of their music. It should be remembered that there is a satellite here in the mud of Pernambuco going directly out to the rest of the world. A similar notion is present in the work of Rio-based MPB artist Fernanda Abreu, who positions Rio de Janeiro, rather than Recife, as "a cardiod center of transnational groove production" (Moehn 2001: 262). In interviews, Chico Science has said that his band needed to gain an international career to avoid having to p ay certain prescribed kinds of music in Brazil.

At the same time, Fernanda Abreu, like some of my consultants in Recife, has stressed "the idea that, starting in the 90s, Brazilian Pop Music mixes, in a more effective manner, 'Brazil' in its language" (from a press kit, publicity office of Fernanda Abreu, 1998, quoted in Moehn 2001: 262). Brazil is a regionally divided country with a rich cultural and musical diversity among states. As such, pop musicians in the country choose to define their local heritage differently depending on where they come from. This situation allows for the diversity of Brazilian culture while it refuses a rigid definition of what it means to make Brazilian music (either as circumscribed by the music industry or cultural critics).

But more than this, constituting part of a global trend toward an increased emphasis on the micro locale as opposed to the nation-state in the construction of musical and cultural identities, *mangue* positions Recife and Pernambuco as more important identifiers than Brazil in the postmodern musical map. Thus, while modernity legitimized the uniform authorities of nation-states, postmodern thought shifts emphasis to the community—or, more precisely, to *communities* (Bauman 1992: 35-36). This, of course, does not discount *mangue*'s relation to Brazil or MPB, but rather reveals a dramatic shift in emphasis. This occurs in a way that did not happen with the samba, bossa nova, or *tropicália*. Although both the urban samba and the bossa nova are inextricably linked to Rio de Janeiro (and indeed because of this connection with Rio), they both came to speak for

Brazil or to represent it in some way to the outside world and to itself. *Tropicália*, too, has come to be a marker of a Brazilian national identity rather than a marker of a regional identity within the Brazilian territory. However, this is not the case with *mangue*. Surely *mangue* has resonated throughout Brazil, has probably had some impact on a national cultural identity, and has come to be associated on some level with the nation in the minds of Brazilian and other listeners. But at the same time, this regionally-based trend points to a shrinking ability for popular music to represent the nation as some unified entity—which it is increasingly not in Brazil and elsewhere—and an expanding ability for it to represent specific regions or communities within nations and across them.

Moreover, this emphasis on the local has become increasingly specific. Within Recife's diverse but coherent music scene, specific communities vie for their place in the largest possible arena of exposure—the world. Members of the hard-core band Devotos do Ódio, for instance, not only position themselves as Pernambucans, but also, more particularly, they project their own neighborhood, the Alto José do Pinho, as the most significant symbol of their identity. In an episode of the "Som da Nota" on Recife's TV Jornal, one member of the Lamento Negro group in Peixinhos reflects on the valuable role of that neighborhood in the Recife scene, and hence in a global arena, claiming, "Peixinhos is in the world!" This could be taken as both an assertion of resistance against the marginality of poor communities as well as an affirmation of the increasingly refined importance of the local in popular music and identity—not only in Brazil, but worldwide.

But concurrent with this increased emphasis on the local is an emergence of the global, and not necessarily as the foreboding homogenizing agent so feared by many scholars and musicians alike. Indeed, as Nação Zumbi and other bands put Pernambuco on the world musical map, they have also mapped music of the world onto Pernambuco in a mutually beneficial process. As such, in Chapter Four I posited the relation between local-global, traditional-modern, and domestic-foreign elements in *mangue* as being a symbiotic, integrated, and blurred one, suggesting a kind of postmodern overlapping of boundaries. The *mangue* movement is testament to the increased importance of both the ever more particular local and the ever more universal global in popular music and ideology. It reveals the articulations of these elements within each other, and a blurring between them, in a postmodern challenge to the supercultural authority of the nation-state to prescribe social and cultural identity. Not rejecting "Brazilianness" by any means, however, *mangue* retains the prerogative to employ modernist and nationalist discourses (such as *mestiçagem* and *antropofagia*) and nationally-associated cultural forms such as the samba among a host of others in the shaping of its sound, style, identity, and ideology.[38]

Mangue and the Global Culture Debate

Entering the recent debate about "world music" and the global economy outlined in the Introduction, I would not categorize the music of bands on the

Recife scene as either always reproducing the hegemony of a certain dominant group, as Erlmann (1996) would have it, or, on the other hand, as the embodiment of unbridled resistance against the "system" on the part of local musicians, as other perspectives may propose.[39] Nor do I see *mangue* as reflecting a kind of platform of contestation for the struggles of various social groups to represent themselves, as other authors have suggested about popular culture.[40] My understanding of *mangue* leaves much room for local expression (see Averill 1995, Bilby 1999), and even resistance, but it does not pit local musicians against any one dominant group or the "system" itself. Rather, I see *mangue* artists as making use of the global cultural system to offer their own localized point of view about the world and artistic expression. Even if this point of view poses a challenge to the dominance of the nation-state to prescribe cultural identity or some of the constricting facets of the culture industry, as authors such as Lipsitz permit, it does not stand in opposition to either "Brazil" or the international recording industry by any means.

Specifically, I regard *mangue* as reflecting and embodying the expanding possibility for subaltern, Third World musicians to project their own localized interpretations of music and culture within a more global system, even if these interpretations are not in opposition to any one hegemonic group. My reading of *mangue* does not ignore the weight of the international music industry or the dominance of U.S.-based musics and influences in Brazil, for example. But it also acknowledges that ever since there was a Brazilian popular music, musicians have been crafting their own creative fusions and hybrids of local and global elements. Such hybrid popular musics may certainly counter established ideologies. They may also be fruitfully seen as simply offering one more valid point of view among many possible ones in the global system, even if there is still an imbalance in which views receive the most exposure.[41] But more than this, these musics (and the cultures that produced them) may take on a special role in a global arena. *Mangue* musicians, as other artists from the periphery of the world system, are acutely aware of the cutting-edge potential for the Third World in relation to the West. As Fred Zero Quatro sings in "Destruindo A Camada de Ozônio" (Destroying the Ozone Layer), "Don't expect anything from the center if the periphery is dead, since what was old in the North becomes new in the South."[42]

Unlike some more overtly accommodating or homogenized forms of pop music, *mangue* in my view stands among some of the most dynamic responses and challenges to the question of cultural imposition, both at the national and international levels. Functioning within a more global network, Recife artists operating on the current scene refuse to be confined by the dictates of an already international Brazilian pop industry at the same time that they selectively use aspects of global, Brazilian national, and more regional discourses or stylistic elements. It is not the "ominous" multinational music industry here that restricts local musicians. To the contrary, it is the more global recording label (but crucially a smaller division of that label) that allows CSNZ to circumvent national prescriptions on their music and in turn to affect music of the nation for the better without the need for massification:[43]

> It's not a question of an ambition. We don't intend for Brazil to fall ill with *mangue beat* fever. We didn't emerge out of nowhere, we've been working at this for at least four years and if we signed with the Chaos label of Sony we were given the possibility of preserving our principles. We won't be the new wave, but the fortification of our work will be able to improve the music of Brazil in general. (Chico Science in an interview with Antônio Carlos Miguel, *O Globo*, March 31, 1994, quoted in Teles n/d: 23)

In their use of collage and fusion and in their assertion of a strong local identity, *mangue* musicians do not stand outside of the "system." Rather, they operate fully and actively within it, adapting elements of globally more dominant styles while injecting their own locally based sounds and images into this system. These local ingredients come to take on a heightened importance both for members or proponents of the movement and for potential consumers in the U.S., Europe, and elsewhere.

The selective use of regional tradition in a contemporary market is an important aspect of the postmodern opportunities for local representation embodied by the *mangue* movement. At the same time, in their affinities with other musics of "resistance" such as rap and heavy styles of rock, *mangue* musicians are crafting their own vision of their place in the world, regardless of how this vision may or may not contribute to socioeconomic betterment or translate into political intention or efficacy. But much more than some kind of safety valve, *mangue* empowers local musicians with the ability to represent their particular realities within a system with an ever more expansive potential for exposure. In line with such a reading, *mangue* pioneers such as Fred Zero Quatro and Renato L. have expressed the ambition that, like Salvador (Bahia) and Jamaica, Recife may be another small, Third World region situated at the periphery of the market destined to garner world recognition (Fred Zero Quatro in his second manifesto of the *mangue* movement *Quanto Vale Uma Vida? Longa Vida Ao Groove!* [How Much Is a Life Worth? Long Life to the Groove!], quoted in Teles n/d: 47).

Along the lines of Slobin's (1992) work, I am willing to see a multitude of possible associations and uses for any given cultural product in the global system, and I certainly would not equate the capacity for cultural representation that I grant to *mangue* musicians with a corresponding degree of socioeconomic empowerment (although unquestionably, *mangue* and the "new music scene" have translated into socioeconomic opportunities for many people in Recife). Nor am I suggesting that there is equal representation of music or points of view in any system; in fact, thus far, compared with other trends on the world market, *mangue* and the "new music scene" have made only a tiny yet promising splash. But, along with other contemporary popular musics, *mangue* does place an emphasis on the local that, contrary to what Erlmann suggests, is much more than a myth created by the West to associate with "otherness" and thereby disguise its own hegemony. Anyone may make sense of, and even affect this local identity in a possibly infinite number of ways; but the participation of multinational labels in the movement—or, so far, any other factor—has not robbed this identity of its ability to represent people in Recife and globally in empowering ways.

In his analysis of Haitian musicians on the world circuit, Gage Averill argues that new markets are "providing them with incrementally improved bargaining positions to record on their own terms" (1995: 358). While he is critical of Western ideologies, replete with time old tropes and stereotypes about the non-Western world, that surround the consumption of Third World pop, Averill maintains that the self-reproducing niche world musicians have been carving in the international arena negates these genres' statuses as novelty items. He argues that the discourses of Third World musicians are affecting how their musics are perceived and genres and audiences are becoming more and more nuanced and refined (ibid.). This optimistic evaluation finds a correlate in the early stages of *mangue*'s ascension on the world stage. The fact that *mangue* musicians did much of their own marketing at least locally, the salience of diversity as a potential buffer to commercial homogenization, the apparent relative freedom granted to the bands that have recorded, and the relative absence of a massification in the movement have further strengthened a sense of local empowerment.

Furthermore, on a related issue, I do not see *mangue* as disembedded from time and space in the way that Erlmann (1996) ascribes to fully postmodern world musics. There is, however, the postmodern sense in *mangue* that the past has become "a synchronic warehouse of cultural scenarios" (Appadurai 1990: 4). CSNZ, for example, have created songs that layer a variety of sounds based on older and current global and local trends; these sounds are part of an endless source of available material to be reworked and refashioned. Referring to the music of his region, Chico Science remarked, "So I saw all of these things that they taught us as folklore, as a manifestation of the past, but it isn't really in his way that you have to see them" (Interview with Luis Claudio Garrido, *Jornal à Tarde da Bahia*, April 30, 1994, quoted in Teles n/d: 30). Yet, the various combinations of influences, a recontextualization of aspects of the past in the present, and the highly dispersed nature of the global music industry do not preclude a grounding of *mangue* in particular social and historical times and spaces.

Perhaps most immediate for certain people in Pernambuco (and especially Greater Recife), *mangue*'s story can be relevant for anyone anywhere on the planet, perhaps particularly so for other subaltern communities. And this is not so solely because *mangue* is at base a commercial product like any other, as Erlmann's theory would have us believe. It is not constructed, as Erlmann proposes—rather problematically—for certain modernized, Third World genres, "around the shock and dislocation an individual from a local, non-Western

Mangue, Postmodernity, and the Global Culture Debate 123

tradition might experience who suddenly finds his or her life-world more or less violently juxtaposed with the world of industrial capitalism" (1996: 476). For the MP3 musician in the 1990s, this is no longer an issue. But neither does *mangue* paint a sonic "pseudopast" or embody a waning historicity that Erlmann ascribes to fully postmodern world music.

Take for example, the opening cut of CSNZ's debut album, titled "Monólogo Ao Pé do Ouvido," which presents an imagined aspect of its past (refer to Appendix 3, Track 1). The lyrics affirm a strong connection to this past, even as a tension is set up between the past and present. The text is recited by Chico Science over the sound of what seems to be an electronically processed or simulated *berimbau* and some *bombo* drums playing a *maracatu nação* pattern called *martelo* (hammer) to which one extra note has been added (refer to Appendix 2, Figure 2, Example 4):

> To modernize the past
> It's a musical evolution
> Where are the notes that were here
> I don't need them!
> It's enough to let everything sound good to the ears
> Fear leads to evil
> The collective man feels the necessity to fight
> The pride, the arrogance, the glory
> Fill up the imagination of control
> They are demons those who destroy the power
> Wild humanity
> Viva Zapata! Viva Sandino!
> Antônio Conselheiro
> All the Black Panthers
> Lampião your image and semblance
> I am certain that they too sang one day.[44]

In these lyrics, there is a strong identification with revolutionary figures from the past, the imperative to modernize this past, and at the same time a kind of postmodern suggestion that we are not bound to a fixed past but rather that we can choose our own relation to it. Accordingly, *mangue* may not have one clear relation to its chosen component influences or historical referents. This is, and perhaps always so, in any music a matter of interpretation to some degree—and even more so in certain recent trends that operate at the crossroads of a multitude of global currents.

Crucially, all of the main influences in *mangue* correspond to specific subscenes in Recife, confirming the "embedded" quality of the music. In the imagery of the movement, the various signals from around the globe are picked up by satellite and reconstituted in the mud of the region. Chico Science's personal cultivation and identification with many of these styles, and knowledge of their cultural and historical significance, further counters the empirically problematic notion of a music "unhinged" from time and space.

Perhaps the crucial difference between *mangue* and more bounded local genres without broad exposure is the *awareness* of the universality of its story—which may be interpreted in multiple ways—rather than some proposed radical break with a past or people. If anything, through its interpenetration of diverse influences and elements, *mangue* enables connections between a history and present in Recife and the rest of the world to be revealed.[45] Here, I wish to reassert the potential role of the subaltern musician in the global system not as merely a comforting symbol of the West's association with the Other (although this dynamic is surely at play), but also as embodying a kind of experience that, even if mediated and reinterpreted in any number of ways, becomes increasingly relevant to the planet.

I wish to challenge the notion that simply through its refashioning of the past that the most postmodern pop can somehow free itself completely of this past or social contexts (whatever these may be). Rather, all current musics exist in the contemporary world with certain connections to the past and orientations toward the future; and all such musics make use of some "tradition" and have some relation to "modernity"—which themselves are not reified but blurred, interpenetrating categories, as I have argued here. As such, Éder Rocha of Mestre Ambrósio told me that *mangue* has

> a connection to the past, which is how this region here was geographically [Recife was constructed on top of the *mangue*] to the present and to the future even more. The relation is exactly this. So when you speak of *mangue beat*, it is searching precisely for the civilization, speaking about the current civilization that lives on top of a *mangue* which is all *caranguejos* [crabs]. (Interview: Rocha 1998)

In a similar way, in referring to the Maracatu Nação Estrela Brilhante, Mestre Valter told me: "We represent real African slaves. We are the Africans. So we transport ourselves to the past, visualize the present and present the future" (Interview: de França 1998). Both *mangue* and *maracatu* incorporate notions of the past into their present music and behavior. Do not all musics to some degree, albeit in different ways?

The notion that any music can break from a sense of history is highly problematic. Ingrid Monson criticizes Jameson's postmodern concept of *pastiche*—which "produces a social experience characterized by 'heaps and fragments,' (1991: 25) and a waning sense of historicity"—precisely because

> There is no distinction between amalgams of incongruous elements, and the network of social interactions which they may or may not set off; nor is there any distinction between unsynthesized collections of borrowed elements which lose their historical referentiality, and those which do synthesize, develop a

social base, and become themselves models for borrowing and reinterpretation. (Monson 1999: 59)

I would question the implication that "unsynthesized" elements lose their historical referentiality while only "synthesized" ones develop social bases. Furthermore, the distinctions between "synthesized" and "unsynthesized" are open to debate. But nevertheless, the particular relation of a music to time and place cannot negate its possible use within and connection to specific social contexts, even ones that are more "disembedded." It is arguable whether humans can ever forget or do away with a sense of past, however that sense is constructed. Rather, what *mangue* and other recent popular trends reveal is perhaps a more relativistic, postmodern notion of the past, whereby artists capitalize on the idea that, in a sense, we are the creators of our own history and sense of collective past. This does not liberate music from a past at all, but instead liberates the artist into actively shaping his or her own vision of that past.

In the end, let us return to the question of *mangue*'s reception and what this might entail for the relations among people via music. I have already argued that *mangue* and Recife's "new music scene" have revealed the boundaries between traditional-modern, local-global, and domestic-foreign as mutually relevant, blurred, and overlapping. Echoing Taylor's (1997: 80-81) reluctance to reduce analysis to a series of opposing binaries (which even Erlmann's article ultimately does), I would like to conclude with the suggestion that the music of CSNZ is evidence of the interpenetration and blurring of Self and Other.[46] As Monson argues for African pop musics, so I see for *mangue*:

> What we see is an increasing interpenetration of them and us whereby the standard oppositions that have been used to describe cross-cultural differentiation—Western/non-Western, cooptation/resistance, modern/traditional, electric/acoustic, bad/good—lose their analytic utility. Yossou N'Dour's explanation of why he uses Western sounds in his music illustrates such interpenetration.... (Monson 1999: 57)

> "In Dakar we hear many different recordings. We are open to these sounds. When people say my music is too Western, they must remember that we, too, hear this music over here. We hear the African music with the modern." (Yossou N'Dour quoted in Taylor 1997: 135)

I submit that among the most convincing recent embodiments of this interpenetration of them and us (and a concurrent questioning of various dichotomies) has been in the music and behavior of Chico Science. Chico did not merely adopt the personae of various local and global artists or traditions like a cloak; he lived these traditions. In a very real sense, Chico was a rapper and an *embolador* [singer of *embolada*], a rocker and a *raggamuffin* singer. He embodied through music the mutual relevance of various cultural traditions, in the process questioning notions of separation between people and cultures.

Although the ways in which this embodiment is manifest have yet to be fully explored worldwide, the case of Recife in the 1990s is evidence that as we approach the twenty-first century, the range of musical and cultural options, and their implications for the formation of identities, are not doomed to a "cultural grey out" but show signs of increasing possibilities. As such, it reveals that in the so-called "Third World" (as anywhere) "traditions" can remain and be asserted at the same time as "modern" culture is critically embraced and utilized. More than that, in the Recife scenario, it is through their relation with one another that both of these already overlapping categories have been assured of a continued relevance.

Mangue artists have refashioned tradition and history within a particular sociocultural context, embedding the local within the global and the global within the local in such a way as to, in the most optimistic of circumstances, "sensually smudge or obliterate . . . some of the us and them, insider, outsider rigidity" (Feld 1995: 122). While this has, of course, not obliterated difference per se, or done away with some of the more ominous aspects that persist in a global cultural system (such as economic and social injustices of various stripes), *mangue* and other contemporary popular musics may be pointing in another direction altogether. In this path, synthesis and hybridity allow for both an increasing assertion of the particular and a new relation among populations otherwise divided by class, race, religion, nationality, or cultural history. This new relation is, in my view, not reducible to a dominant group's "relief from [its] own alienation through identification with exoticized others" (Monson 1999 57) or to a subaltern, neo-imperialistic mimicking of the dominant's culture. But nor is it one that presents local identities as offering counterhegemonic attacks to the system from all sides. The primary "resistance" embodied in *mangue*, in my opinion, instead resides precisely in the fact that local musicians in Recife, many of them of an underprivileged social background, are actively and critically part of the system. They are projecting their own sense of themselves and their sociocultural situation into a network of information that has made them a part of the world—and the world a part of Recife—as never before. In turn, this unprecedented dynamic interaction with a global system has had a reinvigorating impact on local realities in Recife and Pernambuco.[47]

Appendix 1

The *Manifesto Mangue*

The first *mangue* manifesto was written by Fred Zero Quatro and was distributed to the Brazilian press in 1991. Below is my translation of the text into English. This version of the manifesto (quoted in Teles n/d: 5-6) is slightly different from the version that appears on the debut CD of Chico Science & Nação Zumbi (*Da Lama Ao Caos*, Sony CD-81594/2-464476, 1995). (See footnote for major difference.)

Caranguejos Com Cérebro [Crabs With Brains]
Mangue—The Concept

Estuary. The terminal part of a river or pond. A portion of the river with salty water. On its margins are found the manguezais, communities of tropical or subtropical plants flooded by the movements of the tides. Through the exchange of organic material between the fresh and salt water, the mangues are among the most productive ecosystems of the world, despite the fact that they are always associated with filth and with rottenness.

It is estimated that around 2,000 species of microorganisms and vertebrate and invertebrate animals are associated with the sixty mangue plants. Estuaries furnish areas for the laying of eggs and for breeding for two-thirds of the annual fishing production of the entire world. At least eighty commercially important species depend on the coastal marshes.

It isn't by accident that the mangues are considered a basic link of the marine food chain. Aside from the mosquitoes and other bugs, enemies of housewives, for scientists the mangues are taken as symbols of fertility, diversity, and richness.

Manguetown—The City

The wide coastal plain where the city of Recife was founded is cut by the estuaries of six rivers. After the expulsion of the Dutch in the seventeenth century, the (ex) "maurician" city [named after the Dutch leader Maurice] grew in a disorderly fashion, at the cost of indiscriminate landfilling and the destruction of its manguezais, which are on the road to extinction.

As a counterpart, the irresistible madness of a cynical notion of "progress," which elevated the city to the position of metropolis of the Northeast, was not slow in revealing its fragility.

It only took small changes in the "winds" of history for the first signs of economic sclerosis to manifest themselves in the beginning of the '60s. In the last thirty years, the syndrome of stagnation, allied with the permanence of the myth/stigma of the metropolis, has only led to the accelerated aggravation of the picture of misery and of urban chaos.

Today, Recife holds the highest index of unemployment in the country. More than half of its inhabitants live in favelas [slums] and alagados [shacks built on stilts in the *mangue*]. And, according to an institute of population studies in Washington, it is today the fourth worst city of the world in which to live.

Mangue—The Scene

Emergency! A shock, quick, or Recife will die of a heart attack. You don't need to be a doctor to know that the simplest way to stop the heart of a person is to obstruct its veins. The fastest way also to obstruct and evacuate the soul of a city like Recife is to kill its rivers and fill up its estuaries. So what is there to do to prevent sinking in the chronic depression that paralyzes the citizen? Is there a way to give back the spirit, delobotomize/recharge the batteries of the city? Simple, just inject a little energy in the mud and stimulate what still remains of the fertility in the veins of Recife.

In mid-'91, an organism/nucleus of research and creation of pop ideas began to be generated and articulated in various points of the city. The objective is to engender an "energetic circuit" capable of allegorically connecting the good vibrations of the mangue with the world network of the circulation of pop concepts. Image symbol: a parabolic antenna placed in the mud.* Or a caranguejo [crab] remixing ÁNTHENA by *Kraftwerk* [a Euro-tech group] on the computer.

The mangueboys and manguegirls are individuals interested in Chaos Theory, *World Music*, Legislation about means of communication, ethnic Conflicts, Hip Hop, Chance, Bezerra da Silva [a Rio-based samba musician originally from Recife], Virtual Reality, Sex, Design, Violence and all the advances of the Chemical applied in the terrain of the alteration/expansion of consciousness.

Mangueboys and manguegirls frequent locales like the Bar do Caranguejo [The Crab Bar] and the Bar do Maré [The Tide Bar].

Mangueboys and Manguegirls are recording the collection "Caranguejos Com Cérebro" [Crabs with Brains], which brings together the bands Mundo Livre S/A, Loustal, Chico Science & Nação Zumbi, and Lamento Negro.

* In the linear notes to *Da lama Ao Caos*, the rest of the manifesto reads as follows: "Mangueboys and manguegirls are individuals interested in charts,

Appendix 1 　　　　　　　　　　　　　　　　　　　　　　　　　　　　*129*

interactive TV, anti-psychiatry, Bezerra da Silva, Hip Hop, midiotia [a made up term that apparently plays on the words for "media" and "idiocy"], artism, street music, John Coltrane, chance, non-virtual sex, ethnic conflicts, and all the advances of the chemical applied in the terrain of the alteration/expansion of consciousness."

Appendix 2

Musical Transcriptions and Analysis

This appendix consists of transcriptions (with figure-by-figure explanations) that are meant to elucidate various musical styles and songs discussed in the body of the dissertation. These are supplemented with charts that show musical influences in *mangue*. Figures that present the basic rhythm of a particular style (e.g., *baião*, *côco de roda*, etc.) are meant as prototypical only. There may be many different patterns allowable for some styles; in such cases, the patterns I feature here were selected based on my experience with these musics. Furthermore, such charts obviously cannot account for the rhythmic variations inherent in such musics. Where appropriate, I have indicated with whom or where I learned specific musical styles or information.

It is my contention here that the musical innovation and complexity of CSNZ come precisely from the sophisticated way in which stylistic elements are juxtaposed, combined, and fused. Although some of the original complexity of each source style may be lost (this may be typical in syncretic popular music; see Manuel 1988: 21), the fusion gains in textural and combinatory richness. For example, the funk and *maracatu* sections of "O Cidadão do Mundo" may not inherit the degree of variation that James Brown or a traditional *maracatu* group has, respectively. But the group's command over the basis of these two styles and the act of juxtaposing them reveal striking similarities, affinities, and overlap between local and global elements. The melody and Chico's multistyled vocal production—which themselves are often fusions of various stylistic elements—further contribute to the originality of the band's music.

Figure 1: Maracatu: Baque de Marcação ("Marking Beat").
This chart provides an example of the basic "marking beat" as played by the *maracatu* "nations" of Recife. This one was learned from the Maracatu Nação Estrela Brilhante in 1998. Other "nations" may use different *caixa* (snare drum) patterns or may not use *abê* (beaded gourd), or whatever, but the basis of this rhythm is constant across the various groups. Like other *baques*, the *baque de*

marcação is defined by the *bombo* pattern, which here is said to "mark" the rhythm. At the same time that some of the *bombos* in an ensemble play this "marking beat," others may *virar* (literally, "turn"), or improvise. These improvisations typically involve playing a sixteenth note-eighth note-sixteenth note figure repeatedly with an accent on the middle eighth note; when this

Figure 1:

Maracatu: Baque de Marcação ("Marking Beat")

Special thanks to Mestre Valter, Neide Alves,
and the Maracatu Nação Estrela Brilhante
for the transmission of this rhythm.

pattern resolves, the player may return to the "marking" rhythm. It is crucial that some *bombo* players "mark" the rhythm at all times. There are three basic sizes of *bombos* used by the *maracatus*: *marcante* (largest), *meião* (middle), and *repique* (smallest). Although in some cases or in some groups (e.g., Nação Pernambuco) these three drums may each have a different rhythmic function, in Estrela Brilhante any size drum could be used either to play the "marking beat" or to improvise. The notated *onguê* (bell) pattern is the foundational one used by the "nations," subject to variation on the part of each player. As in other African-based Brazilian rhythms, notated sixteenth notes are not played evenly but are "swung," whereby the middle two sixteenth notes of each beat are condensed; this produces a feel that approaches a triplet. This is noticeable particularly in the *ganzá*, *abê*, and *caixa* patterns.

Appendix 2   133

Figure 2:

Maracatu: Bombo Parts for Other Baques

Ex. 1. Baque de Arrasto (Dragging Rhythm)

Ex. 2. Martelo (Hammer)

Ex. 3. Baque de Parada (Stop Rhythm)

Examples 1-3 may be played with the same ganzá, abê, caixa, and gonguê basic patterns as featured in the baque de marcação; see "Maracatu: Baque de Marcação (Marking Beat)."

Special thanks to Mestre Valter, Neide Alves and the Maracatu Nação Estrela Brilhante for the transmission of these bombo rhythms.

Ex. 4. Bombo part for "Monólogo Ao Pé do Ouvido" by Chico Science & Nação Zumbi (one note is added to "Martelo")

Figure 2: Maracatu Bombo Parts for Other Baques.

Examples 1-3 demonstrate the defining *bombo* patterns for some of the other *baques* played by Estrela Brilhante (with correlates in other "nations"). There are specific songs (*toadas*) that are sung with particular *baques*.

Figure 3:

"Da Lama Ao Caos" Basic Groove

"Da Lama Ao Caos" (Chico Science)

Performed by Chico Science & Nação Zumbi
From "Chico Science Mangue Star"
(TV Jornal/TV Viva)

Special thanks to Maureliano of Via Sat and Jorge Martins da Silva
of Cascabulho for the transmission of this rhythm.

Figure 3: "Da Lama Ao Caos" Basic Groove.
This hybrid soul/funk-*maracatu* rhythm is explained in the text (see "Mangue Style and Ideology" in Chapter Five). With respect to the *bombo* part, as Jorge Martins da Silva of Cascabulho pointed out to me, since funk and *maracatu de baque virado* share a very similar rhythmic vocabulary, each cell of this pattern could be heard as coming from either funk or *maracatu*. The defining notes of the *maracatu baque de marcação* (the dotted eighth notes a sixteenth note after beats 3 and 4) are played here without the lighter left hand strokes on beats 3 and 4 as is done traditionally (see Figure 1). On the one hand, this omission of the left-hand strokes highlights the essence of the *maracatu* pattern, but on the other, it positions this pattern closer to a typical funk bass drum pattern. The manipulation of the subtle connections and even ambiguities between styles is part of the genius of the multivalent sound of CSNZ.

Appendix 2

Figure 4:
"A Cidade" Basic Groove

[Musical score with parts for Elec. Gtr. 2, Elec. Gtr. 1, Synth, Elec. Bass, Ganzá, Caixa, and Bombo]

Electric Guitar 2 (with distortion) and
synthesizer (with quick digital delay) are in
the refrain section only

Figure 4: "A Cidade" Basic Groove.

The *bombo* and caixa patterns of this song are another example of a hybrid funk-*maracatu*. As in "Da Lama Ao Caos," the *bombo* pattern for "A Cidade" works perfectly well as a funk bass drum pattern, while its various cells may also be found in *maracatu*. As in the "Da Lama Ao Caos" *bombo* part, notice here the prominence of the two eighth notes that begin each bar (a typical rock, soul, or funk rhythmic cell) and the dotted eighth on the "e" of 3 or 4 (defining notes of the *maracatu baque de marcação*). In measures 3 and 4, the eighth note offbeat on the "and" of 2 is sometimes used by some "nations" instead of the dotted eighth beginning on the "e" of 2 that is found in Estrela Brilhante's *baque de arrasto* (see Fig. 2, ex. 1); see Figure 7 for CSNZ's use of this traditional *bombo* variation.

"A Cidade" (Chico Science)

Performed by Chico Science & Nação Zumbi
Da Lama Ao Caos (Sony CD-81594/2-464476)

The electric instruments in "A Cidade" (two electric guitars, synthesizer, and electric bass) work within the A Dorian mode (a G major scale from A to A), highlighting the A minor 7 and secondarily B minor 7 chord. A modal scheme that centers on one or two chords is typical not only of much funk or rock but also of much northeastern Brazilian folk music. The electric bass and electric guitar 1 parts exhibit typical rock or funk riffs. Electric guitar 2 plays a sparse distorted pattern that recalls heavy styles of rock. The synthesizer's A minor-B minor diads, processed with a quick digital delay, recall electronic dance music in their sound and rhythm. Already in its rhythm section, this song references at least four distinct styles: *maracatu de baque virado*, funk, hard rock, and electronic dance music. Notably, this is accomplished with economy:

Appendix 2

minimal parts that point to particular styles or combine styles are compounded for a cohesive unified effect. The distorted guitar solos by Lúcio Maia in the instrumental interludes reveal a strong Jimi Hendrix influence (use of the wah-wah pedal, pentatonic minor scale, emphasis on the sonority of the instrument, etc.).

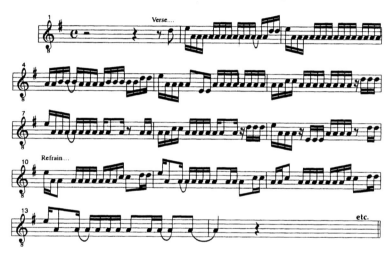

"A Cidade" (Chico Science)

Performed by Chico Science & Nação Zumbi
Da Lama Ao Caos (Sony CD-81594/2-464476)

Figure 5: "A Cidade" Vocal Melody Excerpt.
The predominant use of sixteenth notes, the heavy repetition of notes, the limited note choice, and modal quality of this melody all suggest a very strong identification with the vocal styles of both the *embolada* (see Figure 12) and with the Jamaican *raggamuffin* (see Figure 13). The chanted quality of the voice and rhythmic vocabulary also point to a connection with rap. In the *embolada* example, as a general pattern the melody starts by iterating the third scalar tone (in an A-flat minor mode), sometimes goes up to the fourth and then descends in a particular way to resolve to the root; all motion is either stepwise or by a third. By contrast, in both the *raggamuffin* and "A Cidade" examples, the melody tends to stress the root note, not the third (both examples are in an A-minor mode;

since not all the notes are present it is a moot point which mode this is). Furthermore, both the *raggamuffin* and "A Cicade" examples feature leaps of a fourth or fifth, making prominent use of the fourth or fifth notes of the mode.

Figures 6-9: "O Cidadão do Mundo" Rhythm Section.

Taken together, these figures present the basic rhythm section groove for the various sections of the song "O Cidadão do Mundo," one of CSNZ's most texturally interesting and musically compelling pieces. **Figure 6** shows the hip-hop (funk) groove used for sections A and A'. This is a rather basic, sparse repeating funk feel with ostinato electric guitar, electric bass, and drum-set patterns (the top line of the drum-set part is the hi-hat, the middle line is the snare drum, and the bottom line is the bass drum). Like "A Cidade," this song is modal. As a whole, the song shifts modal centers in a kind of atonal way; the A/A' section is in an E-flat mixolydian mode, with the accompaniment iterating an E-flat 9 sound. **Figure 7** shows the *maracatu de baque virado* feel for sections B and B'. This feel is at base a traditional rendering of the *maracatu* rhythm: the low bell plays the foundational *gonguê* pattern (see Figure 1) while the high bell plays a traditional

Figure 6:
"O Cidadão do Mundo" Rhythm Section: Hip Hop

"O Cidadão do Mundo"
(Lyrics by Chico Science; music by CSNZ-Eduardo BIDlovski)

Performed by Chico Science & Nação Zumbi
Afrociberdelia (Sony Latin CDZ-81996 2-479255)

Appendix 2   139

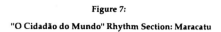

Also contains: analog bass synth sound and horns in transition bars (16-19; 42-45)

"O Cidadão do Mundo"
(Lyrics by Chico Science; music by CSNZ-Eduardo BIDlovski)

Performed by Chico Science & Nação Zumbi
Afrociberdelia (Sony Latin CDZ-81996 2-479255)

gonguê pattern that has, for reasons unknown, become associated even more than the first pattern with the *maracatu* outside of its original environment. *Bombo 1* plays a typical variation on the basic "marking beat" (see Figure 1), while *bombo 2* takes what could be an example of *virando* or "turning"—that is, improvising around the "marking beat"—and makes this into another ostinato pattern. The *maracatu* section's only other instrument aside from the voice and percussion is a very low-pitched analog bass synthesizer sound relatively low in the mix. In the instrumental transition bars back to A or to C, horn parts play off a G9 or G13 (no 11) chord, shifting the modal center temporarily from E-flat mixolydian to G mixolydian. **Figure 8** depicts the accompaniment for the majority of section C, which has the funk drum-set groove from section A and a *berimbau* (a single-stringed bow associated with the martial art-dance *capoeira*), whose constantly changing line alternates between A and B-flat pedal points. This play between the notes "A" and "B-flat" on the *berimbau* roughly parallels the contours of section C's vocal melody (a *ragamuffin-embolada*), which moves between the notes "A," "B-natural," and "B-flat." Only the first four bars of the *berimbau* melodic line are notated here as an example. **Figure 9** represents the accompaniment for the last five measures of C (and the entire piece). These measures feature a condensed version of the funk drum-set groove and *bombo* drums doubling the drum-set bass drum figure underneath distorted heavy metal-style electric guitars playing rhythm and lead within a G minor chordal framework. The *berimbau* from the *raggamuffin-embolada* remains, albeit buried somewhat in the mix, providing a sus2 (the note "A") over the G minor guitar chord.

Figure 8:
"O Cidadão do Mundo" Rhythm Section:
Raggamuffin-Embolada

"O Cidadão do Mundo"
(Lyrics by Chico Science; music by CSNZ-Eduardo BIDlovski)

Performed by Chico Science & Nação Zumbi
Afrociberdelia (Sony Latin CDZ-81996 2-479255)

Figure 9:
"O Cidadão do Mundo" Rhythm Section:
Heavy Metal

Also contains: berimbau and distorted electric guitar

"O Cidadão do Mundo"
(Lyrics by Chico Science; music by CSNZ-Eduardo BIDlovski)

Performed by Chico Science & Nação Zumbi
Afrociberdelia (Sony Latin CDZ-81996 2-479255)

Appendix 2

Figure 10: "O Cidadão do Mundo" Vocal Melody

142 Appendix 2

Appendix 2   143

"O Cidadão do Mundo"
(Lyrics by Chico Science; music by CSNZ-Eduardo BIDlovski)

Performed by Chico Science & Nação Zumbi
Afrociberdelia (Sony Latin CDZ-81996 2-479255)

Figure 10: "O Cidadão do Mundo" Vocal Melody.

Figure 10 is a complete notation of the vocal melody of "O Cidadão do Mundo." As an overview, the A/A' and B/B' sections of the piece feature a melody that could be a traditional *toada* (song) in the *maracatu nação* tradition. First, the melody is modal. More specifically, it is in a mixolydian mode, which is typical for much northeastern music. The vocal line emphasizes the particular essence of this mode by relying heavily on the defining flat seven tone; this tone is known in Brazil as the *sétima nordestina* (northeastern seventh). It also dwells on two other important chord tones, the third and fifth, as resting places. Another feature that circumscribes this melody within a *maracatu* framework is its reliance on and repetition of certain stock rhythmic cells that fall easily within the *maracatu de baque virado* rhythm. My colleague David Rumpler brought to my attention how *maracatu* melodies are not as free as the phrasing in samba melodies, which can sometimes "float" more independently over the rhythm section. This limited rhythmic vocabulary emphasizes especially the sixteenth note-eighth note-sixteenth note isorhythm.

The melodic-poetic quality of section C recalls both the northeastern *embolada* and Jamaican *raggamuffin*. Musically, these affinities are manifest in the almost unrelenting use of sixteenth notes (even more typical of *embolada* than of *raggamuffin*, which varies a bit more), insistent note repetition, the limited note choice (here, only three notes: A, B-natural, and B-flat). Stepwise motion and the use of quick vocal glides (a common Middle Eastern trait found in the Northeast of Brazil from the Moorish influence on Portuguese music) further reinforce the *embolada* connection. Not having carried out a thorough musicological study of the *embolada*, I cannot comment on the note choices here as being typical or not. At least compared to the traditional *embolada* as notated in Figure 12, this example does not feature a third, which may be uncommon in *embolada*. In any case, it is interesting to note that there is a certain ambiguity in some of the pitches, which becomes more pronounced as the *embolada* progresses. At first, Chico alternates between "A" and "B-natural." Soon, this alternation becomes between "A" and "B-flat." Beginning in measure 52, the "A" notes begin to lose their specific pitch and begin to sound even closer to the "B-flats," which are still nevertheless distinct. The entire melodic nature of this section explores the more "non-Western" aspects of northeastern music: the interplay between the "B-naturals" in the voice and "B-flats" in the *berimbau*, the chromatic and microtonal aspects of the notes, and the use of quick vocal glides that are typical of *embolada*. (The *raggamuffin* example as shown in Figure 13 also reveals a kind of modal ambiguity, whereby the "C-natural" used in measure 2 becomes a "C-sharp" in measures 3-5.)

The quality of Chico's voice throughout the piece is quite gruff, made even more so by a kind of electronic distortion. This gruffness may reference both *raggamuffin* and some styles of *embolada*, but it is also, of course, found in many styles of rock music. This latter connection is made clearer when, after completing the *embolada*, Chico screams a phrase in the style of a heavy metal or hard-core vocalist. The rendering of a *maracatu*-like melody with a distorted vocal production over a funk groove, or the singing of a *raggamuffin-embolada* over a funk groove with *berimbau* exemplify the links made among various stylistic influences in the music of CSNZ. The particular combination of rock, rap, *embolada,* and *raggamuffin* references in Chico's vocal production—such that the borders between these references become hazy—renders his singing style unique.

Below, I elucidate the complex juxtaposition of broad stylistic influences in the vocal line and rhythm section of "O Cidadão do Mundo":

Chart of Stylistic Influences in "O Cidadão do Mundo"

	Vocal Line		**Rhythm Section**
A/A'	Maracatu-like melody with distortion effect	+	Funk groove
B/B'	Maracatu-like melody with distortion effect	+	Maracatu groove
C	Raggamuffin-Embolada with distortion effect	+	Funk groove with Berimbau
End of C	Shouted text in harsh voice with distortion effect (in heavy metal style)	+	Condensed funk groove

Appendix 2   145

"Mateus Embaixador" (Antônio Carlos Nóbrega)

Performed by Maracatu Nação Pernambuco
Nação Pernambuco (Velas 11-VO16)

Figure 11: "Mateus Embaixador" Vocal Melody.

This *maracatu de baque virado* song created by trained musician Antônio Carlos Nóbrega is much like a typical *toada* of the *maracatu* "nations." This is manifest in its modal quality (mixolydian), its emphasis on chordal tones of the tonic chord (C, E, G, and B-flat), and its reliance on stock rhythmic cells such as sixteenth note-eighth note-sixteenth note; dotted eighth note-sixteenth note; and sixteenth note rest-eighth note-sixteenth note. Compare this piece with the vocal melody for sections A and B in "O Cidadão do Mundo" (Figure 10) for the latter's similarity to traditional (or neo-traditional) folk music.

Figure 12: "Côco de Embolada (Desafio)."

This example of a musical "duel" (*desafio*) between two singers (Pinto and Rouxinol) in the *embolada* style is included as a sample on the album *Fome Dá Dor de Cabeça* by Cascabulho (Mangroove MR 0020). Some of the salient features

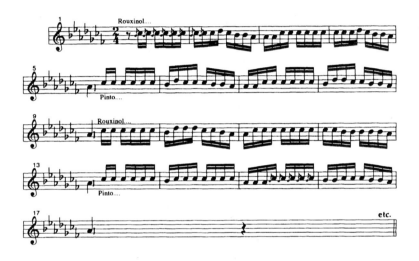

Figure 12:

Côco de Embolada (Desafio)

Snippet of a desafio (duel) in the embolada style

Performed by Pinto e Rouxinol, K7 Emboladas
From Cascabulho, Fome Dá Dor de Cabeça
(Mangroove MR 0020)

of the melody include its minor modal quality, its reliance on almost constant sixteenth notes, its use of relatively few notes within a small range (A-flat, B-flat, C-flat, and D-flat), its heavy repetition of pitches, its use of vocal glides, its largely stepwise motion, and its formulaic progression of notes in a phrase. The broad outline of this progression begins on the third tone (C-flat), sometimes touches the fourth (D-flat), and then moves stepwise down to "resolve" to the tonic (A-flat). In each singer's four-bar verse, there are two of these phrases. The rhythm of this piece is a *côco* played on *pandeiros*.

Appendix 2 147

Figure 13: "Mr Loverman" Vocal Excerpt.
 This example of Jamaican *raggamuffin* (dancehall reggae) vocal melody by Shabba Ranks shows some of the same features as the *embolada* in Figure 12: its minor modal quality (an A minor mode "contradicted" by a few C-sharps), its reliance on sixteenth notes, its use of relatively few notes (1, 2, 3, and 5: A, B, C or C-sharp, and E), its heavy repetition of pitches, its stepwise motion, and its formulaic phrases. This example differs from Figure 12 in its increased use of leaps of a third or fourth, its use of the fifth tone instead of the fourth, its ambiguous third tone, and its slightly more varied rhythmic vocabulary

Figure 13:

"Mr Loverman" Vocal Excerpt

An example of Jamaican raggamuffin
(dancehall reggae) vocal melody

"Mr Loverman" (R. Gordon-M. Bennett-H. Lindo)
Performed by Shabba Ranks with Chevelle Franklin
Rough & Ready - Volume 1
(Epic EK 52443)

(including a sixteenth note triplet typical of *raggamuffin*). Although this *raggamuffin* is sung over a slow hip-hop groove, in its original context the style often makes use of a persistent rhythmic cell in the accompaniment (dotted eighth-sixteenth tied to eighth-eighth) that one also finds in the *côco de embolada* (as well as in many other genres). This example of *raggamuffin* was chosen precisely to show the connections between this style, *embolada*, and the music of CSNZ. A more in-depth comparison of *embolada* and *raggamuffin* would be an intriguing pursuit, both for the further elucidation of these influences in Chico Science's vocal style and for its own sake.

Figure 14: Basic Baião Rhythm.

This chart provides a basic *baião* rhythm. Aside from the triangle part, all of the other instrumental patterns are more variable. The patterns notated here are typical. Together with the triangle rhythm, the basic feel of the *baião* comes from the strokes on the top head of the *zabumba* (a thin bass drum with two heads)—a dotted eighth-sixteenth note ostinato.

Figure 14:

Basic Baião Rhythm

KEY:
T = thumb
F = fingers
H = heel of hand

+ = closed stroke (for zabumba: mallet pressed into head)
   (for pandeiro: finger pressed into back of head)
o = open stroke (for zabumba: open mallet stroke)
   (for pandeiro: head played open)
x = left hand plays thin stick (bacalhau) on bottom
   head of zabumba

D = downstroke
U = upstroke

Special thanks to Jorge Martins da Silva
of Cascabulho for the transmission of this rhythm

Appendix 2   149

Figure 15:

Basic Forró Zabumba Pattern

This basic zabumba pattern, as well as other rhythmic variations
and a quicker tempo, distinguishes the forró
from the baião. Otherwise, the baião and forró share
some of the same instrumental patterns.

Special thanks to Jorge Martins da Silva
of Cascabulho for the transmission
of this rhythm and this information.

Figure 16:

Bombo Part for "Recife Veneza" by Via Sat

This rhythm economically combines defining aspects of
both the forró zabumba pattern (pickup 16th-dotted 8th-16th) and the
maracatu nação bombo pattern of the baque de marcação
(dotted 8ths a 16th note after beats 3 and 4).

"Recife Veneza" (authors not listed)
Performed by Via Sat (CD-demo)

Figure 15: Basic Forró Zabumba Pattern

Although *forró* means a party where northeastern dance musics are performed, it is also an umbrella term for many of these dances (all played with the core instrumentation of *zabumba, triângulo,* and *sanfona,* or accordion). But more specifically, *forró* refers to a variation of the *baião* with a quicker tempo and other related rhythmic patterns. This *zabumba* pattern—with a sixteenth pick-up note and the open and closed tones reversed from the *baião*—is one of the features that distinguishes the *forró* from the *baião*.

Figure 16: Bombo Part for "Recife Veneza" by Via Sat.

The *bombo* pattern for the song "Recife Veneza" by the *mangue*-type band Via Sat economically combines defining aspects of the above *forró zabumba* rhythm (pick up sixteenth-dotted eighth-sixteenth) and the *bombo* pattern of the *maracatu baque de marcação* (strokes a sixteenth note after beats 3 and 4).

Figure 17:

Côco de Roda: Basic Rhythm

KEY:
Bombo - played with 2 thick wooden sticks
(same as maracatu de baque virado)
Regular notes played on head
x = notes played on the rim of the drum

Special thanks to Jorge Martins da Silva
of Cascabulho for the transmission of this rhythm.

Figure 17: Côco de Roda: Basic Rhythm.

There are at least several different styles of *côco*, a common black northeastern music and dance style. This *côco de roda* ("circle *côco*," referring to the formation of the dance) comes from the Pernambucan coastal region. Other instruments may include conga, handclaps, and so on. The *pandeiro* and *bombo* are prototypical. Many other patterns are possible. The *bombo* line in particular depends on the melody of the song and constantly varies. The *bombo* pattern here is a common riff used; in practice, this riff would be combined with both other patterns and "open space" where the sticks would iterate the basic eighth-sixteenth-sixteenth note ostinato on the rim of the drum with no strokes on the head. According to Jorge Martins da Silva of Cascabulho, one of the features that distinguishes the *côco* of Dona Selma from that of Zé Neguinho (refer to Appendix 3) is the former's incorporation of congas. These are played

Appendix 2 *151*

like the *ilú*, a drum used in *Candomblé*. The *côco* features responsorial vocals between a soloist and chorus. The dance involves a strong step with the right foot on the first beat of each 2/4 measure.

Figure 18:
"Rio, Pontes & Overdrives" Basic Groove

"Rios, Pontes & Overdrives"
(Chico Science-Fred Zero Quatro)

Performed by Chico Science & Nação Zumbi
Da Lama Ao Caos (Sony CD-81594/2-464476)

Figure 18: "Rios, Pontes & Overdrives" Basic Groove.
In live performance, Chico Science highlighted the *côco* connection in this song by saying the word "*côco*" and dancing the *côco* step ("Chico Science Mangue Stars," TV Viva/TV Jornal). But, in fact, this CSNZ song contains a rhythmic basis that borrows from various regional folk styles. According to Maureliano of the band Via Sat (Interview: Ribeiro 1998), the *bombo* rhythm is a *baião* and the *caixa* (snare drum) part is based on the *rojão*, a northeastern dance rhythm in the line of *baião*, *xote*, *xaxado*, etc. The accent on the "and" of 2 in the second beat of the *caixa* also duplicates the most basic rhythm of the thin stick (*bacalhau*) played on the bottom head of the *zabumba* drum in the *baião*. How could this composite rhythm then be mistaken for a *côco*? According to

Maureliano, in the *agreste* region of Pernambuco "the rhythm of the *côco* . . . is equal to that of the *baião*. What changes are elements like this: [in the *côco*] there isn't accordion, it uses handclaps, there's no triangle, things like this" (ibid.). The use of the triangle in this song recalls the *baião*, as does the bell 1 pattern, which reverses the high and low tones found in the *agogô* pattern of the *baião* in Figure 14. While the quarter-note rhythm of bell 1 points to the *baião*, the eighth note rhythm in bell 2 is suggestive of a number of *gonguê* patterns for the *maracatu de baque virado*. (See Guerra-Peixe 1980: 71 for several different *gonguê* patterns observed in the 1950s in the Maracatu Nação Elefante.) The bells in "Rios, Pontes & Overdrives" sound like differently pitched cow bells; traditionally, in the *maracatu*, different tones are coaxed out of the *gonguê* (a long, flat single bell) by striking the stick alternately closer to the mouth or farther away from it.

Figure 19:

Basic Ciranda Rhythm

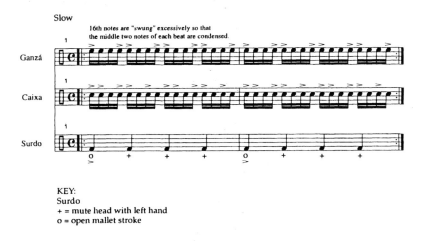

KEY:
Surdo
+ = mute head with left hand
o = open mallet stroke

This basic ciranda rhythm was transcribed from
a performance of Lia de Itamaracá at the
1998 Abril Pro Rock festival in Recife.

Figure 19: Basic Ciranda Rhythm.
The *ciranda* is a typical dance of northeastern Brazil, performed with a circle of participants who join hands and move counterclockwise. This basic

Appendix 2

ciranda rhythm was transcribed from a performance of a legendary singer in the tradition, Lia de Itamaracá. The dancers step inward on the accent of the bass drum (here, a *surdo*).

Figure 20: "A Praieira" Basic Groove.

This song is a reinterpretation of the *ciranda* rhythm combined with a rock-funk feel. The tempo of this song is much quicker than the very stately, slow *ciranda* of Lia de Itamaracá. Although the *ganzá* and *caixa* patterns are, to my ears, well within a traditional mold, perhaps most conspicuously different is the lack of an accent in the drum pattern (here played by *bombos*). This pattern features a straight four quarter note pulse that suggests an affinity with

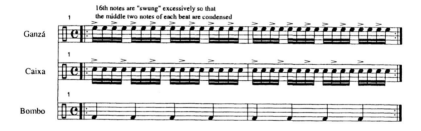

Figure 20:

"A Praieira" Basic Groove

"A Praieira" (Chico Science)

Performed by Chico Science & Nação Zumbi
Da Lama Ao Caos (Sony CD-81594/2-464476)

various kinds of rock or pop dance musics. The *caixa* pattern's accents in this song are a condensed version of those accents of the previous example. The *ganzá* part here places a primary emphasis on the "and" of each beat and a secondary one on the downbeats, while the corresponding pattern in the previous example accents only the first and last sixteenth notes of each beat; the sixteenth notes of both rhythms are "swung" excessively such that the middle two notes of each beat are condensed and slightly rushed.

Figures 21 and 22: Flow Charts of Primary Musical Influences in *Mangue*'s Two Principal Bands

Figure 21: Mundo Livre S/A

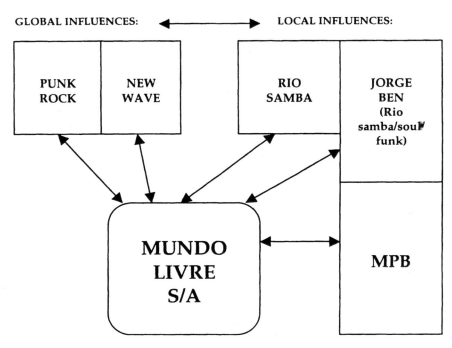

  These two charts show some of the primary stylistic influences in the music of the two major *mangue* bands, Mundo Livre S/A and Chico Science & Nação Zumbi (Figures 21 and 22, respectively). The two-way arrows between the global influences and these bands are not meant to suggest that *mangue* is as important to these styles as these styles are to *mangue* by any means; after all, proportionally, *mangue* borrows more from global influences than these influences borrow from *mangue*. But, at the same time, throughout their histories and in their various local manifestations, global styles are impacted by many local musics (themselves inextricable combinations of local and supra-local elements). As such, the two-way arrows show how, even in a small way, *mangue* has made a contribution to the development of global music in general and to specific global styles, even if this contribution remains largely unnoticed. In a similar way, even if the flows are not identical in each direction, there is a dialogic relation between *mangue*, its various local influences, and MPB as a whole. As CSNZ incorporated elements of local folk traditions in its music, these

Appendix 2

traditions and their practitioners have been directly impacted in the process. And even though Mundo Livre's work has not, as far as I know, directly influenced either Rio's samba tradition or Jorge Ben, the potential for this influence is there. Just as CSNZ and Mundo Livre have been shaped by their Brazilian peers and forebears, both of these bands have in turn inspired many recent and established Brazilian pop artists and, indeed, have helped shape the course of MPB as a whole. In a general sense, these charts depict the interactive quality of local and global that I have highlighted throughout the dissertation.

Figure 22: Chico Science and Nação Zumbi

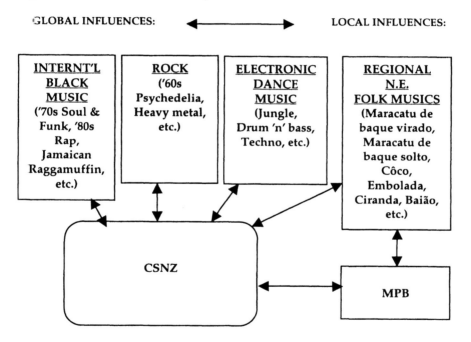

Appendix 3
Song Notes

The following song notes are meant as an aid in understanding the sonic and lyrical aspects of some of the music discussed in this work. Ideally, the reader should purchase the various CDs listed here (refer to the Discography for addresses of music shops or band web sites). There are two basic ways of utilizing these notes. The reader may read the dissertation in a linear fashion, and, whenever applicable, listen to a given track (or set of tracks) and read the accompanying notes. Alternatively, the reader may choose to go through this list, cross-checking each cut or set of cuts with the appropriate sections of the dissertation. As a package, the CDs and notes should serve as a useful, independent supplement to the rest of the dissertation. Even without the CDs, however, some of the notes may be useful. Refer also to Appendix 2 for transcriptions and musical analyses of various songs and styles.

1. Monólogo Ao Pé do Ouvido" (Chico Science). From: Chico Science & Nação Zumbi, *Da Lama Ao Caos* (Sony CD-81594/2-464476). This piece is discussed in the last section of the last chapter of the dissertation. **(See also Appendix 2, Figure 3.)**

2. "Maracatu Atômico" (Jorge Mautner-Nelson Jacobina). From: Chico Science & Nação Zumbi, *Afrociberdelia* (Sony Latin CDZ-81996 2-479255).

3. "Se Zé Limeira Sambasse Maracatu" (Siba). From: Mestre Ambrósio, *Mestre Ambrósio* (Videolar 199.000.855). These two pieces highlight the use of the *maracatu de baque solto* rhythm, albeit in different ways. CSNZ's cover of "Maracatu Atômico" adds this rhythm in the refrain (and a snare drum part from the *maracatu de baque virado* in the verse) to a funk foundation. Mestre Ambrósio's song, by contrast, is a more traditional rendering of the *baque solto* rhythm and song form, complemented with electric guitar

157

embellishments by Nação Zumbi's Lúcio Maia. These divergent approaches to the use of folk sources can be explained by the distinction between "from the outside in" and "from the inside out" (made in the "Mestre Ambrósio" section of Chapter Four).

4. "Pé de Calçada" (Siba). From: Mestre Ambrósio, *Mestre Ambrósio* (independent).

5. "Xodó de Sanfoneiro" (Gerson Filho-João Silva). From: Cascabulho, *Fome Dá Dor de Cabeça* (Mangroove MR 0020, independent). Special participation: Jacinto Silva (voice). These next two pieces jointly represent the two types of *forró* music mentioned in the dissertation (see, e.g., the "Mestre Ambrósio" section in Chapter Four). Mestre Ambrósio plays here the *forró de rabeca*, featuring the *rabeca* fiddle, while Cascabulho (with guest singer Jacinto Silva) presents the *forró* with accordion. **(See also Appendix 2, Figures 14 and 15.)**

6. "Clementina De Jesus no Morro da Conceição (Delírios da Ressurreição)" (Silvério Pessoa). From: Cascabulho, *Fome Dá Dor de Cabeça* **(Mangroove MR 0020, independent).** This song uses the *maracatu de baque virado* rhythm (see the "Regional Folk Artists and Associations" section in Chapter 4). The lyrics imagine the resurrection of the late great samba singer Clementina de Jesus within the context of the *maracatu* "nation" tradition on the Immaculate Conception Hill, one of Recife's most famous *favelas*. Notice the brief changes to a rock feel. This song would also exemplify the "from the inside out" approach mentioned in the "Ethnography of the Recife Music Scene" chapter.

7. "Folia Geral" (Bernardino José). From: Nação Pernambuco, *Nação Pernambuco* (Velas 11-VO16). This song presents Nação Pernambuco's interpretation of the *maracatu de baque virado* rhythm (see "Folklore and Recife's Middle Class" in Chapter Four).

8. "A Cidade" (Chico Science). From: Chico Science & Nação Zumbi, *Da Lama Ao Caos* (Sony CD-81594/2-464476). **(See also Appendix 2, Figures 4 and 5.)**

9. "Da Lama Ao Caos" (Chico Science). From: Chico Science & Nação Zumbi, *Da Lama Ao Caos* (Sony CD-81594/2-464476). These next two CSNZ songs are discussed in Chapter Five under the heading "Mangue Style & Ideology." They both feature composite soul-funk/*maracatu de baque virado* rhythms. The studio version of "Da Lama Ao Caos" heard here is slightly

Appendix 3

different from the live video version analyzed in Appendix 2. (See also Appendix 2, Figure 3.)

10. **"Minha Ciranda" and "Frevo Ciranda" (Capiba); "Lia de Itamaracá" (public domain). Arrangement: Edson Rodrigues. From: Antúlio Madureira,** *Perré-Bumbá* **(independent).**

11. **"A Praieira" (Chico Science). From: Chico Science & Nação Zumbi,** *Da Lama Ao Caos* **(Sony CD-81594/2-464476).** The medley by Antúlio Madureira presents some orchestrated versions of popular *ciranda* songs. The next example by CSNZ readapts the *ciranda* rhythm into a rock/funk context. Notice the bass drum attack on the "one" of the four-beat rhythm in the traditional *ciranda* versus the even four quarter-note bass drum pulses in CSNZ's adaptation. (See also Appendix 2, Figures 19 and 20.)

12. **Sample of** *côco de embolada***, Pinto e Rouxinol, K7 Emboladas. From: Cascabulho,** *Fome Dá Dor de Cabeça* **(Mangroove MR 0020, independent).** Here's a snippet of a *desafio*, or duel, between two singers—Pinto and Rouxinol—in the *embolada* style (a musical-poetic form typical of Northeast Brazil). The rhythm, played on the *pandeiro* frame drum, is a *côco*. Here is a sampling of some of the verses, which rhyme in Portuguese, translated into English:

> **Rouxinol:** "Pinto, I've been asleep until now, 'cause I'm gonna get you on my turn. If you don't sing nothing, why did you try to record?"
> **Pinto:** "Careful my friend, with me you can't. Prepare your music more 'cause Pinto's gonna make it rough."
> **Rouxinol:** "Respect my mustache because I'm your professor and I'm your superior, even in the way that you walk!"
> **Pinto:** "You may be a singer and sing in your place, but in my territory, you only leave when you get hurt!"

(See also Appendix 2, Figure 12.)

13./14. **"Mateus Enter" (Lyrics: Chico Science; Music: CSNZ)/"O Cidadão do Mundo" (Lyrics: Chico Science; Music: CSNZ-Eduardo BIDlovski). From: Chico Science & Nação Zumbi,** *Afrociberdelia* **(Sony Latin CDZ-81996 2-479255).** For these pieces, which open CSNZ's second CD, refer to the "Mangue Style and Ideology" section of Chapter Five. Near the end of "O Cidadão do Mundo," listen to how Chico Science takes the *embolada* and fuses it with other global influences—Jamaican *raggamuffin*, rap, heavy metal—in his vocal production. The form of this piece juxtaposes funk, *maracatu de* *baque virado*, and heavy metal sections (see an outline of the form in Chapter Five, p. 110). **(See also Appendix 2, Figures 6-10.)**

15. "A Rolinha." From: Dona Selma do Côco, *Cultura Viva*. SC 100.001.

16. "Pau de Quiri" (Zé Neguinho do Côco). Zé Neguinho do Côco, from: Cascabulho, *Fome Dá Dor de Cabeça* (Mangroove MR 0020, independent). These two songs present two of the most visible and respected performers of the *côco* (*coquistas*) of Pernambuco: Dona Selma do Côco and Zé Neguinho do Côco. Dona Selma's "A Rolinha" (one of the most popular tunes for the Recife/Olinda Carnival 1998) plays on the double entendre of *rolinha* as both bird and cock and on the sexual meaning of "to eat" (which can also mean "to fuck"): "I don't go to your house so you won't go to mine/You have a big mouth and you're gonna eat my hen/Get, get, get my *rolinha*." "Pau de Quiri" (a type of tree) by Zé Neguinho also uses bird imagery, albeit very differently: "My canary singer/Where do you want to make your nest/In the first tree of the forest on the last little branch/I didn't want to leave because the forest is very dark and the wood is very hard, it's very bad to leave/Axe cutter, sharpen the axe/To cut the quiri wood." **(See also Appendix 2, Figure 17.)**

17. "Côco Dub (Afrociberdelia)" (Chico Science). From: Chico Science & Nação Zumbi, *Da Lama Ao Caos* (Sony CD-81594/2-464476). This next piece by CSNZ uses a *côco*-identified rhythm to explore more experimental electronic territory, in the vein of Jamaican dub music (note: the rhythm of this song bears more similarity to a *baião* rhythm than to a *côco*, despite the title). Purportedly, a critic of Spin magazine claimed that this song was everything that English "jungle" music (electronic dance club genre of London) wanted to be but never was (in Teles n/d: 23). **(See also Appendix 2, Figure 18 for the transcription of a similar rhythm.)**

18. "Recife Veneza." From: Via Sat (CD demo). In "Recife Venice" (a play on Recife's hopeful nickname the "Brazilian Venice"), the *mangue*-type band Via Sat paints a critical picture of Recife, highlighting pollution, prostitution, etc., and referencing some of the cities' neighborhoods: "Boa Viagem, Piedade, Candeias, Ipsep, Center of the City/A lot of iron, will she be able to take it?/A lot of cement, will I be able to take it?/Things happen in Recife/Things happen in the Brazilian Venice." The bass drum figure of this song is an economical hybrid of the *forró* (a variation of the *baião*) and *maracatu de baque virado* bass drum rhythms (first half: *forró*; two offbeats in second half: *maracatu*). **(See also Appendix 2, Figure 16.)**

Appendix 3

19. **"Free World"** (Lyrics: Zero Quatro; Music: Mundo Livre S/A). From: **Mundo Livre S/A,** *Guentando a Ôia* **(Excelente Discos 011060-2).** This song by Mundo Livre S/A also references neighborhoods of the city, showing the expanse of *"Manguetown"* (i.e., Recife): "From Rio Doce to Piedade/From Barra de Jangada until Casa Caiada. . . . Save Zero Quatro/Save/Save the music." Notice the use of samba rhythmic elements and instruments (*cavaquinho, pardeiro,* and *tamborim*) in a rock/funk context.

20. **"Eu Tenho Pressa"** (Cannibal-Neilton-Celo). Devotos do Ódio. From: *Abril Pro Rock* **(Columbia 758.434/2-490151).**

21. **"Ruas da Cidade."** Faces do Subúrbio. From: *Enjaulado: Música Para Ouvir Trancado#* **(independent).** The next two songs by two of the biggest bands on the Recife scene—Devotos do Ódio (The Devotees of Hate) and Faces do Subúrbio (Faces of the Suburbs)—present straight hard-core rock and protest rap styles, respectively, borrowed from foreign models. "Eu Tenho Pressa" says: "I have an urgency to overcome/I have an urgency to be successful [or avenge]/Living like this I'm going to die/Living like this I'm going to kill."

Over a jazz upright bass line, scratchy record, and other samples, and a hip-hop groove, MCs Tiger and Brown of Faces do Subúrbio critique the social conditions of Recife and Brazil in "Ruas da Cidade" (Streets of the City). Here are some lines translated into English; upper case words are shouted by both MCs (notice how a sampled line in English "I can feel" precedes the first spoken line of the song — RECIFE):

"RECIFE! A beautiful city/But I can't believe that it still happens. . . . Whoever lives on the street doesn't have any security/Adults, adolescents, especially CHILDREN!!/Here in Brazil it's already become a scene/Many crimes, people assassinated, many deaths. . . . There's no hope of being in first place, this killing of children,* they're the CHILDREN!!. . . . Some of them rob because they can't work and others sniff glue. . . . I want to see who it is that is GOING to help THIS COUNTRY, this WHOLE people who are very UNHAPPY. These children will certainly be the marginals of the future WHEN THEY GROW UP!!/STREETS OF THE CITY, STREETS OF THE CITY!!. . . ."

*This line resembles an *embolada*: {Não tem nenhuma esperança estar em primeiro lugar esse assassinato de criança}, são as CRIANÇAS!!

22. **"Vô Imbolá"** (Zeca Baleiro). From: **Zeca Baleiro,** *Vô Imbolá* **(Polygram 011297-2).** Zeca Baleiro, from Maranhão in northern Brazil, is being lauded as the best new thing in MPB. Along with other current Brazilian bands and performers, Baleiro clearly shows a strong affinity with Pernambuco's

and performers, Baleiro clearly shows a strong affinity with Pernambuco's *mangue* movement, if not a direct influence from it. In this opening title cut of his CD "Vô Imbolá" (I'm going to sing *embolada*/improvise/mix), Zeca uses the *embolada* vocal style in his own pop fusion. The words, which rhyme in Portuguese, reference various local and global influences in his music. Here is one verse (English words are in boldface):

"I'm going to sing the *embolada*, my binge, my guitar, my **riff, Bob Dylan,** *banda de pife*,* Luiz Gonzaga, **Jimmy Cliff**/Poetry doesn't have an owner/Joy doesn't have a trademark/When I get my money I'm going to Recife/Because there the sun is great/It was speaking Brazilian that I learned how to sing *embolada*."

*Note: the "*banda de pife*" (from *banda de pífanos*) refers to a typical drum and fife band from the northeastern Brazilian interior.

Appendix 4
Fieldwork Account

Recife and Olinda, Pernambuco, Brazil: January 27-June 25 1998

AUDIO RECORDINGS

1. *Candomblé* ceremony. Recorded by Philip Galinsky and Neide Alves. Sítio de Pai Adão, Água Fria. Toque for Ogum. 4 tapes of 90 minutes each. April 18, 1998.

2. Maciel Salu e Rodrigo Costa (Caçapa) (Chão e Chinelo). Recorded by author. Cidade Tabajara. Original songs and "Asa Branca" by Luiz Gonzaga with *rabeca* (fiddle) and *viola* (lute). Included with the interview of May 13, 1998.

3 José Severino Vicente (Zé Neguinho do Côco). Recorded by author. Morro da Conceição. Original songs with *pandeiro* (frame drum), voice, foot stamps, handclaps. Included with the interview of June 3, 1998.

VIDEO RECORDINGS

1. Maracatu Nação Estrela Brilhante in the 1998 Carnival. Recorded by author. Presentation for the community of the neighborhood at the Pólo Cultural, Alto José do Pinho. Approx. 10 minutes (1 tape). February 23, 1998.

2. Maracatu Nação Estrela Brilhante in the 1998 Carnival. Recorded by author. "A Noite dos Tambores Silenciosos" (Night of the Silent Drums). Pátio do Terço, Bairro Santo Antônio (Center of Recife). Approx. 50 minutes (2 tapes). February 23, 1998.

3. Maracatu Nação Estrela Brilhante in the 1998 Carnival. Recorded by author. Presentation in the Terreiro de Santa Barbara (Nação Xambá) [*Candomblé* temple]. Beberibe, near Olinda. Approx. 50 minutes (2 tapes). February 24, 1998.

LESSONS/CLASSES
1. *Candomblé* class with Dito D'Oxossi. Alto José do Pinho. Involved lectures on *Candomblé*, playing *atabaque* drum and singing, and attending ceremonies. Periodic attendance.

2. Lesson in *maracatu* percussion with Neide Alves, member of Maracatu Nação Estrela Brilhante.

3. Percussion lesson (covering *baião, forró, côco, maracatu,* and *mangue*) with Jorge Martins da Silva, member of Maracatu Nação Estrela Brilhante and the band Cascabulho.

PERFORMANCES
1. Played *repinique* drum with Patusco, a samba *bloco*. Rehearsals and street parade. Carnival 1998. Olinda.

EVENTS ATTENDED
These include: the 1998 Carnival in Recife/Olinda; Abril Pro Rock '98 (local music festival featuring rock and other international styles, *mangue*, and regional folk music); *Festas Juninas*, the June Festivals, important regional festivals (in Recife and Caruaru); and many other music events in clubs and outdoor festivals throughout Recife and Olinda.

FORMAL INTERVIEWS CONDUCTED
1. Renato Lins, DJ and host of radio program *Mangue Beat*. Interview by author, January 30, 1998, Olinda. Tape recording.

2. Zé da Flauta, producer. Interview by author, February 5, 1998, Recife. Tape recording.

3. Dr. Mário Souto Maior, folklorist. Interview by author, February 10, 1998, Recife. Tape recording. Fundação Joaquim Nabuco.

4. Eduardo Fonseca, anthropologist. Interview by author, February 10, 1998, Recife. Tape recording. Fundação Joaquim Nabuco.

5. Éder Rocha, percussionist for the band Mestre Ambrósio. Interview by author, February 17, 1998, Recife. Tape recording.

6. Paulo André Pires, producer and impresario. Interview by author, March 6, 1998, Recife. Tape recording.

Appendix 4 165

7. Pupillo, drum-set for the band Nação Zumbi. Interview by author, March 9, 1998, Recife. Tape recording.

8. Fred Zèro Quatro, vocalist, guitarist, and *cavaquinho* player for the band Mundo Livre S/A. Interview by author, March 10, 1998, Recife. Tape recording.

9. Mestre Bernardo, musical director of Nação Pernambuco. Interview by author, March 31, 1998, Recife. Tape recording.

10. Maureliano Ribiero and Hamilton Tenório, percussionist and guitarist, respectively, for the band Via Sat. Interview by author, April 13, 1998, Recife. Tape recording.

11 Alessandra Leão, percussionist for the band Comadre Florzinha. Interview by author, April 15, 1998, Recife. Tape recording.

12. Dito D'Oxossi, practitioner of and authority on *Candomblé*. Interview by author and Neide Alves, April 21, 1998, Recife. Tape recording.

13. Jorge Martins da Silva, percussionist for the band Cascabulho. Interview by author, April 23, 1998, Recife. Tape recording.

14. Mestre Meia-Noite, director for the Centro de Apoio à Communidade Carente "Daruê Malungo" in Chão de Estrelas (Center of Support to the Poor Community). Interview by author, April 28, 1998, Recife. Tape recording.

15. Ariano Suassuna, Secretary of Culture for Pernambuco. Interview by author, May 9, 1998, Recife. Tape recording.

16. Oni, guitarist for the band Faces do Subúrbio. Interview by author, May 12, 1998, Recife. Tape recording.

17. Maciel Salu and Rodrigo Costa (Caçapa), *rabeca* player and percussionist, respectively, for the band Chão e Chinelo. Interview by author, May 13, 1998, Cidade Tabajara. Tape recording.

18. Mestre Salustiano, folk musician. Interview by author, May 13, 1998, Cidade Tabajara. Tape recording.

19. Mestre Valter Ferreira de França, percussion director for Maracatu Nação Estrela Brilhante. Interview by author and Neide Alves, May 14, 1998, Recife. Tape recording.

20. José Teles, journalist. Interview by author, May 20, 1998, Recife. Tape-recording.

21. Maureliano Ribiero and Hamilton Tenório, percussion and guitarist, respectively, for the band Via Sat. Interview by author, May 22, 1998, Recife. Tape recording.

22. Dona Rita, Seu Francisco, and Jefferson França (family of musician Chico Science). Interview by author, May 30, 1998, Olinda. Tape recording.

23. Sílvio Romero Costa Lima, producer. Interview by author. June 2, 1998, Recife. Written notes.

24. José Severino Vicente (Zé Neguinho do Côco), folk musician. Interview by author, June 3, 1998, Recife. Tape recording.

25. José Antônio de Souza Filho, DJ. Interview by author, June 5, 1998, Recife. Written notes.

OTHER FORMAL INTERVIEWS USED
1. Siba and Hélder Vasconcelos, members of the band Mestre Ambrósio. Interview by Tânia Lima, August 22, 1997, Recife. Transcript.

2. Chico Science and Paulo André Pires, musician and producer-impresario. Interview by Marty Lipp, date unknown, New York. Tape recording.

3. Carlos Alberto Medeiros, Chief of Cabinet for SEAFRO (Secretary for the Defense and Promotion of the Afro-Brazilian Population). Interview by author, July 21, 1994, Rio de Janeiro. Tape recording. SEAFRO.

Notes

Preface

1. Translation by the author. All subsequent translations in the dissertation are also by the author unless otherwise indicated.

Chapter 1: Introduction

1. *Antropofagia* was proposed by the São Paulo poet Oswald de Andrade in his *Manifesto Antropófago* (1928) and introduced into Brazilian popular music by the *tropicalistas*. Both *antropofagia* and *tropicália* are explored further in Chapters Three and Five.

2. Throughout this dissertation, I use "new music scene" and "Recife scene" interchangeably. Some acts on this scene were directly influenced by the pioneering *mangue* bands Chico Science & Nação Zumbi and Mundo Livre S/A. Other groups, such as Mestre Ambrósio and Nação Pernambuco, were developing more or less concurrent musical projects. Some bands, such as Devotos or even Mundo Livre S/A, predate the articulation of *mangue*. Some people refer to virtually all of the new music on the Recife scene as *"mangue."* At the other end of the spectrum, some reserve the term for the pioneering work of Chico Science & Nação Zumbi and Mundo Livre S/A. Still others categorize *mangue* as any kind of fusion music on the Recife scene. (See Chapter Two, pp. 61-66 for a more detailed definition of *mangue* and an examination of the movement's relation to the "new music scene.")

3. Although I do impose my own theoretical lens in my choice and understanding of these terms, I attempt to show how members of the scene label and theorize these and similar concepts as well, which they do in a variety of ways. Although there are sure to be discrepancies between these *-emic* and *-etic* approaches, I hope to have presented a cohesive, somewhat well rounded, and

mutually supportive inclusion of my own theoretical terminology, conceptualizations, and insights and those of my consultants.

4. This dissertation represents the first in-depth scholarly treatment of the *mangue* movement and "new music scene" of Recife in English. My work was preceded by journalist José Teles's book on the career of Chico Science (Teles n/d), anthropologist Tânia Lima's as-yet-unpublished paper on environmental aspects of *mangue* for the Joaquim Nabuco Foundation in Recife, and journalist Pedro Rampazzo's (n/d) unpublished paper on the use of regional elements in Pernambucan pop in the '90s for a University course. I am also aware of a scholar from Brasília who was preparing to research the representation of *mangue* in the mass media of southern Brazil for her master's degree in sociology.

5. Rampazzo (n/d) also finds a similar kind of interaction among performers of various kinds on the Recife scene in his paper.

6. Another kind of blurring of the domestic and foreign is in the identity of particular musics. I discuss this in the body of the dissertation.

7. The following literature review is more a representative sampling of some major trends in Brazilian popular music studies rather than a comprehensive listing and evaluation of sources.

8. As Vianna states, his book analyzes "the invention of the samba as national authenticity, showing how the authentic is always an arbitrary phenomenon . . . and how diverse social groups, with not coincidental intentions, participated—transculturally—in the fabrication of this authenticity" (1995: 173).

9. Tinhorão claims that the evolution of the urban samba of Rio de Janeiro can be linked with various social classes to which the genre spoke throughout its history (1986: 130-131). As Tinhorão observes, in the 1920s, the fledgling urban samba was associated with professional and semi-professional composers such as Donga and Sinhô in the city's center. Later in the Estácio neighborhood, the samba rhythm was taken back to its roots with a cohort of composers from the lowest social classes. In the 1930s and '40s the genre was associated with a generation of professional composers in the environment of radio and record companies and came to be played by "semi-erudite" salon dance orchestras. As a response to this middle-class *samba-canção* (samba-song), composers from the "popular" (i.e., lower class) sectors made the contrary move in the 1930s, syncopating the samba even further in the form of the *samba-de-breque* (break-samba). Meanwhile, Tinhorão observes, some isolated composers from the slums such as Nélson Cavaquinho continued to cultivate a *samba-canção* closer to popular sources—that is, more "samba" than "song." Finally, when the *samba-canção* practiced by the professional middle-class composers had been exhausted of its possibilities (and had its rhythm "diluted") by hybridizing with other styles such as the *bolero* or *balada*, Rio's middle class university culture in

the 1950s reformulated the samba with the inspiration of jazz, yielding the bossa nova (ibid.: 157).

10. Although I cannot adequately address here the complex issues of the cultural politics of race in Brazil, a short explanation is in order. Whereas conservatives and leftists alike have regarded social class as the most salient factor in Brazilian social life, racial distinctions were long considered not only insignificant, but also not even worth discussing (Skidmore 1985). Despite both clear examples of discrimination and the fact that most dark-skinned Brazilians fall into the lowest socioeconomic brackets of society, there has been a culture of silence around the racial question in Brazil, supported by the widespread, elite-sanctioned belief in a supposed "racial democracy." The inclusion of non-whites in the sociocultural conception of the nation (through the ideas of *mestiçagem* and the racial democracy) has been cited as one of the reasons these groups have been historically unable to articulate an agenda of social justice (see Yúdice 1994). Winant (1994) has produced an excellent assessment of both racial dynamics in Brazil and the literature addressing this topic.

11. Like Tinhorão, Lopes depicts the history of the samba as a battleground for competing aesthetic interests, although he defines these interests less in class terms than in racial/cultural/national terms. Nonetheless, there is an implicit class dimension to his work since the black popular expressions he aims to valorize are the products of poor communities, while the foreign influences that he pits these against are, in his estimation, supported by both multinational interests and the Brazilian elite. Lopes sidesteps an investigation of competing black identities in his 1993 essay by depicting young black Brazilians' identification with international music such as hip-hop and reggae as a misguided search for identity. Lopes attributes this (at least in part) to elite efforts to deny Afro-Brazilians a positive sense of their heritage and to bourgeois and elite support of these foreign musics. Although no scholar has been as pointed as Lopes in addressing race, nationality, and music, other writers have expanded the scope of racial identity as it relates to music, particularly in a series of 1990s publications. My own research into the *pagode* samba (Galinsky 1995, 1996), like that of Lopes, presents a particular genre as the site for the negotiation of competing aesthetics and ideologies. However, where my approach differs is in allowing for a more flexible sense of black identity. I see the more traditional and more international strains of the *pagode* movement as representing two distinct kinds of black Brazilian ideologies—where, at least in this case, the former is characterized as more resistant and the latter as more accommodating to commercial influences. While I allow for the possibility of resistant expression through international influences (primarily in Brazilian rap or the reggae influence in the Afro-Bahian *blocos afro*, but also possibly even in the commercial 1990s *pagode*), I do not, at least in these studies, look to such influences as oppositional alternatives to an established identity. Other authors (discussed below) take this sort of approach.

12. Hermano Vianna's *O Mundo Funk Carioca* (1988) was the pioneering work on the "funk balls" of Rio youth.

13. Despite its interesting insights, this work presents a theoretical approach with which I take issue (see Galinsky 1998). In her attempt to rectify popular Afro-Brazilian and Western academic ways of thinking, Browning brilliantly posits the notion of a corporal intelligence in black Brazilian dance. However, I dispute Browning's semiotically problematic next step borrowed from literary theory. She suggests that cultural forms "write their own meanings," which may be "read" (i.e., learned) by anyone simply through participation (Browning 1995: xi, xxii). In my view, "meanings" of cultural forms are not a priori qualities but context dependent, ascribed by particular people within particular sociohistorical contexts. Browning's approach ironically allows the foreign scholar a dangerous amount of leeway to speak in place of the communities under study.

14. Other authors who have explored the relationship between race, gender, and popular culture include Alma Guillermoprieto (1990) and Richard G. Parker (1991). Both authors focus on the figure of the *mulata*, a woman of mixed black and white racial types (in U.S. terms, a light-skinned black woman), who in Brazilian culture represents an erotic ideal. For Parker, the *mulata* paradoxically embodies "the living expression of racial mixture" in Brazil (1991: 153) serving, in Guillermoprieto's view, to perpetuate the myth of the racial democracy and to present miscegenation in a harmless light (1990: 180). In her assessment of the relationship between black women and white men in Brazil from a "black" point of view (see ibid.: 179-187), Guillermoprieto sees the *mulata* as existing only in her *relation* to white men (to the black community she is simply black). This is evident in the Carnival, where, the author notes, black men dressed as *malandros* (the rogue figure whose archetype is a pimp) "offer" sexy *mulatas* (the archetypal whore is a *mulata*) to an audience understood to be white and male (even though it is not exclusively that). As a key symbol of the samba and Rio Carnival, the *mulata* then is historic proof of the white man's power—not only "to wrest the *mulata*'s black mother away from her black partner" (ibid.: 180), but also to define her sexuality.

15. Very few works treat gender as a separate factor of analysis. Examining images of masculinity, Oliven (1993) regards popular song in Brazil as one of the only public instances in which the man allows himself to talk sincerely about his feelings in relation to women. There, instead of showing an explicit image of power and superiority, the man confesses anguish, weakness, pain, and desire. The article examines lyrics of samba compositions of the 1930s, '40s and '50s. The relationship between work, money, and women appear as interlinked themes because, as Oliven argues, the relations of work, the dissemination of salaried work, and a redefinition of sexual roles occurred in this period of urban-industrial development along with the change from a patriarchal family to a more nuclear one. In Oliven's analyses, the woman is necessary to the man, but

is also the cause of his suffering: vengeance, as the result of abandonment and betrayal, is thus a central theme of many sambas from this period.

16. Carvalho relies on the interpretation of song texts as one of his primary means of analysis, offering hard data and a useful first overview of black identities. However, several important factors are left out of his analysis. For one thing, Carvalho mostly bypasses the issue of international (particularly black North American and Caribbean) musical influence and how this impacts Afro-Brazilian identities. Secondly, he leaves untreated the whole realm of secular Afro-Brazilian music such as samba (instead subsuming this under the syncretic cult model, which makes use of these genres in a religious context).

17. I discuss these texts in more detail in Chapters Four and Five of the dissertation.

18. "Global," "global culture," and "globalization" are words that crop up many times in the dissertation. These terms are meant to reference the growing fluidity of peoples, media, technologies, economies, ideologies, political power, social relations, and cultures across nationally-defined borders (see Appadurai 1990, Slobin 1992).

19. This is partly because much of the best known northeastern pop music has been produced in the South and many northeastern performers have left their place of origin to make a huge impact on the national scene. Indeed, many of the most influential popular musicians in Brazil have been of northeastern (largely Bahian) background (e.g., Dorival Caymmi, João Gilberto, Caetano Veloso, Gilberto Gil, Gal Costa, Maria Bethânia, Simone, Luiz Gonzaga, Jackson do Pandeiro, Alceu Valença, and so on). The *mangue* trend thus represents the emergence of one of several main northeastern states that has long supplied the national scenario with talent or until recently, kept well-hidden cultural secrets. The growth in the last several decades of an Afro-Bahian music scene in Salvador represents a similar development.

20. Timothy D. Taylor challenges the privileging of such binary categories as complicity and resistance, which are questionable in their ability to address the complex "lived situations" of members of a particular society (Taylor 1997: 80-81).

21. For example, it would be problematic to assign any one particular racial or class identity to Chico Science & Nação Zumbi, whose members are of diverse racial and socioeconomic backgrounds and whose music and discourse embrace not only more Afrocentric styles and ideas but also nationalist ones such as *mestiçagem* (miscegenation). This ambiguity is, in fact, fascinating and worthy of study. Nonetheless, I see these racial and class factors in *mangue* as subsumed under a wider -*emic* ideological framework (which I elucidate in Chapter Five) that centers around issues of local and global.

22. The popular and commercial use of "world music" is as a marketing label for music that falls outside of established categories in Europe and North America (see Taylor 1997). Born from a meeting of record executives in England in the summer of 1987 who sought to market music from other cultures

in Britain (see ibid.: 2-3), this label is fraught with controversy, lumping a host of diverse musics from various cultures into one generic bin. "World music" is also infused with old tropes about the primal "authenticity" of non-Western cultures based on expectations that these cultures and their musicians remain sources for a primal, original essence (see ibid.). In his book *Global Pop: World Music, World Markets*, Timothy Taylor unravels these various notions of authenticity and Western perceptions of Third World cultures, as he uncovers the Western-dominated economic structures that support them. This dissertation does examine *mangue*'s articulation of local and global interplay, but it does not analyze *mangue* as "world music" in the commercial sense. Although Chico Science & Nação Zumbi toured parts of Europe and the U.S. in the so-called "world music" circuit, they, or *mangue* as a whole, cannot easily be labeled "world music." As Chico Science remarked, "We have a vision of music of the world, without intending to make world music" (interview with Antônio Carlos Miguel, *O Globo*, March 31, 1994, quoted in Teles n.d., 23). I have preferred to look at the music of the *mangue* movement more on the terms of its creators rather than to impose a discourse that they themselves do not engage in and even reject.

23. I do not critique all of the important aspects of this body of literature in this Introduction or in the dissertation as a whole. Rather, I outline here only some of the issues that were most pertinent in my work.

24. Even though Yúdice's analysis pits samba and a supposed "consensus culture" against imported black music from the U.S. (which he does not regard as necessarily resistant), this is not really an "either-or" proposition. In my own research on the samba in Rio de Janeiro in 1993 and 1994, I found that these musics were not mutually exclusive in black Brazilian identities at all. For example, I interviewed Carlos Alberto Medeiros (1994), a black rights leader in Rio, who told me that these musics co-exist in black communities. According to Medeiros (ibid.), many youth who dance to funk also go to samba during Carnival time, and moreover, as they get older, black youth tend to dance more to samba and MPB (*Música Popular Brasileira*) than to funk. Perhaps samba has had to give up some of its space for other modes of expression, but this has always been the case anyway. Indeed, samba's position as a "national" music is a social and ideological construction (see Vianna 1995).

25. Flávia de Gusmão wrote a second article about me and my research in the *Jornal do Commércio*, and near the end of my stay a small segment on my research (including an interview with me) was featured on the SBT channel in Recife, produced by TV Jornal.

26. The latter festival is dominated by various kinds of *forró* music. The famous *São João* (Saint John's Day) party in Caruaru, for example, featured a wide range of *forró* music, from roots *forró* to a kind of *forró*-rock to highly commercialized pop *forró*.

27. This crowd of mostly female musicians and researchers from the Federal University of Pernambuco was one of the main crowds that I worked with during my stay.

28. According to Joseph Page in *The Brazilians*, the recent development in Recife and the Northeast in general has only significantly affected the region's affluent: "Yet the signs of progress throughout the Northeast and the new Recife mean only that a considerable degree of economic progress has bettered the condition of the region's haves, who were able to take advantage of the 1969-73 'Brazilian Miracle,' the tax incentives that facilitated the creation of new industry in the region, and the opportunities Brazilian financial markets provided for investing money. What trickled down to the have-nots was hardly enough to make a meaningful change in the lives of a substantial number of them" (1995: 195).

29. I do not mean to lump recent Bahian and Pernambucan popular music trends into the same category at all; I only wish to emphasize that both are from the Northeast. In fact, there are great differences between Bahian *axé-music* and acts from the Recife scene. Aside from significant musical and cultural differences between the two, the former has been for several years, along with the *pagode* samba, among the most dominant popular music trends in the nation, garnering massive media attention and sales. *Mangue* and other Recife acts, on the other hand, are commercially much more insignificant, occupying a more marginal position in the national mass media (although the local media in Pernambuco have covered Pernambucan bands and trends devotedly). As such, the Recife scene is, despite its growing interest and impact outside of Pernambuco, still a kind of alternative scene, while many Bahian *axé* and regional *pagode* groups have been projected from a local scene in Salvador onto a network of national mass exposure. Another striking difference is that many traditionalists and music aficionados lambaste both *axé* and the current *pagode* for being commercial music of the "lowest quality," while many Recife bands and artists have been regarded highly by the nation's music critics.

30. Even though historically many of the country's most popular singers and composers have come from Bahia and the Northeast, not all of these singers necessarily present a strong, overtly northeastern identity. Of course, Alceu Valença and the northeastern wave of the 1970s and '80s, as Luiz Gonzaga and Jackson do Pandeiro, certainly promoted a kind of northeastern identity. In general, various regions of Brazil have had their spotlight in the national scenario, and this spotlight shifts from era to era even as Rio affirms its (contested) role as the primary representative of Brazilian national culture. In the 1990s, where various regions have experienced a renaissance in their recuperation of roots within a process of musical innovation, there has been a strong focus on the Northeast. This emphasis on the Northeast is also represented in other realms of Brazilian culture such as tourism, cinema, literature, etc.

31. See Vianna 1995 for a discussion of one dominant national project (that of Gilberto Freyre and the Rio de Janeiro samba) and how this has been challenged in recent decades. I also discuss some of these issues in Chapter Five.

Chapter 2: "Da Lama Ao Caos"

1. S/A stands for *sociedade anônima* (anonymous society) in Portuguese and is used in Brazil as a kind of classification of a business. S/A is similar to "limited," except that for the former, it is not known who the owners of the company are, or how many there are. Despite these differences between the terms, I have chosen the more familiar "limited" (ltd.) as the English translation.

2. The *mangue* movement's connection to the local environment is discussed at various points further in the dissertation. See, for example, Chapter Five (under the heading "Mangue Style and Ideology") for more information about Josué de Castro's influence on *mangue* as well as some of the natural and geographical aspects of the movement.

3. As for sources, this chapter is indebted to the recently released fanzine style booklet that traces the career of Chico Science called *Meteoro Chico* (n/d), organized and edited by Recife journalist José Teles. *Meteoro Chico* contains interviews with and sound bites by Chico Science, eulogies and information provided by friends and musicians, the two manifestos of the *mangue* movement, complete lyrics from both of the band's CDs, a chronology of the band's history, original text by Teles, and various previously published newspaper articles and press releases. This first codified history of *mangue* is synthesized here with the perspectives of various local musicians, producers, and others whom I formally interviewed in Recife and with my own interpretations.

4. Since the time fieldwork was conducted (1998), the band has shortened its name to "Devotos" (Devotees), dropping "do Ódio" (of Hate).

5. In Chapter Three I discuss other significant movements and tendencies that predate *mangue*, addressing their relation to *mangue* and assessing the peculiar role and contribution of *mangue* to the lineage of fusing local and global sounds in Brazilian popular music. Here, I simply "set the stage," as it were, by discussing some general and musical conditions of Recife in the 1980s prior to the emergence of *mangue*. All of the information and quotations in this section ("Setting the Scene: Recife in the 1980s"), except for my own interspersed comments, are derived from Teles n/d: 13-14.

6. This rock boom will be addressed in more depth in Chapter Three.

7. A friend of Chico Science's told me this in an informal conversation.

8. Hard-core (or hardcore) is a style of rock that came after punk. According to *The Rolling Stone Encyclopedia of Rock & Roll* (edited by Jon Pareles and Patricia Romanowski), "By the early Eighties, though, punk had

turned into American and British 'hard-core' movements. The music was louder, harder and faster, the politics more nihilistic than ever and the use of dress codes (leather) and hairstyles (the Mohawk) was more pronounced than ever" (1983: 450). The dress codes of hard-core in Recife are notably different. Not surprisingly, mohawks and leather are not typical, and Cannibal of Devotos do Ódio wears his hair in dreads. The peculiar manifestation of hard-core in Recife is touched on in Chapter Four.

9. This was the basic formation of Lamento Negro and other *blocos afro*. *Tambor*, meaning generically "drum," may refer to the *bombos* that CSNZ eventually used, but at least in an early video of the band (the song "A Cidade" in "Chico Science: Mangue Star"), percussionists from Lamento are shown playing the *surdo* drums that the *blocos afro* use. The visual of the percussionists at this time, and even the drum rhythms, bore a closer resemblance to the *samba-reggae* of Olodum.

10. The band was very disorganized in the beginning. As an example, Toca Ogan played with CSNZ at the first Abril Pro Rock festival (described later in this chapter) in 1993 after not having shown his face in rehearsals for more than three months (Teles n/d: 11). Having assumed vocals in Loustal when Chico left, Jorge du Peixe was invited to join CSNZ right before Sony Music executives came to Recife to see the band perform at the Som das Águas club; for lack of space, he ended up playing *bombo* drum (ibid.). Canhoto (snare drum) left the band after their first international tour (see note #14); Pupillo, who plays drumset, replaced him.

11. Gabriel of the band Coração Tribal replaced Dengue on bass for this gig (Teles n/d: 11).

12. Some of these distinctions are clarified in Chapter Four.

13. For the latter definition, see Éder Rocha's distinction between his group, Mestre Ambrósio, and *mangue* in Chapter Four.

14. For instance, the percussionist for Mundo Livre, Otto, has lived in France and speaks French fluently (Interview: Teles 1998). This contrasts sharply with the story of Canhoto, former snare drummer for Nação Zumbi and resident of Peixinhos. Prior to the band's first European tour, Canhoto exclaimed to impresario Paulo André Pires that he had always dreamed of seeing Paraguay. Apparently, Canhoto suffered such a culture shock on that tour that he started to become a burden to the group and finally had to quit (Teles n/d: 19). The ways in which the *mangue* phenomenon united diverse social groups of the city will be touched on later in the dissertation.

15. The following information and quotations in the "Mundo Livre" section are derived from my interview with Fred Zero Quatro (1998).

16. Fred's original idea was to be called "Zero Quatro," but people have insisted on using his baptized name together with the code numbers, hence he is now known as Fred Zero Quatro.

17. The *guitarra baiana* is a miniature electric guitar used in Bahian pop music, especially in the context of the *trio elétrico* ("electric trio"), a popular kind of sound truck during Carnival in Salvador (and now other cities) on top of which an electric band plays.

18. In the '90s, *pagode* mainly refers to highly commercial varieties of samba. On *pagode*, see Galinsky 1994, 1995, and 1996.

19. Chapter Three further elucidates some distinctions between Brazilian rock of the '80s and *mangue*.

20. Paulo André Pires called Chico the scene's "greatest exponent" (Interview: 1998).

21. Antonio Nobrega is a trained Pernambucan musician who was at the forefront of the *Movimento Armorial*, which sought to create erucite interpretations of the region's folk culture. According to DJ José Antônio de Souza Leão Filho, Antônio Nóbrega originally called *mangue* crap but is now an advocate of *mangue* (Interview: Filho 1998).

Chapter 3: *Mangue* in the Context of Brazilian Pop Music History

1. As Dunn elaborates, "In some ways Tropicália was akin to a postcolonial critique in that it recognized the peripheral position of Brazil in the world economy, but also challenged static notions of national culture" (Dunn 2001: 89). Dunn regards Tropicália and the subsequent work of Caetano Veloso and Gilberto Gil as inaugurating a "critique of prescriptive ideologies of national identity . . . in the realm of popular music, responding to and inspiring new expressions of Brazilian modernity inscribed within global countercultural and Afro-diasporic dynamics" (ibid.: 89, 91).

2. Bossa nova is a softer, middle class variation of the samba that emerged in Rio de Janeiro in the late 1950s, becoming the most influential international pop music trend in the early '60s (until the arrival of the Beatles). For more information on bossa nova, see, e.g., Behague 1973, Castro 1990, McGowan and Pessanha 1998, and Dunn 2001.

3. Besides the composer-performers Veloso and Gil—who are two of Brazil's most beloved popular artists—the movement's central figures included singer Gal Costa (one of the country's most renowned vocalists), composer-performer Tom Zé, lyricists Torquato Neto and Capinam, the rock band Os Mutantes (The Mutants), bossa nova muse Nara Leão, and the conductors Rogério Duprat and Júlio Medaglia. With a foot in both the classical and experimental electronic music camps, São Paulo native Rogério Duprat was the musical director and arranger of most *tropicália* works, functioning much like George Martin did for The Beatles. In fact, The Beatles directly inspired some of Duprat's orchestral ideas. For more information on *tropicália*, see, for example, Calado 1997, McGowan and Pessanha 1998, Marzorati 1999, Dunn 2001, and Harvey 2001.

4. From the movement's musical manifesto "Tropicália" (Caetano Veloso), quoted in Schreiner 1993: 170. The "monument upon the central plateau of the country" is a reference to the newly constructed, ultra-modern capital of Brasília. The bossa is a reference to bossa nova, a soft, modern middle-class form of samba, which is juxtaposed with the old rustic abode of Brazil's poor, the *palhoça*, or thatched hut.

5. *Choro* is a genre of instrumental music that originated in Rio de Janeiro in the latter part of the 19th century and that continues to thrive today. Noel Rosa (1910-1937) was one of the samba's most renowned composers. *Música caipira* is folk music from the interior of southern, southeastern, and central Brazil.

6. As John J. Harvey writes: "The Tropicalists challenged the dualism of *engajado/alienado* ["engaged"/"alienated," referring to the nationalistic protest singers versus the rock singers of the Jovem Guarda]. To bridge the gap between 'national' and 'international,' the Tropicalists used such procedures as playing electric instruments together with traditional Afro-Brazilian instruments (e.g., *berimbau*). Their musical and performative styles fused rock elements with popular Brazilian forms such as the *samba-de-roda*, *baião*, *marcha*, *frevo*, as well as rhythms associated with folkloric dances such as the *bumba-meu-boi* and *maracatu*. Inspired by the critical revision of Brazilian modernism undertaken by the concrete poets, the Tropicalists incorporated Oswald de Andrade's idea of cultural cannibalism in order to create hybrid arts that challenged the restrictive political and aesthetic dualisms of the time" (Harvey 2001: 109).

7. Gilberto Gil dedicates his CD *Quanta* (Mesa 92778-2) to Cássia Eller, samba musician Zeca Pagodinho, and in memoriam Chico Science; on this CD Gil interprets Gordurinha's "Vendedor de Caranguejo" (Crab Vendor), which has a northeastern theme. Caetano Veloso sings his own "Livros" from the album of the same name (Polygram 536584 2), which is in a *maracatu de baque virado* rhythm.

8. This is more or less how the saying went. I heard this from producer Fred Lasmar at the bar Soparia.

9. This distinction between "international" and "Brazilian" is not so clear-cut. Indeed, Brazilian popular music itself—as really all popular music in the world—is an inextricable fusion of various domestic and foreign influences.

10. José Teles told me that the first time he saw a *bombo* drum (from the Afro-Pernambucan *maracatu*) being used in a pop format was in a Lenine show in 1982 (Interview: Teles 1998). In the 1990s, CSNZ expanded on this idea, making the incorporation of *bombos* in a rock band format a pervasive trend in Recife. Today, Lenine remains at the artistic forefront of the current MPB and has performed with notable Rio percussionist Marcos Suzano (including at the Brazilian Music Festival in Central Park's SummerStage in 1997). Compared with CSNZ, for example, Lenine's sound is less aggressive and more akin to a classic MPB aesthetic, albeit with a stronger regional orientation, sharing some similarities with the recent work of Gilberto Gil.

11. On one level, the comically exaggerated comparison of the era of Alceu Valença or of *mangue* to the "sugar cane cycle" (which refers to the colonial period in which sugar cane was Brazil's primary economy) simply highlights the sheer length and utter dominance of Valença's previous reign in Pernambucan music, confidently asserting the new reign of Chico's own movement, *mangue*. On the other hand, as David Rumpler pointed out, referring to the pre-Valença era of Pernambucan music as the "sugar cane cycle," which carries connotations of something archaic and dated, suggests that music before Valença's rise to stardom was considered old-fashioned by Valença's generation. It also affirms that as the first Pernambucan musician of visibility to incorporate the global pop and rock explosion that began in the '60s and fuse this with his regional heritage, Valença represented a pivotal turning point for modern Pernambucan music. (David Rumpler, personal communication, 1999) By the same token, Chico announces that, just like the "sugar cane cycle," the time of Alceu has ended; indeed, by the 1990s, the music of Alceu and his generation had become out-moded for young Pernambucans and had to make way for *mangue*, the next dominant phase of Pernambucan music.

12. Some artists, such as Elomar and Vital Farias, produced guitar-based representations of northeastern music that are largely acoustic. For a representative sampling of some of the main artists from the northeastern wave (plus other MPB artists interpreting songs with a northeastern flavor), listen to the compilation *Nordeste Brasil* (Verve 845 327 - 2), 1990.

13. Valença has worked with both rural and urban Pernambucan sounds, whereas CSNZ has relied on such styles as *maracatu de baque virado*, *côco*, and *ciranda* from the urban coast (Recife).

14. From this perspective, *mangue* was not a predetermined movement but the result of a group of self-aware people shaping their historical moment within a given set of conditions. I would agree with this assessment. In Chapter Five, I allow much room for individual and group agency in my assessment of *mangue*, which has refashioned tradition, locality, and a sense of history.

15. This synopsis of Brazilian rock history is derived from Cáurio 1988: 250-265 and McGowan and Pessanha 1998: 185-201.

16. See Harvey 2001 for a discussion of Os Mutantes.

17. The Paralamas do Sucesso were an exemplary band that in the later 1980s enlarged their early rock and ska sound to include such Brazilian rhythmic influences as samba and in some instances regional northeastern idioms *xaxado*, *afoxé*, *côco*, *baião*, and the northern *lambada* along with other Caribbean touches (reggae-dub and Haitian *compas*). For this phase of the band's career, listen to *Selvagem?* (1986) and especially *Bora Bora* (1988). However, in their recent performance at Central Park SummerStage in New York City (July 1999), Paralamas played material that combined mostly rock, ska, and reggae. The band did include a cover of a CSNZ song ("Manguetown")

in the show but at least in this version, the song did not contain any overt "Brazilian" references.

18. Of course, local-global fusion is characteristic of all Brazilian popular music, but here I have focused only on several movements within the last thirty or so years of Brazilian popular music history.

19. Jorge Ben incorporated soul and funk musics, important ingredients in CSNZ's sound, into MPB in the 1960s and '70s.

20. I develop this argument later in the dissertation by contending that in a postmodern way, *mangue* posits Pernambuco and Recife as even more important identifiers than Brazil in its style and ideology, albeit without rejecting a sense of "Brazilianness" (see Chapter Five).

Chapter 4: "É do Caralho Ser Pernambucano, Pôrra!"

1. *Afoxé* is a secularized manifestation of *Candomblé* music and dance, featured during Carnival and other festive occasions. The *maracatu* is a Pernambucan music and dance style that will be discussed in depth later in the chapter. Samba is Brazil's most famous, nationally known folk/popular music and dance genre. *Pagode* (originally meaning a party where samba is played) refers to various samba trends in the 1980s and '90s; regarding the latter, see Galinsky 1994, 1995, and 1996.

2. Although the origin of this style is international, the band's lyrics, which speak about daily existence in Recife, are decidedly local. Of course, the larger question here is how bands work with these particular international idioms in their adopted contexts.

3. I put the words "local" and "global" in quotes because I wish to question the a priori assumption that any music can be neatly categorized as one or the other. I explore this issue more in the next chapter.

4. *Nação*, or "nation," refers to an ethnic or pseudo-ethnic grouping of Africans in Brazil during the slave period. Often these "nations" were derived from the ports out of which Africans were shipped rather than from ethnicities, serving in effect as trade names (see Kubik 1979; Browning 1995: 23). However, Afro-Brazilians have reclaimed these designations as a way of identifying cultural affinities (Browning: ibid.) as opposed to ethnic affiliations per se. Hence, for example, a house (i.e., temple) of *Candomblé* that is said to be of one of the Yoruba "nations" and that is characterized by Yoruba practices may be frequented by Afro-Brazilians whose ancestors came from diverse regions in Africa as well as by Brazilians of various races (see Kubik 1979; Browning: ibid.). The *maracatu* associations that parade during Recife's Carnival are also referred to as "nations." I discuss the history and present of the *maracatu* "nations" later in the chapter.

5. At a subsequent Nação Pernambuco performance in the parking lot of a shopping mall, a woman in the audience remarked to me that the group is better

than the old *maracatu* "nations" precisely because the dancers have a classical training and hence, "better technique."

6. I am making a distinction here between a *maracatu* "nation" (*nação*), which has a historical lineage and an obligation to *Candomblé*, and a *maracatu* "band" (*banda*), which performs in the style of the *maracatu nação* but has neither of these two defining qualities. Another such *maracatu* band is Badia, composed exclusively of women and probably the most popular such group after Nação Pernambuco.

7. Unlike the *maracatu de baque virado*, which is an urban, coastal rhythm performed by the Afro-Brazilian *maracatus nação*, the *maracatu de baque solto* is from the *zona da mata* region of Pernambuco and is believed to have both African and indigenous cultural origins. The two styles sound markedly different and have distinct histories. I examine these traditions, especially that of the *maracatu nação*, later in this chapter.

8. The word "stylized" (*estilizado*) was used by some people on the scene (e.g., traditionalists) to refer to the kinds of reinterpretations of *cultura popular* ("popular" here refers to the folk culture of the lower classes) by groups such as Nação Pernambuco. It seemed to have a pejorative connotation, as in a fake or fabricated imitation of, or a non-traditional elaboration on, the "real thing."

9. For his part, Chico Science was supposedly enamored of the Nação Pernambuco and their new way of playing the *maracatu*. According to journalist Pedro Rampazzo, who became a member of Nação Pernambuco, "I met Chico Science during a presentation of Nação Pernambuco. At the time he told me he liked the attitude of the group a lot, that is, the way we played maracatu, which was very different from the traditional maracatu groups" (Rampazzo n/d).

10. A figure such as Antônio Carlos Nóbrega, a trained Pernambucan musician, for instance, appears to be highly regarded by a diverse national (and international) public for his refined reinterpretations of regional folk styles. Crucially, Nóbrega is not in danger of replacing the position of folk artists in the minds of Pernambucans; to the contrary, he seems to have garnered the respect of such artists. As one indication of this, Mestre Valter, percussion director for the Maracatu Nação Estrela Brilhante (The Shining Star Maracatu Nation) had one of Nóbrega's CDs playing in the background at his home when I arrived to interview him. Valter had high praise for *mangue* as well (a fact that will be discussed later), but he countered the idea that the Nação was responsible for the recent resurgence of *maracatu* and Pernambucan culture (Interview: Ferreira de França 1998).

11. Taking advantage of the newly created music scene, traditional "nations" such as Estrela Brilhante have also begun to perform at functions outside of the Carnival season.

12. Living in Rio or São Paulo, the two most important centers for Brazil's national music industry, is almost a necessity for any Recife band that wants to create a nationally viable career.

Notes to Chapter 4

13. The traditional northeastern folk sources that the band draws from comprise *cavalo-marinho, forró de rabeca, maracatu rural* (i.e., *maracatu de baque solto*), *cantoria* (poetic genres accompanied by the *viola*, a double-coursed steel string lute), *côco*, Umbanda (a local syncretic religion), *banda de pífanos* (drum and fife music of the interior), and *maracatu nação* (i.e., *maracatu de baque virado*) (see Murphy 2001a: 247-248).

14. The information in this paragraph on Mestre Ambrósio's early history is derived from Murphy 2001a: 248-249.

15. This portion of Mestre Ambrósio's history is derived from my interview with Éder Rocha (1998).

16. These are some of the musicians who have contributed to a re-exploration of regional music in 1990s Brazil. All of the artists mentioned have worked within regional Brazilian traditions, blending them to various degrees with international elements.

17. In my discussion of *tropicália* and *mangue* in Chapter Three, I explore a similar distinction (offered by DJ-journalist Renato L.), but with regard more specifically to the purported musical backgrounds of the *tropicalistas* and *mangue* musicians. According to Renato L., the *tropicalistas* began careers in Brazilian music and sought to interact with international styles of the 1960s while the *mangue* musicians began as rock, funk, soul or rap fans and later sought to integrate elements of their local tradition with these adopted styles (Interview: Lins 1998). According to the model presented above, then, we might be tempted to conclude that if *mangue* embodies a "from the outside in" approach, then *tropicália* represents "from the inside out." However, we need to make a clear distinction here between musical background/trajectory and resultant musical sound. The model offered by Mestre Ambrósio and cited by John Murphy should be taken to refer more to the *resultant sound* of a particular group or artist rather than to their musical background and trajectory. As such, although its proponents began careers in Brazilian music and later sought out global influences, *tropicália* cannot be accurately regarded as musically comprising a Brazilian stylistic basis with added global influences. Rather, as in *mangue*, global pop forms the musical basis of much *tropicália* to which are added regional and national references. Likewise, from the perspective of musical background/trajectory, the members of Mestre Ambrósio did not start only on the "inside." As I pointed out in Chapter Three, most Brazilian popular musicians in the end have had significant experience with both local and global styles by the time they create their "sounds." Moreover, as I also pointed out earlier, the Brazilian music that Caetano Veloso and Gilberto Gil began their careers in, bossa nova, was already a thorough and deliberate fusion of "local" and "global" elements (i.e., samba and North American pop and jazz). This calls into question the rigid distinctions between "local" and "global" or "domestic" and "foreign" in the first place. To summarize: Independent of the diverse musical background and trajectories of the musicians, Mestre Ambrósio's music

differs from both the sounds of *mangue* and *tropicália* in that its basis is in regional folk music complemented with international references. By contrast, *tropicália* and *mangue* present either the opposite proportions, a basis in global sounds with local references, or a more even fusion between "local" and "global" traits. From a theoretical point of view, we can glean from this discussion: 1) given their diverse and eclectic musical backgrounds and trajectories, there are various possible ways Brazilian popular musicians can arrive at a particular sound; 2) there are many possible combinations and proportions of influences that can make up a given sound; and 3) there are various ways we can interpret the identity of these various influences and the sound as a whole ("local" and "global" being only one set of markers).

18. Various other bands that work predominantly with the regional rhythms (e.g., Cascabulho, Comadre Florzinha) have solidified relationships with traditional performers, and must contend with the same sorts of issues.

19. Just who can claim to be part of this group is contested. Different people whom I interviewed, for example, placed Chico Science in both a middle class and a lower middle class (and hence "poor") category to correspond with their particular interpretations of Chico's relation to the *classes populares*. For instance, Maureliano and Hamílton of the band Via Sat (Interview: 1998) saw Chico initially as a somewhat suspect middle class outsider looking to learn more about the local folk culture; despite the odds, they told me, Chico became a local hero to many poor youth in Recife. By contrast, to support his belief that Chico had the local culture running "in his blood," impresario Paulo André Pires (Interview: 1998) emphasizes Chico's humble background. Of course, these assessments of Chico's social class are not merely ideological since social class is a relative concept: compared to the low class backgrounds of Maureliano and Hamílton, Chico was firmly middle class, while from the perspective of Paulo André Pires and other more privileged Pernambucans, Chico was "poor." What is interesting to me is how social class is used to support various ideological views on cultural heritage.

20. The sheer number of *oficinas* (workshops) and ongoing classes for poor youth or a wider public being offered by different groups and musicians on Recife's scene during my period of fieldwork was striking.

21. The idea of musicians "researching" their "own" traditions presents an interesting situation that complicates the foundational notion in anthropology and ethnomusicology of "insiders" and "outsiders." For one, it should be recognized that there may be different levels of these categories. For instance, the son of an expert folk musician probably has a different relation to the folk music of his region than a middle class University student even though both may be credible "native" performers. Secondly, there may be "insider" and "outsider" qualities simultaneously in any given individual. For example, a scholar or musician from another state or even country (presumably an "outsider") may acquire some insider knowledge or status. At the same time, a native to a particular region may not know much about certain aspects of his or

her "roots," although in other respects this person may claim insider status. What I think this research activity on the part of Recife musicians shows is that many people involved in the music field in the city are extremely self-aware and are as such reinvestigating and engaging with what they see as their heritage. Bands such as Mestre Ambrósio, Cascabulho, CSNZ, and many others exemplify this active "self-discovery" by Pernambucans of their local cultural heritage. This observation runs counter to the traditional idea in anthropology of the "native" who does things a certain way but is not necessarily self-aware or analytical about his or her own culture.

22. In one of the oldest texts on the subject, Pereira da Costa claims that the Institution of the King of the Congo did not last much beyond the middle of the nineteenth century, leaving only a dramatic play called the Auto dos Congos (1908: 270). In this play, Africans, generally slaves, presented a story that took place on a stand where a king sat on a throne surrounded by his court; besides dialogue, the Auto dos Congos had its own music and dance (ibid.). According to musicologist César Guerra-Peixe (1980: 20), the Auto dos Congos began to decline. With the elimination of its theatrical aspects, the procession (*cortejo*) from this play remained and turned into the *maracatu* (ibid.).

23. "At the moment, however, it is opportune to reveal that in our investigations in a Maracatu, we distinguish the word 'Afoxé,' or better 'Afoxé of Africa' as a remote label of the *folguedo* [word meaning party or cultural expression, here referring to *maracatu*]—an expression remembered today only by some of the most expert participants. We know that the word 'Afoxé'—from the Sudanese **àfohsheh**—indicates in Bahia the type of Maracatu from Salvador [the capital of Bahia state] and referred to, as Arthur Ramos explains, the profane parties of the Bahian **terreiros** [houses of worship in the Candomblé religion]. The word appeared in Recife, certainly, in virtue of the religious influence that the Sudanese [e.g., Yoruba] exerted on the Bantu [e.g., peoples from the Congo-Angola region of Africa]. 'Nação' would be then the label for the group administered by the black governor; 'Afoxé,' or 'Afoxé de África,' the profane-religious party carried out by the **nação in the** opportune **moment**. The authors that concern themselves with the Maracatu of Recife do not register 'Afoxé' in their notes, making us suppose that the expression has been restricted to the environment of its participants" (Guerra-Peixe 1980: 25-26; bold-face in the original).

24. Currently there are also *afoxé* groups in Pernambuco; whether these were based on the ones from Bahia or not is unclear. Some people on Recife's music scene claimed that the *afoxé* as an institution originated in Pernambuco not Bahia. This statement, regardless of its potential validity, is evidence of the intense cultural rivalry between Pernambuco and Bahia.

25. As far as instrumentation the *afoxés* utilize *atabaque* (Afro-Brazilian religious drums), *agogô* (double metal bell), and *xequerê* (beaded gourd) while the *maracatus* employ *bombo* (bass drum), *caixa* and *tarol* (snare drums),

gonguê (single metal bell) and in some cases, *mineiro* (shaker) and *xequerê* (known in Pernambuco as *abê*).

26. The first written reference to the *maracatu*, however, apparently dates back to 1845. On July 1 of that year, the *Diário de Pernambuco* newspaper of Recife announced the escape of a slave who "on Sundays is accustomed to selling green vegetables in the *maracatu of the coconut trees*, in Aterro dos Afogados" (Quoted in Silva 1988: 3). What exactly the "*maracatu* of the coconut trees" refers to, however, is not clear.

27. Why a practice originally associated with one sub-group of Afro-Brazilians (the *Congo* "nation," of Bantu African derivation) was later identified, including by its practitioners, as that of another (the *Nagô* "nation," associated with the Yoruba of present-day Benin) is not entirely clear. Indeed, if the *maracatu* is identified with the *Nagô*, how can one explain its historical association with the coronation ceremonies of "kings of the Congo"? I cannot offer a definitive explanation here, although several possibilities deserve mention. First, since the concept of "nation" was originally employed by the authorities and then reclaimed by Afro-Brazilians themselves, it makes sense that the authorities could have referred to the groups associated with the precursor to *maracatu* as pertaining to one "nation" (the "*Congo* nation"), while later, members of the *maracatu*, in identifying their own cultural affinities, could have chosen to link their practice to another "nation" (*Nagô*). Both groups have used the idea of "nation" in Brazil for different purposes, hence the possibility for such discrepancies. It is even conceivable that the Institution of the King of the Congo, as well as the Auto dos Congos—antecedents to the *maracatu*—were, despite their names, not necessarily linked to members of any one particular "nation." Guerra-Peixe alludes to such a possibility when he claims that "Possibly the disappearance of the institution of the King of the Congo and the decline of the auto dos Congos led the kings to fill the gaps in their processions with the members of the *nações*. And the use of the **nações** is such that it would have induced the lower-class people of Recife to call the Maracatu "nation"—words which still today are employed in the same sense to mention the retinue" (1980: 20). In other words, an enduring link between the regal procession and a particular "nation" may not have crystallized until the formation of the *maracatu* proper. A second possibility is that both the *Congo* and *Nagô* "nations" in Recife could have had a mutual influence in the formation of the current practice of *maracatu*. One could speculate that while the royal court procession aspect of *maracatu* was derived from a *Congo* "nation" activity, the religious and possibly other facets were the providence of the *Nagô* (Guerra-Peixe suggests this mutual influence; see endnote 23). Given the interpenetration of diverse African cultures in Brazil, this is a strong possibility. Finally, one should consider the possibility that in general the "nations" are fluid concepts. Guerra-Peixe suggests, for example, that the term "*Nagô*" in its association with *maracatu* simply indicates "African": "The

people of the traditional Maracatu [*maracatu nação*]—'Nagô,' as they say, in the sense of 'African'—is constructed, in the majority, by initiates of the Xangôs [*Candomblé* temples]" (1980: 23). All of these possibilities of course remain speculative, and further research would be needed to clarify this issue.

28. According to one source, the entire entourage of the *maracatu* consists of: the *damas de paço* (ladies of the palace); the *rei e rainha* (king and queen), each with a *dama de honra* (lady of honor); the *príncipe* and *princesa* (prince and princess); the *ministro* (minister); the *embaixador* (ambassador); the *duque* and *duquesa* (duke and duchess); the *conde* and *condessa* (count and countess); the *conselheiro* (councilor or advisor); the *soldados* (soldiers); *vassalos* (vassals); the *baianas* (females dressed as women from Bahia state); the *lançeiros* (lancers); and the *porta-bandeira* (flag bearer). Following the procession are the *guarda-coroa* (crown guard); the *corneteiro* (bugler); the *baliza*(?); the *secretário* (secretary); the *batuqueiros* (drummers); and the *caboclos de pena* (Indian-identified characters with feathers) (Soares et. al. 1996: 34).

29. The historical emphasis on the crowning of the black king in the Institution of the King of the Congo presents a stark contrast to the primacy of the queen in the *maracatu*. This difference is likely tied to the crucial role of the *Candomblé* in the *maracatu* versus the earlier manifestation of the tradition, which at least in its official capacity was mandated by Christian brotherhoods and connected to the political workings of the state. It is not known what the roles of the queen and of *Candomblé* in general were in this early stage, particularly in the festive domain of the "nations" (i.e., the regal processions and the Auto dos Congos). While even today this connection to *Candomblé* remains largely secretive for the *maracatu* "nations," it is likely that in the past, to the extent that they were present, aspects of Afro-Brazilian religion in the festivity were kept even more hidden from the authorities for reasons of personal safety.

30. The *baque solto* associations are also referred to as "*maracatu de orquestra*" or "*maracatu de trombone*" for their inclusion of brass instruments along with percussion, or even, though more rarely, "*maracatu moderno*"; Katarina Real (1990) has coined the term "*maracatu rural*" (rural *maracatu*) for these groups.

31. Guerra-Peixe supposes that the term "*baque virado*" came from the number of bass drums used in the ensemble: "In the old Maracatus, infallibly more than one zabumba [now called *bombo*] participated—at minimum, three. For this reason, its percussion rhythm is called "toque dobrado" or "baque dobrado"—or yet, "toque virado" or "baque virado" [turned rhythm] (1980: 65). This contrasts with the *baque solto* (*solto* can mean "loose," "free" or "alone" in Portuguese) in which only one bass drum is used (ibid.). Why the use of more or fewer *bombos* should warrant these respective names is unclear. The name *baque virado*, aside from designating the percussion music in general of the *maracatu nação*, also refers to a specific rhythm, among others, performed by

this group. Thus, for instance, Guerra-Peixe claims that the old *maracatus* utilized only two *baques* or rhythms—*luanda* and *baque virado*, the latter permitting rhythmic variations that are used to animate the music at certain moments (ibid.). Based on my own research with Estrela Brilhante, the concept of *virar*, "to turn," refers to the syncopations that the *bombos* play (whether in the *baque virado* or other *baques*).

32. Two of the biggest acts on the Recife scene—the hard-core band Devotos do Ódio (Devotees of Hate) and the rap group Faces do Subúrbio (Faces of the Suburbs)—come from the Alto José do Pinho.

33. The highly commercial *pagode* samba of the 1990s has been one musical trend that has bridged all social classes in Rio and Brazil.

34. I am suggesting here that one of the effects of a full-fledged commercialization in at least certain Brazilian popular musics has been the appearance of "traditional" and more "commercial"/"international" strands of a genre or practice. These divergent practices are connected to separate ideological camps that differ in their idea of what constitutes an acceptable modification of "tradition." This situation was one of my findings in the *pagode* samba scene of Rio de Janeiro, for example (see Galinsky 1994, 1995, 1996); a similar situation has occurred in Bahia with the original *blocos afro* and *afoxés* versus the 1990s pop trend known as *axé music*. The boundaries between these two broadly defined varieties of a musical practice may, of course, be very fluid and flexible. But the point is that they are often strongly articulated, and typically the debate revolves around the issue of "selling out" to commercialism or to international influences. Indeed, the special trait of *mangue* in this regard is its fusion of "traditional" and "commercial"/"international" elements in an experimental way that not only is accepted by both pop and regional folk music camps, but also that has revitalized both of these camps. It is in this sense that I argue later in this chapter that the Recife scene articulates a symbiotic relationship among these diverse influences. I do not wish to suggest that *pagode* or Bahian pop have *not* demonstrated a mutual affinity among their diverse influences; surely they have. Furthermore, at least the original *pagode* samba helped to revalorize older samba music and musicians while it spawned more commercial and international tendencies. Rather, I am pointing out that *pagode* and Bahian popular music have divided into more "commercial" and more "traditional" camps (however these have been construed) that have created polemics in these scenes. In Recife, partially because its scene has been shaped around the idea of diversity with a widely divergent plethora of musics, and because the full commercial potential of the scene has yet to be exploited, these divisions have not been as manifest there. It remains to be seen whether members of the Recife scene will be able to maintain their experimental edge and a sense of mutual affinity among diverse elements and musical camps as it commercializes. With the arrival of multinational music labels in Recife in 1993 for the Abril Pro Rock festival, this test is surely not far off. I would speculate

that this musical diversity on Recife's scene—so long as it is upheld—may act as a counteragent to a homogenization and overt commercialism of its music (one of the principle complaints of traditionalists). Another counteragent to these processes would surely be the adherence to certain musical principles in the face of commercial alternatives. So far, it appears that at least certain Recife bands, in spite of major label participation (Sony released CSNZ's first two CDs and has released Mestre Ambrósio's second), have remained firm to their musical principles.

35. This is not to say that the folk artists themselves did not play a role in their own renewed popularity. Rather, the *mangue* initiative (and related projects) served as a catalyst for the appreciation of the folk culture in general, which has impacted the careers of a number of folk artists. Certain musicians are more explicit in their assessment of the situation. For instance, Mestre Valter of Estrela Brilhante attributes a renewed valorization of the *maracatu* to Chico Science personally (see Mestre Valter's quote later in this chapter).

36. Undoubtedly the biggest *côco* song in 1998 was Dona Selma do Côco's "A Rolinha" (a double entendre that can mean "little bird" or "cock") (refer to Appendix 3, Track 15). However, as Paulo André Pires pointed out to me, it was the more commercialized cover version of this song by Banda Pinguim, rather than Dona Selma's original, that was receiving the most airplay at the time (Interview: Pires 1998).

37. "Us" could mean various things, including Estrela Brilhante, the *maracatu* community, or practitioners of Pernambucan traditional music. I would need to confirm with Valter whom he was referring to.

38. It is precisely for a perceived selfishness and lack of recognition of the pioneers that samba traditionalists in Rio critique the 1990s crop of *pagode* samba artists that have been topping the charts nationally. Traditionalists also tend to regard this music as overly commercial, of bad quality, and impure.

39. I refer to such genres as heavy metal, rap, *raggamuffin*, jungle, and so on as "alternative" because they are not mainstream within the context of the Brazilian music industry.

40. The samba genre, already characterized as Brazil's "national music," is seen by traditionalists within the samba community as deserving a central space in the media and culture in its "traditional" form. For particular reasons of "preservation," certain lines are drawn around this tradition, presenting much more of a dichotomization between the "traditional" and the "modern." Since the *maracatu*, for instance, does not already have the same visibility as the samba (though its practitioners surely demand a space for it), the incorporation of its rhythm in a sensitive manner within a global pop context is a way for it to gain exposure and prestige. Of course, there are still those in Recife who argue vociferously against the use of the folklore in this way, but compared to the situation with the samba in Rio, it seemed to be less of a common position.

41. It also speaks to the huge success of rock music in Brazil and its adoption as a pervasive homegrown style. But at the same time, the use of non-Western folkloric elements in the world music of Western pop musicians may also lend their rock or pop bases a more "universal" identity. The West may have long had the power to create a universal culture, but this situation may be changing. "Third World" cultures are also recognized—even idealized—as being able to create more global musics and cultures that are in turn embraced by at least some segments of Western culture as embodying some kind of universality. I expand on this idea further in the next chapter.

42. As José Antônio de Souza Leão Filho observed, in Europe and the U.S. artists add bits of "world music" to styles such as techno or psychedelic, to make these styles a bit different. In Recife, it's the opposite: The "root" is already there and is being mixed with whatever comes from the outside. These are opposite processes, but both could, according to José Antônio, be considered world music. As such, *mangue* is part of a worldwide movement (Interview: Filho 1998).

43. See Appendix 3, Track 21. Even Faces do Subúrbio, classified as an "Americanized" rap group (Interview: Pires 1998), does not belie their local heritage. On "Ruas da Cidade," one line in particular sounds, whether intentionally or not, very reminiscent of the local *embolada*. More recent work by the band has consciously incorporated this *embolada* influence.

44. For an excellent summary of the music scene and social issues connected to the Alto Zé do Pinho, see Teles 2001: 242-254.

45. Of course these images are themselves in part a façade for a more complex reality, and indeed, in the U.S. some of the media-inforced barriers between "white" and "black" genres have been countered by both mainstream and more underground bands, particularly as rap and heavy rock have grown closer together. It has also been acknowledged that rap has a huge white audience in the United States.

Chapter 5: *Mangue*, Postmodernity, and the Global Culture Debate

1. Gage Averill came up with this particular reading of the film (personal communication, 1999). This paragraph paraphrases Averill's interpretation.

2. Indeed, the works of Jorge Amado are centered on this region, particularly Bahia.

3. This space that postmodernist discourse allows for subalterns—one that is often characterized by collage and hybridity and the potential for universal appeal—is also characteristic of black-identified hip-hop culture.

4. I have mentioned the *côco*, *ciranda*, and *maracatu* previously. The *caboclinho* is a local "Indian"-identified Carnival tradition.

5. These aspects in *mangue* are no longer shocking opposites in typical modernist fashion (modernity has often been associated with shock and

Notes to Chapter 5

dislocation), but, as I argued in Chapter Four, have become integrated, overlapping, and interpenetrating. This situation marks somewhat of a break with *tropicália* where such juxtapositions embodied the shock that its Bahian creators felt in their encounter with São Paulo. (Though this does not preclude a postmodernist reading of *tropicália*; the lines between modernism and postmodernism in the Brazilian context are themselves fluid.) Thirty years later in *mangue* and other contemporary MPB, these juxtapositions have in a postmodern way become less a mark of dislocation and more one of integration and location. In such an analysis, however, I do leave room for expressions of difference and resistance within this integration, particularly as artists worldwide assert the primacy of the local within the global. Revealing the interpenetration of local and global, these assertions of local difference are also, paradoxically, increasingly relevant for the rest of the planet. I develop this line of thought further in this chapter.

6. The origin of the *bombo* drums used in the *maracatu* is open to debate, and whether or not they came directly from Africa is not clear. Also, there have certainly been some changes in the way the drums have been made over time; Mestre Valter of the Maracatu Nação Estrela Brilhante described some of these to me in our interview (Ferreira de França 1998).

7. The *caboclo de lança* is considered to be the protector, and is also one of the characteristic figures, of the rural *maracatu de baque solto* groups that parade in the Carnival of Recife and Olinda (Pinto 1996: 107). "*Caboclo*" in Brazil refers to a *mestiço* of white and indigenous mixture or to a representation of the "Indian" in the context of Afro-Brazilian religion. One of the most powerful current symbols of Pernambucan culture, even used on TV commercials to represent the state, this figure holds a spear, carries bells on his back, and wears a large wig consisting of hundreds of colorful strips of cellophane. It is interesting to note how the *caboclos de lança* already utilize sunglasses in addition to red or black face paint; Pinto claims that these are used as a disguise, since in former times, the *caboclos de lança* would attack members of rival groups and remain unknown (ibid.). In a sense, then, the *caboclo de lança* figure was "ready made" (complete with sunglasses) to be used in a pop format. Pupillo suggests this idea that the *caboclo de lança* and other folkloric elements are already modern, hip, and cutting edge in a quote later in this chapter. One could argue that as an important traditional element refashioned within a more potentially global arena, this figure also takes on a kind of postmodern role.

In his 1995 appearance at Central Park SummerStage in New York City, Chico came onto the stage at one point in this dress and performed the characteristic dance of the *caboclo de lança*; he also appears in this costume in the band's video for the song "Maracatu Atômico."

8. This may be true, but Chico himself, as well as Pupillo, has downplayed a political element in the band's music. Chico discusses the name

of the band and the question of politics: "The Brazilian people are very miscegenated and it is from there that the name (of the band) comes. I think that it's a revolutionary denomination. Since Zumbi [leader of the famous runaway slave society, Quilombo dos Palmares] was a great revolutionary. Not that there's anything political there, besides I don't expect anything from politicians, I don't expect them to be heroes, because the heroes were the guys who fought against the system and ended up marginalized" (Interview with Paulo Paniago in the *Jornal de Brasília*, April 13, 1994, quoted in Teles n/d: 26). Although *mangue* may embody in part a lower class perspective, I am reluctant to characterize it as symbolizing the identity of any one social group, considering the participation of diverse groups and individuals in the movement.

9. This "stench," as Paulo André Pires pointed out to me, is not a reference to garbage but to the smell of the *mangue* itself, which, particularly on sunny days, is not a pleasant smell (Interview: 1998). On the other hand, the "stench" referred to in the song could also be interpreted as the smell of garbage or even as symbolic of a rotten social situation.

10. This association may signal the postmodernist proposition by *mangue*'s creators of a "techno-ecology" in which technology and nature are not only compatible, but also even part of one another (see CSNZ's explanation of *afrociberdelia*, below). This would reverse the modern relation between technology and nature in which the former is used to dominate the latter. Gage Averill raised this interpretation as a possibility (personal communication, 1999).

11. " Rivers and bridges" is a reference to the infrastructure of Recife.

12. The title of this song combines the local and folkloric with the global and technological. Mateus is one of the principal characters in both the *bumba-meu-boi* and *cavalo-marinho* folk plays. In the latter, he symbolizes a "black man in search of work" (Soares et. al. 1996: 162). "Enter" is a reference to computers.

13. Veludinho, cited in the last chapter, was an important figure in the *maracatu nação* tradition. Zumbi is a legendary hero of black resistance in Brazil, who was the leader of the most famous runaway slave colony—the *Quilombo dos Palmares*. "Mestre Salu" is a reference to Mestre Salustiano, one of Pernambuco's most esteemed folk musicians.

14. Even the name of the band, Nação Zumbi, highlights this traditional-modern interaction. Zumbi, as mentioned, is a legendary hero of black resistance in Brazil, and the term "nation" links the band to the *maracatu, Candomblé*, and a traditional notion of Afro-Brazilian identity. At the same time, as Bruno Lims (brother of Renato) pointed out to me, the name of the band may have been inspired by Africa Bambaata's Zulu Nation, a formative New York rap band s own links to an African identity (personal communication, 1998).

15. Specifically, diversity (the biodiversity of the *mangue* and the cultural diversity of the city) and chaos are two features these realms have in common. The idea of "chaos" in *mangue* ideology is explored later in the chapter.

16. The postmodern worldview entails the "dissipation of objectivity," as well as the surrender of the dominant position of the West in the world (Bauman 1992: 35). As Buell argues, the ensuing crisis of the West in its recognition of being just one among many cultures, means opportunities for peripheral cultures and communities (1994: 326). For Buell, postmodernism is more empowering for the Third World (with its basis in syncretism) than the idea of modernity, in which "developing" nations have had to play a game of "catch up" (ibid.:327). But at the same time, postmodernism—to be sure, as modernity—is not exactly the same for the West as for the Third World. Whereas for Jameson, First World postmodernism reflects the fact that everything at last has been modernized, Buell's notion of "peripheral postmodernism" "thrives on incomplete modernization, the result of modernization from the top down" (ibid.:335). Peripheral postmodernism exposes the idea that the nation, in Buell's case, Brazil, "is itself unreal, a fantastic, illegitimate construct . . . a sign of the disappearance of the real—in postmodern pastiche and simulacra" (ibid.: 330-331). In this "unreal" pastiche, the pre-modern and postmodern can be merged in the "absurd," such that, for example, natives from the Amazon can coexist with satellite dishes, challenging clear-cut ideas about time, space, and culture that were more secure in modernity.

17. One could see this "relevance" as another aspect of the West's fascination with the Other. While not denying this relation, my argument here makes room for another view that allows for a breakdown of divisive categories such as traditional/modern, self/other, etc. I present this idea near the end of this chapter.

18. Traditionally this is done as a contest between two singers who play *pandeiro* (Brazilian frame drum with inverted jingles) each of whom tries to "outdo" the other with his (or her) verses.

19. As a set of reactions to modernity, modernism already bears some similarity to postmodernism—especially in the Third World, where the contradictions of modernity are even more remarkable than in the West. In this sense, Third World communities (as well as subalterns of the West) have arguably long recognized and made use of some of the concepts and discourses that have more recently been subsumed under the Western rubric of "postmodernism."

20. As stated in Chapter Three, an explicit cultural cannibalism gained widespread currency in MPB through the work of the *tropicalistas*, becoming, like *mestiçagem*, a story Brazilians repeatedly tell themselves about who they are. Although *antropofagia* entered the musical realm in the late 1960s, syncretism has always characterized Brazilian popular music, as it does all forms of music on some level.

21. A similar sort of "cannibalistic" play is at work in other current MPB. For instance, Carlinhos Brown, a versatile and influential popular artist from Salvador, Bahia, speaks about this eating cycle on his latest album, *Omelete Man* (1998). As Frederick Moehn notes, "In the song, 'Tribal United Dance,' Brown sings, /'I'm eternal matter/succulent cannibal/ether now.' Brown is an omelet of syllables, words and musical styles; now and eternally ethereal. He ironically calls himself a succulent cannibal and offers himself up for consumption *em caso de fome* [in case of hunger]" (Moehn 2001: 265). This reference to food and eating also has a strong sexual connotation in Brazilian popular culture (see Parker 1991).

22. With the disintegration of the bounded nature of nation-states and increasing globalization of the world through complex "global cultural flows" (Appadurai 1990), borders between communities are constantly being reconfigured. Old boundaries are not effaced, but are reassembled in strategic, situational ways (Buell 1994: 341). As Frederick Buell states, "a use of borders, not to separate, but to connect has become the basis for assembling new coalitions to negotiate the postnationalist fragmentation and restructuring of the world system—to negotiate a set of global patterns so complex that chaos theory has had to be invoked to describe it" (ibid.). Hence, postmodernity and postmodernism regain the plurality of chaos that the perpetrators of modernity had sought to subvert into order. But according to Chaos Theory, this "chaos" is really just a different kind of order.

23. But, again as Chaos Theory informs us, disorder is also paradoxically ordered.

24. As Jorge Martins of the band Cascabulho pointed out to me, both funk or soul and *maracatu* share some of the same rhythmic vocabulary (personal communication, 1998), making the "unraveling of musical codes" (Slobin 1992) a somewhat subjective endeavor. Indeed, the two offbeat notes that define the *maracatu* aspect of the *bombo* part are also heard in funk (Jorge Martins da Silva, personal communication, 1998). These notes, if perceived as such, may be a more informed aspect of local identity. The very use of the *bombo* drums by the band is a more conspicuous local element here. In some other CSNZ songs, however, the *bombos* play more complete *maracatu* or *côco/baião* patterns, for example.

25. A similar *maracatu*-funk hybrid is used in the *bombo* and *caixa* parts of the song "A Cidade" discussed above (see Appendix 2, Figure 4).

26. Paulo André Pires says that the vocal of this song may sound like a *raggamuffin*, but it is, in fact, an *embolada* (Interview by Marty Lipp: Chico Science and Paulo André Pires n/d).

27. Some critics started to praise Brazil's mixed-race heritage as early as the 1910s (see Skidmore 1974: 167). *Mestiçagem* could be seen as an answer to an earlier racial ideology called *branqueamento* (whitening), the influence of which is still strong in Brazil (see Skidmore 1974). "Whitening" was a

peculiarly Brazilian response on the part of the elites to the so-called "Negro problem": that is, how the black element of the nation's population would be rectified with, and integrated into, the fabric of society. According to *branqueamento*, the black race would "naturally" disappear into the white race through miscegenation, a suggestion that rested on the assumptions that white genes were stronger than black ones and that people would choose lighter partners than themselves, presumably for reasons of socioeconomic mobility. Of course, "whitening" also depended on the Brazilian version of racial classification in which African (and indigenous) blood could be mixed with European blood to produce intermediate—in this case, "whiter"—results. The European immigration campaigns launched in nineteenth century Brazil furthered the aims of the "whitening" objective.

28. Despite its progressive intentions, Freyre's project has been criticized for disguising racial inequities in Brazil. The Freyre-derived idea of the "racial democracy"—founded on the belief that the social and genetic racial intermingling initiated by the Portuguese has led to a state of racial harmony in Brazil (see Margolis 1992)—has held and continues to hold a pervasive sway with Brazilians of various races, even as it has been debunked by many as a myth that obscures racism in the country. Some have even suggested that Freyre's theory unwittingly strengthened the "whitening" agenda (see note 27 above) by revealing how the primarily light-skinned elite had simply gained valuable cultural traits from intimate contact with the other two races (Skidmore 1974: 192). Furthermore, Freyre argued that poverty, not race, degenerates humans, and that consequently, discrimination in Brazil falls along economic, not racial, lines (Browning 1995: 6)—another point which has ended up obscuring the racial question in Brazil.

29. It is certainly not the only image reproduced in the samba. A kind of Afrocentrism—itself linked to a celebration of the national—is another competing (and overlapping) discourse in the samba world. Moreover, the inherent racial contradictions in Brazil are highlighted in the samba, which Vianna (1995) claims was "constructed" by many social groups as a national symbol. Even if it is praised as a product of mixture (or as a black expression), some of the earliest representatives of the genre were white Brazilian singers such as Carmen Miranda and Francisco Alves. Co-option or manipulation of the samba and other popular genres by the predominantly white Brazilian elite problematizes the samba's associations with a black or mixed-race identity.

30. See Note 28 above.

31. The traditional Brazilian racial classification is more fluid than the U.S. one. It accounts for many intermediate categories between "white" and "black," the uses of which can vary depending on many other factors (such as class, region, etc.). Because of this fluidity—and the possibility of "racial mobility"— many potential adherents of a black movement could be lost. There has been a growing trend for more and more Brazilians to identify as *negro* (black), and with it a tendency toward the more "defined" bi-polar racial categorization

system of the United States. This system makes who is black and who is white clearer, and consequently it makes mobilizing a black movement more workable. Refer to Winant 1994 for an overview of racial politics in Brazil.

32. As Vianna states, "The discourse of the *mestiço* homogeneity, created in Brazil through a long process of negotiation, which reached its climax in the 1930s, rendered determined 'decisive acts' possible and accepted (as for example, the parade of the samba school with sponsorship of the State), inventing a new way to struggle with the problems of ethnic heterogeneity and the erudite/popular confrontation" (Vianna 1995: 154). Later on, Vianna points out that "The concept of transculturalism is a currency in current ethnomusicological debates, helping to explain heterogeneity. My objective, in studying the samba, although inspired by the studies cited above [e.g., Nettl 1985 and Frith 1989], is another one. This book can be seen as an attempt to show that transculturalism is also useful to help us understand the invention of homogeneity" (ibid.: 174).

33. This is the outgrowth of an earlier trend. Particularly since the late 1960s and the 1970s, many non-white Brazilians have challenged the "racial democracy" view (as well as the persistent "whitening" ideology) in the face of a government that continues to deny that any racial problem exists in Brazil. As Barbara Browning indicates: "But since the 1970s, there has been a steady tide of resistance rising among young blacks who got the big picture. They've been telling each other another story. Popular accounts of race relations in Brazil, which hold that abolition never took place in a meaningful way (a 'false abolition' leading to the favela as modern slaves' quarters), are grounded in historical and demographic realities" (1995: 7).

34. For a discussion of the *bloco afro* movement of Bahia and the articulation of links across the African diaspora in this movement, see Crook 1993 and Risério 1981. Rio's core samba community has generally been reluctant to participate in this exchange with international styles out of a concern for preserving the samba tradition. However, many younger samba musicians and fans also appreciate funk and other black international musical forms. Some bands (such as the Rio-based Funk 'n Lata) blend samba with funk and rock, and even a few of Rio's *escolas de samba* have recently incorporated funk breaks into their samba arrangements for Carnival.

35. Yúdice (1994) sees these youth movements of marginalized, black and mulatto urban poor as testament to the contradictions inherent in Brazil's recent path to redemocratization (which is really only valid for middle and upper class citizens). As such, these tendencies diverge from the national "consensus" culture of samba and Carnival supposedly upheld by previous generations of blacks. Unlike Bahia's *blocos afro*, or even socially engaged Brazilian rap, however, Rio funk expression (which is mostly in the form of dancing to pre-recorded black American music of several different genres) is not explicitly political. Instead, it provides a new, alternative social space for disempowered youth.

36. Yúdice's analysis pits samba and a supposed national "consensus" culture against imported funk. In my own research, however, I found that these musics were not necessarily mutually exclusive in black Brazilian identities at all. For example, I interviewed Carlos Alberto Medeiros (1994), a black rights leader in Rio, who told me that these musics co-exist in black communities. According to Medeiros, many youth who dance to funk also go to samba during Carnival time, and moreover, that as they get older black youth tend to dance more to samba and MPB than to funk. Also, Yúdice's analysis downplays or even ignores the resistive potential of samba to boost his assertion that funk is an alternative.

37. Frederick Buell's analysis of the film *Bye Bye Brazil* offers a similar view of Brazil: "And *Bye Bye Brazil*'s characters are, every bit as much as postmodern ethnics in North America, 'others' who are not backward, but cutting-edge, even (as with the Indians) 'always already' postmodern" (1994: 332).

38. According to Frederick Buell, "Modernism becomes one more code afloat in the hyperreal sea of codes that the postmodern sponsors" (1994: 332).

39. I use the term "global culture debate" here to reference the recent discussions about particularly Third World musical products and their function within a kind of global cultural network or system (e.g., the international music industry and media, the Internet). This debate is fueled by questions about the extent to which such musics can truly represent the musicians who perform or create them and to what extent these musics may be "resisting" against the system.

40. As Peter Manuel points out, "Scholars like Richard Middleton and Stuart Hall stress the importance of analyzing popular culture neither as pure resistance nor as superimposition, but as the arena of negotiation, and 'the ground on which the transformations are worked.' . . . Because of the potentially contradictory nature of popular music expression, it should not be dismissed as either an undiluted *vox populi*, or as superimposed, monolithic, dominant ideology" (Manuel 1988: 14). Although I am in agreement with the idea that multiple viewpoints may be expressed through music (as Slobin [1992] also maintains), I would question whether popular culture can necessarily be reduced to an "arena of negotiation" between the ideological positions of "dominant" and "dominated." With its complex array of affiliations among various social groups, the case of the Recife scene certainly suggests otherwise.

41. Even Erlmann permits a special role for diversity in his vision of the global cultural system: "But if the global culture of commodities depends on the homogenization of cultural diversity to realize the value of any particular product, it cannot afford to blind itself entirely to this very diversity as its primary source of raw material, of new images" (1996: 478). Where my perspective differs from Erlmann's is in my refusal to reduce this diversity of local expression to merely a disguised manipulation by a dominant group.

42. Music by Zero Quatro/Tony Regalia/Fábio Malandragem and Lyrics by Zero Quatro. From Mundo Livre S/A, *Guentando a Ôia* (Excelente Discos, 011060-2, 1996).

43. *Mangue* has been embraced by many at both the regional and national levels, and its entrance into the global culture industry has been proudly regarded as a triumph for local musicians. As a point of comparison, Jocelyne Guilbault presents *zouk* music of the French Creole-speaking islands of the Caribbean in a completely different way: "What has come out most strongly in public debates and in my own interviews has been the ways in which zouk actually threatens [individual or national] identity. Zouk has indeed raised many fears in the islands. For a start, its inclusion of many features of the dominant musics on the international market (the use of the rhythm box, e.g.) has been interpreted as a sign of the gradual homogenization of local practices and therefore an erosion of the cultural uniqueness of the islands" (Guilbault 1993: 202). By sharp contrast, *mangue*'s use of international elements—albeit, more "alternative" global genres—has, in fact, helped *enable* the cultural uniqueness and diversity of the region (i.e., Pernambucan folk culture) to be better represented and to flourish. And where my reading of *mangue* depicts musicians' associations with the "system" (for example, the Sony Music connection) to be liberating, and even an aspect of resistance (see below), Guilbault reveals these associations in *zouk* to be debilitating: "In that same vein there is thus the fear that local musics are being exploited and taken over by the system. For that reason, the signing by the group Kassav of a contract with CBS in 1988 has met with much suspicion. This new collaboration has been seen less as a step forward in reaching a wider market than as a sellout of Antillean music to the multinationals. The compromises that had to be made by Kassav in the choice of, say, the songs and the performers to be used on the two 1988 and 1989 albums produced under the contract (Phoenix horns, e.g., were added to Kassav's own brass section) have been perceived by many musicians and other observers as putting at stake the integrity of the group. Along the same line, the enormous production of zouk recordings and the ensuing connection of zouk with commerce has also been received with mistrust, based on the implicit belief that commercialism necessarily precludes artists from contributing to a culture of resistance" (ibid.: 202-203). The case of CSNZ's relation with Sony has been markedly different. Based on comments by Chico Science, the band was allowed to pursue, for the most part, the artistic direction they wanted to on their recordings. Moreover, the lack of a large-scale massification of *mangue* recordings has not generated a local fear of a sellout to the system. To the contrary—unlike the case of Kassav—CSNZ's and other Recife bands' signing with multinational labels has been enthusiastically taken precisely as "a step forward in reaching a wider market."

44. Zapata and Sandino are Latin American political heroes of Mexico and Nicaragua, respectively. Lampião and Antônio Conselheiro are revolutionaries

of the northeastern Brazilian *sertão*. Lampião was a legendary bandit-hero who championed the poor and dispossessed of the region. Conselheiro (the "Counselor"), was a rebel preacher who founded the town of Canudos in Bahia, which challenged the sovereignty of the government, leading to a bloody war at the end of the nineteenth century.

45. The same may be true for any music. In fact, it was one of the objectives of the *mangue* musicians to reveal the universality of genres such as *maracatu* through their incorporation into hybrid pop music. Likewise, both types of music in Erlmann's world music taxonomy, the "modernizing" and fully "postmodern" genres, may have such universality. A more important distinction between these two categories that Erlmann proposes (as opposed to the time-space one) may be that the former are more bound to specific communities and the latter less clearly so. Milton Nascimento's exploration of Amazonian themes in his album *Txai* (1990) creates a kind of "pseudopast" in the words of Erlmann because the history of the Amazon is not a history of which Nascimento himself has been a part until then. But this does not mean that this music is somehow detached from time or space any more than any other music is (or is not). In fact, it may thereafter become a part of a history or multiple histories (even the history of the indigenous people he worked with). Other "postmodern" genres may exist in more ephemeral or shifting social contexts, such as the dance club. But who is to say that history is not inscribed in these genres?

46. I realize that Self and Other is simply another set of binaries; however, my aim here is to show how these, as the other "binaries," are not necessarily opposed let alone even discrete entities.

47. In line with my conclusions here and with the work of Averill (1995) and Monson (1999), Kenneth Bilby reasserts the importance of the local in globalizing patterns. Just as I have argued for seeing *mangue* as firmly grounded in Pernambucan history, contexts, and realities (not disembedded from these things) even as it embraces and ascends into the world, Bilby presents a similar picture in Surinamese popular music: "The revelation of unsuspected cultural richness in out-of-the-way places such as Suriname may prompt us to cast a critical eye at the increasingly fashionable tendency in some quarters to focus on patterns of globalization at the expense of the local sites in which specific systems of meaning continue to be generated. While there is no denying the magnitude of the changes wrought worldwide by transnationalism in its various guises, there is also no denying that identities in many parts of the world continue to be constructed upon historically-deep, culturally-specific foundations, albeit from increasingly eclectic materials. We would do well to remind ourselves that giving the global its due ought not mean losing sight of the local. Perhaps popular musicians in Suriname, not to mention other parts of the Caribbean or the wider world, have something to teach us in this regard" (1999: 285-286).

Glossary

Abê: A synonym in Pernambuco for the *xequerê*.

Afoxé: Rhythm and song form derived from *Candomblé*; also a type of *bloco afro*, predominantly in Salvador (Bahia), but also in Recife (Pernambuco), and other cities, that plays this music during Carnival. Typical instrumentation includes the *atabaque*, *xequerê*, and *agogô*.

Afrociberdelia (from Africa + Cibernetics + Psychedelia): A phenomenon described by Chico Science & Nação Zumbi on their CD of the same name: "The art of mapping the primal genetic memory (which in the 20th century was called 'the collective unconscious') through electrochemical stimulus, verbal automation, and intense bodily movement to the sound of binary music." Also used by gangs and in street slang more informally to mean: a) "Creative mixture of tribal and high-tech elements: 'It may be said that the novel The Embedding by Ian Watson, is a precursor to afrociberdelic science fiction.' b) "Disorder, a mess in high spirits . . .: 'The party was scheduled to begin at ten, but afrociberdelia only happened there around two o'clock in the morning.'"

Agogô: Two or more bells of different sizes welded together and played with a stick, of Yoruba origin.

Agreste: Rural, rustic, wild, uncultivated, rough; the geographical region of Pernambuco and other northeastern states in between the *zona da mata* and the *sertão*.

Alfaia: A local synonym for the *bombo* drum used in the *maracatu nação* of Recife.

Antropofagia: "Anthropophagy" or "cannibalism"; a nationalist theory developed by modernist poet Oswald de Andrade in his 1928 *Manifesto Antropófago* (Cannibalistic Manifesto) that urges Brazilians to borrow from or "cannibalize" diverse foreign cultural influences in their art and re-elaborate them within a national framework.

Atabaque: Conical, single-headed drum used in *Candomblé*, similar to the Cuban conga drum.

Auto dos Congos: A play that ostensibly evolved into the *maracatu*. See *congada* and *maracatu nação*.

Axé-music: Label for polished, commercialized versions of Bahian roots music, particularly the music of the *blocos afro* and *afoxés*.

Bahia: State in Brazil's Northeast, a center of black Brazilian culture. An alternate name for the city of Salvador, Bahia's capital.

Baião: Northeastern music and dance form typical of the *sertão* (arid interior) traditionally played with accordion, triangle, *pandeiro*, and *zabumba* bass drum. Created and popularized nationally by Luiz Gonzaga in the 1940s.

Banda de Pífanos: Typical drum and fife ensemble of the northeastern interior.

Batuque: Name for secular dances from the Congo-Angola brought to Brazil by Bantu Africans; generic term for any Afro-Brazilian secular dance accompanied by percussion; an Afro-Brazilian religion in Northern Brazil; a drum used in *jongo*.

Baque: Lit., "thud" or "thump"; one or another rhythmic variations as performed by the *maracatu nação* (e.g.s, *baque de marcação*, *baque de martelo*, *baque de parada*, etc.)

Baque de Marcação: The most basic rhythm as played by the *maracatu nação* (see Appendix 2, Figure 1).

Baque de Martelo: "Hammer rhythm"; a common rhythm played by the *maracatu nação* (see Appendix 2, Figure 2).

Baque de Parada: "Stop rhythm"; a common rhythm played by the *maracatu nação* in which the *bombo* part features a pause (see Appendix 2, Figure 2).

Baque Virado: "Turned or turned-around rhythm"; can refer to a specific *baque* as well as to the *maracatu* rhythm in general. (See *maracatu de baque virado*.)

Berimbau: Musical bow from Bahia of probable Angolan origin, made from a flexible wooden stick, metal string, and hollowed-out, half-open gourd resonator. Played together with the *caxixi*. Used especially to accompany *capoeira*.

Bloco: "Bloc"; generically, any group of people that goes out on the streets to parade with music during Carnival.

Bloco afro: Afro-Brazilian Carnival group, primarily in Salvador, Bahia; plural: *blocos afro*.

Bombo: Double-headed wooden bass drum with goatskin heads and ropes for tensioning, used in the *maracatu nação* and other northeastern folk traditions.

Bossa nova: "New way"; softer, subdued style of samba (and less frequently other genres) developed by middle-class composers in Rio's Copacabana neighborhood in the late 1950s. Featuring harmonic affinities with cool jazz and 20th century classical music, bossa nova was widely popular in Brazil and internationally from the late 1950s until 1964.

Brega: Pejorative term for "tacky" romantic pop music.

Bumba-meu-boi: One of the best known folk plays of Northeast Brazil, the theme of which centers on the death and resurrection of a bull. In Pernambuco, it is celebrated during the Christmas season and in Carnival. Instrumen-tation includes the *rabeca*, *zabumba*, *ganzá*, *canzá*, *viola*, and *pandeiro*. Related to the *cavalo-marinho*.

Caboclo/a: Acculturated Brazilian Indian (*índio*); Brazilian of part white, part indigenous ancestry; of or pertaining to the acculturated Brazilian native; representations of the Native Brazilian in Afro-Brazilian religion.

Caboclinho: Lit., "little *caboclos*," or sons of *caboclos*; a folk form of indigenous origin that is perhaps the oldest dance of Brazil, first registered in 1584 (Soares et. al. 1996: 179). With music and dance, it represents a drama symbolizing battles, hunts, and harvests. Participants dress up as "Indians" and some mark the rhythm by pulling the strings of bow and arrows. Instrumental ensemble includes *pífano*, maracas, *caixa*, small *surdo*, etc. Performed at the Carnival in Recife/Olinda.

Caboclo de lança: Spearthrowing character with large headdress made of many colorful cellophane strips, face paint, sunglasses, and bells on his back. One of the main figures in the *maracatu de baque solto*.

Caipira: An inhabitant of the country, particularly one with little education and rustic, "backward" ways; of or pertaining to such a person; of or pertaining to the *Festas Juninas* or to the typical dress of these festivals.

Caixa: Snare drum.

Calunga: A type of doll that is connected to the *Candomblé* and carried by the *damas de paço* (ladies of the palace) in the procession of the *maracatu nação*.

Candomblé: Afro-Brazilian religion of primarily Yoruba and Fon and Bantu derivation, with Catholic influence. Of all the Afro-Brazilian religions, it maintains the strongest links to its African sources.

Cantoria: A variety of poetic genres performed with accompaniment of the *viola*; a term in Northeast Brazil to describe the event at which such music is played.

Canzá: See *reco-reco*.

Capoeira: Afro-Bahian martial art and dance form brought to Brazil by enslaved Bantu Africans from Angola. In actuality, played as a game to the musical accompaniment of the *berimbau, pandeiro, agogô, atabaque,* and other instruments.

Glossary 203

Carimbó: Afro-Brazilian song/dance from northeastern state of Pará. Features 2/4 meter, a quick tempo, percussion accompaniment, and circle dance with soloists in center.

Catimbó: Lit., "ridiculous man" or "backlander" (see *caipira*); also, an Indigenous Brazilian spiritist cult (Real 1990).

Carnival (Port., *carnaval*): Four days of merrymaking before Ash Wednesday; celebrated in Catholic countries and in New Orleans.

Cavalo-marinho: A "musical play that portrays life on the sugar plantation in song, poetry, dance, and dramatic action" (Murphy 1998). A distinct variant of the *bumba-meu-boi*, this play is most predominant in the *zona da mata norte* (north woods zone) of Pernambuco state, but is also representative of the state of Paraíba. The play contains various characters, all depicted by men in costumes. The public gathers around the performers in a circle and participates in the spectacle. The main melodic instrument is the *rabeca*; other instruments are the *pandeiro*, *canzá* (or *reco-reco*), and *ganzá*.

Cavaquinho: Portuguese four-string ukulele-like instrument with seventeen frets, usually tuned D-G-B-D. Common throughout Lusophone world. Used in *samba*, *choro*, and other genres in Brazil.

Caxixi: Samll wicker basket with pellets inside; played with the *berimbau*.

Charme: Term for contemporary R&B from the U. S., popular among black youth in Rio. Hits from the U. S. are imported and played at *charme* parties.

Chocalho: Shaker.

Choro (or chorinho): Genre of instrumental music developed in Rio de Janeiro in late nineteenth century out of European dance musics (polkas, waltzes, etc.), played with Afro-Brazilian rhythmic influences.

Ciranda: Children's circle dance of Portuguese origin; folk song and dance of Pernambuco State in which participants form a circle, hold hands, and dance counterclockwise; a form of rural *samba* from the state of R o de Janeiro.

Côco: Afro-Brazilian song and dance form of the Northeast with purported indigenous Brazilian influence in the dance step (i.e., a lateral stomp of the right foot, first to the right side and then to the left side, always on the first beat of the two-beat phrase). In the *côco de roda* (circle *côco*), a circle of participants is formed and dance pairs take turns in the center, executing the characteristic dance step while meeting to give each other *umbigadas* (belly bounces), a choreographic trait linked to the Congo-Angola region of Africa. Musically characterized by binary meter, call-and-response vocals, and percussion accompaniment (*ganzá, pandeiro, bombo*, handclaps, etc.).

Côco de embolada: See *embolada*.

Congada (or *congo*): Processional dance that blends African and Iberian influences and often includes characters who represent African royalty. See also *maracatu nação*.

Cortejo: Procession.

Cultura Popular: "Popular culture"; a term used in Brazil to refer to folk culture or the culture of the lower classes.

Dama de paço: "Lady of the palace"; one of the main characters in the *maracatu nação*. Carries the *calunga*.

Desafio: Improvisatory lyrical duel between two contestants characterized by rhyming and bravado. Probably of Portuguese origin.

Drum 'n' Bass: A contemporary style of electronic dance music. See also *jungle*.

Embolada: Poetic-musical form of the northeastern coast, used with the *côco* rhythm (this is called the *côco de embolada*). Characterized by 2/4 meter, stanza-refrain structure with stanzas often improvised, short note values, small musical intervals, and tongue-twisting lyrics. Often performed by two singers, each with a *pandeiro*, in the form of a *desafio*. Vocal quality bears a similarity to Arabic music, likely tied to the Moorish influence in Portugal. See also *repente*.

Glossary

Escola de samba: "*Samba* school"; neighborhood organization often based in a *favela* or low-income area of Rio and other cities that puts on an annual *samba* parade for Carnival with selected theme, complete with elaborate floats, costumed dancers, and song with the accompaniment of a large percussion section called a *bateria*. Also often functions as a community center or mutual aid society, providing other social services for its community.

Favela: Slum.

Festas Juninas: "June Festivals"; a series of parties corresponding to saints days in June. Typical of the Northeast of Brazil. Associated with specific foods, music (*forró*), and dress. The most famous of these parties is *São João* (Saint John's Day).

Forró: Generic term for northeastern dance music styles; dance at which this music is played; specific variation of the *baião*. This is the typical music of the June Festivals (*Festas Juninas*) in the Northeast (e.g., Pernambuco and Paraíba).

Forró de rabeca: *Forró* music performed with the *rabeca* instead of accordion. Typical of the *zona da mata* region of Pernambuco.

Frevo: Quick, syncopated Carnival dance, rhythm, and song form derived from the *marcha*. Probably the best known rhythm from Recife.

Ganzá: Shaker.

Gonguê: Large, flat metal bell played in the *maracatu nação*.

Habanera: Slow, duple-meter Cuban song and dance form. One ingredient in the formation of the *maxixe*.

Ilú: Type of Afro-Brazilian religious drum.

Irmandade: Catholic religious brotherhood.

Jongo: Afro-Brazilian counterclockwise circle dance of Bantu derivation, found in southeastern Brazil.

Jungle: Contemporary style of electronic dance music developed in London.

Lama: Mud.

Lambada: Popular music hybrid of the late 1970s and 1980s that blended Dominican *merengue* with the Afro-Brazilian *carimbó*, along with other Caribbean influences. Characterized by a quick 2/4 meter and syncopated rhythms. Also a close, erotic dance for two partners that developed at the same time, incorporating elements from *merengue*, *samba*, *maxixe*, and *forró*.

Litoral: coast, coastal, seaboard.

Lundu: Song and dance of Angolan origin brought to Brazil by enslaved Bantu Africans. Important progenitor of many urban forms, including *samba*.

Macumba: Syncretic twentieth century Afro-Brazilian religion of Rio; also generic label for many Afro-Brazilian religions.

Mãe de santo: "Mother of the saints"; head priestess in Afro-Brazilian religions.

Mangue: mud-flat, swamp; mangrove. The name for a pop culture movement (*o movimento mangue*) that originated in Recife, Pernambuco in the early 1990s; also refers, in a general sense, to the music and other cultural products associated with this movement; in slang, can refer to a red-light district.

Mangue beat: The name Brazilian journalists in the South gave to the *mangue* movement. This was supposedly a misunderstood transliteration of *mangue bit*.

Mangue bit: The name journalists originally gave to the *mangue* movement. It references both local geography of the region (the swamps, or *mangue*) and high technology (bit, as in computer bits).

Mangueboy: A male adherent of the *mangue* movement.

Manguegirl: A female adherent of the *mangue* movement.

Glossary

Manguetown: A name for Greater Recife in the *mangue* movement slang.

Manguezal: Synonym for *mangue* (as in swamp).

Maracatu: The name for two distinct folk music/dance genres and popular associations of Pernambuco State (see below); in the popular language, a crazy combination of things.

Maracatu de Baque Solto: Lit., "*maracatu* of the loose/free/alone rhythm"; Afro-indigenous association from the sugar-cane *zona da mata norte* (north woods zone) region of the Pernambucan interior that parades during Carnival in Recife and for other occasions. The accompanying orchestra employs percussion and brass and plays in a very fast kind of *marcha*. Thought to have emerged much after the *maracatu nação* tradition (1930s?). Also refers to the rhythm of this association.

Maracatu de Baque Virado: Lit., "*maracatu* of the turned rhythm"; another name for the *maracatu nação*. Also refers to the rhythm of the *maracatu nação*.

Maracatu de Orquestra: See *maracatu de baque solto*.

Maracatu Nação: "*Maracatu* nation"; plural: *maracatus nação*. Afro-Pernambucan association based in the city of Recife that parades as a syncretic royal court during Carnival and other occasions. Linked to the *Nagô* "nation" and to *Candomblé*. Believed to have derived from the processions of the *Rei do Congo*. Performs a slow, syncopated percussion rhythm (played on *bombo, caixa/tarol, gonguê, ganzá*, and sometimes *abê*) that is known generically as *maracatu* or *maracatu de baque virado*. Specific variations of this rhythm (called *baques*) include the *baque de marcação, baque de martelo, baque de parada*, etc.

Maracatu Rural: "Rural *maracatu*"; another name for the *maracatu de baque solto* given by anthropologist Katarina Real (1990).

Marcha (marchinha): Quick-tempo Brazilian march in binary meter. Influenced by ragtime and the one-step in the 1920s. Along with *samba*, a very popular Carnival genre, especially in Rio de Janeiro.

Marcha-rancho: Slower variation of the *marcha* with more melodic development, played by the *ranchos* during Carnival.

Maxixe: Afro-Brazilian music and dance form of the late nineteenth and twentieth centuries representing a blend of *lundu, polka, tango,* and *habanera.* Precursor to the urban *samba* and considered the first dance of national origin.

Mestiçagem: A modern Brazilian theory elaborated principally by Gilberto Freyre in the 1930s that celebrates the tri-ethnic heritage (Native, Portuguese, and African) of Brazilian culture.

Merengue: Popular Afro-Dominican dance and music genre in fast 2/4 meter.

Mineiro: A synonym in Pernambuco for *ganzá.*

Modinha: Considered the first song form of Brazilian national origin. A fusion of the Portuguese *moda* with the Brazilian *lundu.*

Moda: Portuguese sentimental song.

Morro: "Hill"; one of the hills around Rio or other cities on which a *favela* (slum) has been built.

Movimento Armorial: An erudite artistic movement born in Recife in 1970 under the direction of writer Ariano Suassuna that reinterpreted the folk traditions of the Northeast. The movement involved ceramics, painting, sculpture, theater, and music.

MPB: (Música Popular Brasileira) "Brazilian Popular Music"; general term for urban Brazilian popular music after *bossa nova* and particularly since the late 1960s that has incorporated diverse musical genres and influences; label for Brazilian popular music in general.

Nação: (plural: nações) "Nation"; ethnic or pseudo-ethnic grouping of Africans in colonial Brazil. Has been reappropriated by black and other Brazilians to mark African cultural (as opposed to ethnic) affinities. For example, in *Candomblé* a house of worship may be said to follow in the lineage of one or another "nation." Also, the *maracatu* groups of Recife are referred to as "nations" (specifically the Nagô "nation").

Glossary

Nagô: Pertaining to the people of southeastern Dahomey (present-day Benin), Africa; the Yoruba; a particular *nação* in Brazil that is traced to the Yoruba.

Novela: Brazilian soap opera.

Pai de santo: "Father of the saints"; head priest in Afro-Brazilian religions.

Pagode: "Joke" or "merrymaking"; (1) a gathering of people to play and sing *samba*; (2) the *samba* music played at this gathering; (3) synonym for *samba*; (4) style of roots *samba* developed in the mid- to late-1970s with a special instrumentation that emerged out of informal, backyard gatherings (*pagodes*) in a low-income Rio suburb called Ramos, becoming a widespread phenomenon and commercial success throughout Brazil in 1980s; (5) a more commercialized version of #4 with added electric instrumentation and other, including international, influences that is very popular in 1990s throughout Brazil. See also *suíngue*.

Pandeiro: Brazilian tambourine (jingles are inverted), of Portuguese origin. Used in *samba*, *choro*, *baião*, *côco*, and other genres.

Pífano: Wooden flute.

Quilombo: Term for runaway slave settlement in colonial Brazil. Most famous is the *Quilombo dos Palmares*.

Quilombo dos Palmares: *Quilombo* established in Alagoas state in 1631. Its population, which ran into the thousands, constructed a community based on African traditions. Destroyed by the authorities in 1697.

Raggamuffin (ragga): Designation for contemporary Jamaican dancehall reggae music.

Rancho: Carnival organization that parades to the *marcha-rancho*. Influenced the *escolas de samba*.

Reco-reco: Wooden or metal scraper.

Rei do Congo: "King of the Congo"; colonial Brazilian practice in which certain members of black communities were crowned king and queen of their particular *nação*. The Congo *nação* was predominant within this tradition. The coronation ceremonies of this practice are considered to be the roots of the *maracatu nação* tradition.

Repente: An improvisatory musical-poetic song form of Northeast Brazil that occurs as a *desafio* (duel) often performed by two singers who accompany themselves on *viola*. This is similar to the *embolada*, except, among other differences, the *embolada* is typically accompanied by the *pandeiro*.

Samba: Brazil's most famous and influential song and dance genre, believed to have derived from the Congo-Angola region of Africa. It is typically played in 2/4 meter with an accent on the second beat of the measure, and is characterized by interlocking, syncopated parts in melody and accompaniment. Modern samba is mainly a blend of African and European traits. Has rural and urban manifestations, each with myriad variations.

Samba-reggae: Hybrid of *samba*, reggae, and other influences, pioneered by the *bloco afro* Olodum in the 1980s in Salvador, Bahia.

Sambista: Someone who sings, plays, dances, or composes samba almost exclusively.

São João: "Saint John's Day"; a popular saint's day in June celebrated in Brazil with typical music, dance, and dress. See *Festas Juninas*.

Sertão: Remote interior areas of Brazil; specific term for arid backlands of the Northeast.

Tango: Popular Argentinean song and dance form that takes its rhythm from the Cuban *habanera* and Argentinean *milonga*.

Tarol: Shallow snare drum used in *escola de samba*, *maracatu de baque virado*, etc.

Terreiro: "Yard," "square"; place where *Candomblé* is practiced; also headquarters of an *escola de samba*.

Glossary

Toada: Generic term for a stanza-and-refrain song with simple melody and brief lyrics often of a romantic or comical nature; the song form used in the *maracatu de baque virado*, among many other genres.

Toque: Generic term for a rhythm or rhythmic variation in *Candomblé* or other Afro-Brazilian musics. See also *baque*.

Trio Elétrico: "Electric trio"; sound truck on top of which electric pop bands perform. Popular in the Carnival (and other festivals) of Salvador, Bahia, and other cities.

Tropicália (tropicalismo): "Tropicalism"; movement in music and art in the late 1960s, pioneered in the musical realm by Gilberto Gil, Caetano Veloso, and others. An important precursor to the *mangue* movement.

Umbanda: Syncretic Afro-Brazilian religion created in the twentieth century with Spiritist influences.

Umbigada: From *umbigo*, or "navel"; invitation to dance symbolized by the uniting of navels of two dancers. Distinguishing feature of rural *lundu* and *samba* as well as many other dances derived from the Congo-Angolan *batuque*, including the *côco*.

Viola: Folk guitar with four or five double-coursed strings.

Violão: Six- or seven-string classical guitar used in many Brazilian popular and folk musics, including *samba*, *choro*, and *bossa nova*.

Xequerê: Hollow gourd wrapped with beads. A Yoruba instrument used in various Afro-Brazilian folk musics.

Xote: Northeastern Brazilian dance and rhythm derived from the schottische. Has a "swung" feel and duple meter.

Xaxado: Northeastern men's line dance.

Zabumba: Shallow bass drum used in northeastern musics such as *baião*, *xote*, etc.

Zona da Mata: "Woods Zone"; the geographical region just inland from the *litoral* (coast) of Pernambuco and other states in the Northeast.

Zona da Mata Norte: Refers to the northern part of the *zona da mata* of Pernambuco. Home to a wealth of regional folk music, dance, and dramatic traditions (*cavalo-marinho, maracatu de baque solto, forró de rabeca*, etc.).

Zona Norte: "North Zone"; working- and middle-class northern zone of Rio de Janeiro situated away from the coast.

Zona Sul: "South Zone"; wealthier southern zone of Rio de Janeiro that is situated closer to the beaches.

Discography

The following list represents a sampling of available music from Recife's current music scene, as well as some other recordings mentioned in the text of the dissertation. All entries are on CD.

Where available, I have included contact telephone numbers or addresses for independent releases as well as e-mail and web sites for bands or artists in general. Other useful addresses (real and cybernetic) are cited at the end of the discography. To keep up to date on releases from the scene, consult these sources.

Mangue and Recife's "New Music Scene":
In its narrowest sense, *mangue* refers to the pioneering work of CSNZ and Mundo Livre S/A, who paved the way for the visibility of all the artists that came to make up Recife's "new music scene" in the 1990s. In its widest application, *mangue* or *mangue beat* glosses practically all of the bands that developed out of this scene. Antônio Carlos Nóbrega, Antúlio Madrueira, and Dona Selma do Côco did not emerge with Recife's "new music scene," but all three, especially Dona Selma, became associated with it.

Cascabulho. *Fome Dá Dor de Cabeça*. Mangroove Records (independent). Tel: (081) 268-1380. http://cascabulho.cesar.org.br.
Chão e Chinelo. *Loa Do Boi Meia Noite*. Independent.
Chico Science & Nação Zumbi. *Da Lama Ao Caos*. Sony CD-81594/2-464476, 1995.
———. *Afrociberdelia*. Sony Latin CDZ-81996/2-479255, 1996.
Coração Tribal. *Coração Tribal*, Virgin, 1997.
Devotos do Ódio. *Agora Tá Valendo*. BMG/Plug, 1997.
Dona Margarida Pereira e Os Fulanos. *Música Pra Pular Brasileira*. Independent, 1998. Tel: (081) 423-6169.
Dona Selma do Côco. *Cultura Viva*. Independent. Tel: (081) 439-5094/977-2610.

———. *Minha História*. Paradoxx, 1997.
Eddie. *Sonic Mambo*. Roadrunner, 1999.
Faces do Subúrbio. *Faces do Subúrbio*. BMG/Plug, 1997.
Madureira, Antúlio. *Perré Bumbá*. Independent, 1997. Tel: (081) 268-7065.
Maracatu Nação Pernambuco. *Maracatu Nação Pernambuco*. Velas 11-V016.
Mestre Ambrósio. *Mestre Ambrósio*. Independent, 1996. E-mail: msaopaulo@u-netsys.com.br. Fax: (011) 572-5659.
———. *Fuá na Casa de CaBRal*. Chaos (Sony) 758.491/2-492195, 1999. www.mestreambrosio.com.br. E-mail: mestreambrosio@uol.com.br.
Mundo Livre S/A. *Samba Esquema Noise*. Banguela Records, 1995.
———. *Guentando a Ôia*. Excelente Discos 011060-2, 1996.
———. *Carnaval na Obra*. Excelente Discos/Abril Music, 1998.
———. *Por Pouco*. Trama, 2000.
Nação Zumbi. *Chico Science & Nação Zumbi*. Chaos (Sony) 789.124/2-490225 & 789.125/2-490244, 1998. www.sonymusic.com.br. Double-CD tribute to Chico Science featuring live material by CSNZ, new studio recordings by Nação Zumbi, and some studio remixes by guest DJs of previously-released CSNZ songs.
———. *Rádio S.AMB.A: Serviço Ambulante da Afrociberdelia*. Ybrazil? Music 2000.
Nóbrega, Antônio. *Madeira Que Cupim Não Rói: Na Pancada do Ganzá II*. Brincante BR 0002.
Otto. *Samba Pra Burro*. Trama 0005, 1998. www.tramamusic.com.
Querosene Jacaré. *Você Não Sabe da Missa um Terço*. Paradoxx, 1998.
Sheik Tosado. *Som de Caráter Urbano de Salão*. Trama, 1999.
Various artists. *Abril Pro Rock*. Columbia 758.434/2-490151. E-mail: abrilpr@truenet.com.br
———. *Enjaulado: Música Para Ouvir Trancado*. Independent, 1997. E-mail: helder@elogica.com.br.
———. *Pernambuco em concerto*. Independent. África Produções. Tel: (081) 424-7354/424-8998. E-mail: africa@hotlink.com.br.
———. *Recife Rock Mangue Nos. 1-3*. Caranguejo Records (independent). Tel: (081) 221-4434.
Via Sat. *Via Sat*. CD demo. Independent. Tel: (081) 222-0655/963-8213.
———. *Via Sat*. Morango Music (independent). Tel: (081) 439-8592.

Other artists mentioned:
Baleiro, Zeca. *Vô Imbolá*. MZA Music 011 297-2, 1999.
Gil, Gilberto. *Quanta*. Mesa (Warner) 92778-2. http://www.gilbertogil.com.br.
Lenine. *O Dia Em Que Faremos Contato*. BMG 7432150211-2, 1997.
Nascimento, Milton. *Txai*. Columbia CT46871, 1990.
Paralamos do Sucesso. *Selvagem?* EMI 062 421 273, 1986.
———. *Bora Bora*. Intuition/Capitol CDP 7 90554, 1989.

Discography

Sa Grama. *Sa Grama*. Independent. Tel: (081) 326-5208.
Timbalada. *Cada Cabeça É Um Mundo*. Polydor 314 522 813-2, 1995.
Valença, Alceu. *Forró de Todos os Tempos*. Oasis 759.101/2-490224. E-mail: alceuvalenca@plugue.com.br. http://www.alceuvalenca.com.br.
Various artists. *Nordeste Brasil*. Verve 845 327-2, 1990.
Veloso, Caetano. *Livros*. Polygram 536 584-2, 1997. http://www.caetanoveloso.com.br. E-mail: caetanoveloso@ibm.net.

Recording shop addresses:
CD Rock/Caranguejo Records (Elcy Oliveira). Av. Conde da Boa Vista, 50 - Edifício Pessoa de Melo - Térreo Loja E, CEP 50060-000 Recife PE BRASIL. Tel: (081) 221-4434/231-7782. Fax: (081) 431-3190. One of the few sources for bands and artists from Recife's new music scene.

Discos Raros. Praça Maciel Pinheiro, 370 - Sala 102 - terçeiro andar. Recife PE BRASIL. Tel: (081) 421-2020. One of the best (and only) locations in Recife for vinyl recordings of historical folk and popular music of the Northeast.

Internet addresses (a very partial list):
Manguetronic. http://www.manguetronic.com.br
Manguenius. http://www.terra.com.br/manguenius
A Ponte. http://www.aponte.com.br
Interview with Chico Science. http://www.uol.com.br/uptodate/up3/interine.htm
Essays on music in Pernambuco. http://www.brazzil.com/cvrjul01.htm

Bibliography

Abramo, Bia. "Da Lama à Fama." *República* (July 1997): 74-77.
Adamo, Sam. "Race and *Povo*." In *Modern Brazil: Elites and Masses in Historical Perspective*, ed. Michael L. Conniff and Frank D. McCann, 192-206. Lincoln and London: University of Nebraska Press, 1989.
Alvarenga, Oneyda. "A influência negra na música brasileira." *Boletím Latino-Americano de Música* 6 (April 1946): 357-407.
———. *Música Popular Brasileira*, 2d ed. São Paulo: Duas Cidades, 1982.
Andrade, Mário de. "O Samba Rural Paulista." *Revista do Arquivo Municipal* 41 (Ano 4): 37-116, 1937.
———. "O Maracatu." Chap. in *Danças Dramáticas do Brasil,* 2d ed., vol. 2. Belo Horizonte: Editora Itatiaia Limitada, 1982.
Appadurai, Arjun. "Disjuncture and Difference in the Global Cultural Economy." *Public Culture* 2/2 (spring 1990): 1-24.
Appleby, David P. *The Music of Brazil*. Austin: University of Texas Press, 1983.
Averill, Gage. "Anraje to Angaje: Carnival Politics and Music in Haiti." *Ethnomusicology* 38/2 (1994): 217-247.
———. "Haitian Music in the Global System." In *The Reordering of Culture: Latin America, The Caribbean and Canada in the Hood*, ed. Alvina Ruprecht and Cecilia Taiana, 339-362. Ottowa: Carleton University Press, 1995.
———. *A Day for the Hunter, A Day for the Prey: Popular Music and Power in Haiti*. Chicago and London: The University of Chicago Press, 1997.
Bakhtin, Mikhail. *Rabelais and his World*. Bloomington: Indiana University Press, 1984.
Banton, Michael. *Racial Consciousness*. London: Longman, 1988.
Bauman, Zygmunt. *Intimations of Postmodernity*. London and New York: Routedge, 1992.
Béhague, Gerard. "Bossa & Bossas: Recent Changes in Brazilian Urban Popular Music." *Ethnomusicology* 17/2 (1973): 209-33.

———. "Brazil, Folk Music, Afro-Brazilian traditions." In *The New Groves Dictionary of Music and Musicians*, ed. Stanley Sadie, vol. 3, 240-243. London: Macmillan Publishers, 1980.

———. "Reflections on the Ideological History of Latin American Ethnomusicology." In *Comparative Musicology and the Anthropology of Music: Essays on the History of Ethnomusicology*, ed. Bruno Nettl and Philip Bohlman, 56-68. Chicago: The University of Chicago Press, 1991.

Benjamin, Roberto. *Folguedos e Danças de Pernambuco*, 2d ed. Coleção Recife, vol. LV. Recife: Fundação de Cultura da Cidade do Recife, 1989.

Benjamin, Walter. "The Work of Art in the Age of Mechanical Reproduction.' In *Illuminations*, ed. Hannah Arendt, 217-251. Translated by Harry Zohn. New York: Schocken Books, 1969.

Berman, Marshall. *All That Is Solid Melts Into Air: The Experience of Modernity*. New York: Penguin Books, 1988.

Bilby, Kenneth. "'Roots Explosion': Indigenization and Cosmopolitanism in Contemporary Surinamese Popular Music." *Ethnomusicology* 43/2 (spring/summer 1999): 256-296.

Browning, Barbara. *Samba: Resistance in Motion*. Bloomington: Indiana University Press, 1995.

Buell, Frederick. "Postmodernism and Globalization." Chap. in *National Culture and the New Global System*. Baltimore: Johns Hopkins University Press, 1994.

Burkholder, Mark A. and Lyman L. Johnson. *Colonial Latin America*, 2d ed. Oxford: Oxford University Press, 1994.

Cabral, Sérgio. *As Escolas de Samba do Rio de Janeira*. Rio de Janeiro: Lumiar, 1996.

———. *No Tempo de Ari Barroso*. Rio de Janeiro: Lumiar Editôra, n/d.

Cahoone, Lawrence E. "Introduction." In *From Modernism to Postmodernism: An Anthology*, ed. Lawrence Cahoone, 1-23. Cambridge: Blackwell Publishers Inc., 1996.

Calado, Carlos. *Tropicália: A História de Uma Revolução Musical*. São Paulo: Editora 34 Ltda., 1997.

Carneiro, Edison. "Folclore do Negro." In *Folclore* (Orgão da Comissão Paulista de Folclore e do Centro de Pesquisas Folclóricas "Mário de Andrade") 2/1 (1953): 28-37.

———. *Folguedos Tradicionais*. Rio de Janeiro: Edições FUNARTE/INF, 1974.

Carvalho, José Jorge de. "Black Music of All Colors: The Construction of Black Ethnicity in Ritual and Popular Genres of Afro-Brazilian Music." In *Music and Black Ethnicity: The Caribbean and South America*, ed. Gerard H. Béhague, 187-206. Coral Gables: University of Miami North-South Center, 1994.

Castro, Josué de. *Of Men and Crabs.* Translated from the Portuguese by Susan Hertelendy. New York: The Vanguard Press, 1970.
Castro, Ruy. *Chega de Saudade: A História e as Histórias da Bossa Nova.* São Paulo: Companhia das Letras, 1990.
Caúrio, Rita, ed. *Brasil Musical.* Rio de Janeiro: Art Bureau, 1988.
Chernoff, John Miller. *African Rhythm and African Sensibility.* Chicago: University of Chicago Press, 1979.
Cohen, Abner. *Masquerade Politics: Explorations in the Structure of Urban Cultural Movements.* Berkeley/Los Angeles: University of California Press, 1993.
Crook, Larry N. "Black Consciousness, *samba reggae*, and the Re-Africanization of Bahian Carnival Music in Brazil." *The World of Music* 35/2 (1993): 90-108.
———. "Turned-Around Beat: *Maracatu de Baque Virado.*" In *Brazilian Popular Music and Globalization*, eds. Charles Perrone and Christopher Dunn, 233-244. Gainesville: University Press of Florida, 2001.
DaMatta, Roberto. *Carnivals, Rogues, and Heroes: An Interpretation of the Brazilian Dilemma.* Translated by John Drury. Notre Dame: University of Notre Dame Press, 1991.
Degler, Carl N. *Neither Black Nor White: Slavery and Race Relations in Brazil and the United States.* New York: The Macmillan Company, 1971.
Dunn, Christopher, *Brutality Garden: Tropicália and the Emergence of a Brazilian Counterculture.* Chapel Hill & London: The University of North Carolina Press, 2001.
———. Co-production and fieldwork. "Return of *Tropicália.*" Afropop Worldwide (radio program), Public Radio International, 18 November 1992. Produced by Sean Barlow for World Music Productions. Co-production by Ned Sublette.
———. "Tropicália, Counterculture, and the Diasporic Imagination in Brazil." In *Brazilian Popular Music and Globalization*, eds. Charles Perrone and Christopher Dunn, 72-95. Gainesville: University Press of Florida, 2001.
Dzidzienyo, Anani. "The African Connection and the Afro-Brazilian Condition." In *Race, Class, and Power in Brazil*, ed. Pierre-Michel Fontaine, 135-153. Los Angeles: Center for Afro-American Studies, UCLA, 1985.
Erlmann, Veit. "The Aesthetics of the Global Imagination: Reflections on World Music in the 1990s." *Public Culture* 8/3 (1996): 467-487.
Feld, Steven. "From Schizophonia to Schismogenesis: The Discourses and Practices of World Music and World Beat." In *The Traffic in Culture: Refiguring Art and Anthropology*, ed. George E. Marcus and Fred R. Myers, 96-126. Berkeley and Los Angeles: University of California Press, 1995.

Frith, Simon. "Introduction." In *World Music, Politics and Social Change,* org. Simon Frith, 1-6. Manchester: Manchester University Press, 1989.
Fryer, Peter. *Rhythms of Resistance: African Music Heritage in Brazil.* Hanover, N.H.: Wesleyan University Press, 2000.
Galinsky, Philip. "*Pagode* Samba: From the Back of the Yard to the Top of the Charts." *The Beat* 13/6 (1994): 46-49.
――――. "Co-option and Cultural Resistance in Brazilian Popular Music: The *Pagode* Samba Movement in Historical Context." M.A. thesis, Wesleyan University, 1995.
――――. "Co-option, Cultural Resistance, and Afro-Brazilian Identity: A History of the *Pagode* Samba Movement in Rio de Janeiro." *Latin American Music Review* 17/2 (fall/winter 1996): 120-149.
――――. Review of *Samba: Resistance in Motion,* by Barbara Browning. In *Yearbook for Traditional Music* 30 (1998): 143-145.
――――. "The 'Atomic *Maracatu*': Tradition and Modernity in the *Mangue* Music of Chico Science & Nação Zumbi." Paper presented as part of the panel "Completely Brazil" (chair: Anthony Seeger) at the Annual Meeting of the Society for Ethnomusicology, Indiana University, Bloomington, Indiana, October 22, 1998.
――――. CD review of *Mangueira: Sambas de Terreiro e Outros Sambas (Projeto Pela Memória do Samba, Arquivo Musical I), Candomblé de Angola: Afro-Brazilian Ritual Music,* and *Drama e Fetiche: Vodum, Bumba-Meu-Boi e Samba no Benim. Ethnomusicology* 46/1 (Winter 2002): 186-189.
――――. "Music and Place in the Brazilian Popular Imagination: the Interplay of Local and Global in the *Mangue Bit* Movement of Recife, Pernambuco, Brazil." In *From Tejano to Tango: Latin American Popular Music,* ed., Walter Aaron Clark. New York: Routledge, 2002.
Guerra-Peixe, César. *Maracatus do Recife.* São Paulo: Ricordi Brasileira Editôres, 1980 [1955].
Guilbault, Jocelyne. *Zouk: World Music in the West Indies.* Chicago and London: The University of Chicago Press, 1993.
Guillermoprieto, Alma. *Samba.* New York: Knopf, 1990.
Harvey, John J. "Cannibals, Mutants, and Hipsters: The Tropicalist Revival." In *Brazilian Popular Music and Globalization,* eds. Charles Perrone and Christopher Dunn, 106-122. Gainesville: University Press of Florida, 2001.
Kubik, Gerhard. *Angolan Traits in Black Music, Games and Dances of Brazil.* Lisboa: Junta de Investigações Científicas do Ultramar, 1979.
Leitch, Vincent B. *Postmodernism—Local Effects, Global Flows.* Albany: State University of New York Press, 1996.

Lins, Renato. "Renato L: 'Mangue não é fusão!'" *Manguenius: Sua Revista Mangue na Internet* (http://www.terra.com.br/manguenius/artigos/ctudo-entrevista-renatol.htm), November 2001.
Lipp, Marty. "Chico Science & Nação Zumbi." *The Beat* 14/6 (1995): 48-9.
Lipsitz, George. *Time Passages: Collective Memory and American Popular Culture*. Minneapolis: University of Minnesota, 1990.
———. *Dangerous Crossroads: Popular Music, Postmodernism and the Poetics of Place*. London: Verso, 1994.
Lopes, Nei. "Pagode, o Samba Guerrilheiro do Rio." In *Notas Musicais Cariocas*, organized by João Baptista M. Vargens. Coleção - Debates Culturais/3. Petrópolis: Editôra Vozes, 1986.
———. *O Negro no Rio de Janeiro a Sua Tradição Musical: Partido-Alto, Calango, Chula e Outras Cantorias*. Rio de Janeiro: PALLAS, 1992.
———. "Afro-Brazilian Music and Identity." *Conexões: African Diaspora Research Project* 5/1 (1993): 6-8. East Lansing: Michigan State University.
———. *Sambeabá: O Be-A-Bá Do Samba*. Unpublished manuscript, n/d.
Maior, Mário Souto and Leonardo Dantas Silva, organizers. *Antologia do Carnaval do Recife*. Recife: Editora Massangana, Fundação Joaquim Nabuco, 1991.
Manuel, Peter. *Popular Musics of the Non-Western World*. New York: Oxford University Press, 1988.
Margolis, Mac. "The Invisible Issue: Race in Brazil." *The Ford Foundation Report* 23/2 (summer 1992): 3-7. New York: The Ford Foundation.
Marzorati, Gerald. "Tropicália Agora!" *The New York Times Magazine*, April 25, 1999, 48-51.
McGowan, Chris and Ricardo Pessanha. *The Brazilian Sound: Samba, Bossa Nova, and the Popular Music of Brazil*. Philadelphia: Temple University Press, 1998.
Moehn, Frederick. "'Good Blood in the Veins of This Brazilian Rio,' or a Cannibalist Transnationalism." In *Brazilian Popular Music & Globalization*, eds., Charles A. Perrone and Christopher Dunn, pp. 258-269. New York and London: Routledge, 2001.
Monson, Ingrid. "Riffs, Repetition and Theories of Globalization." *Ethnomusicology* 43/1 (winter 1999): 31-65.
Moura, Roberto. *Tia Ciata e a Pequena África no Rio de Janeiro*, 2nd ed. Rio de Janeiro: Coleção Biblioteca Carioca, 1995.
Mukuna, Kazadi wa. *A Contribuição Banto na Música Popular Brasileira*. São Paulo: Globo, 1979.
Muníz, Júnior. *De Batuque a Escola de Samba: Subsídios para a História do Samba*. São Paulo: Símbolo, 1976.
Murphy, John and Sérgio "Siba" Veloso. "Self-Discovery in Brazilian Popular Music: Mestre Ambrósio." Draft of a chapter for publication in

Brazilian Popular Music & Globalization (eds., Charles Perrone and Christopher Dunn, New York and London: Routledge, 2001), October 21, 1998.

Murphy, John. "Self-Discovery in Brazilian Popular Music: Mestre Ambrósio." In *Brazilian Popular Music & Globalization*, eds., Charles A. Perrone and Christopher Dunn, pp. 245-257. New York and London: Routledge, 2001a.

———. "Regional Identity, Cultural Politics, and the Circulation of Musical Ideas: Alternative Popular Music in Northeast Brazil." Paper presented as part of the panel "Popular Music in Brazil: Nationalism and Globalization" (chair: Philip Galinsky), Society for Ethnomusicology meeting, Detroit, October 27, 2001b.

Neto, Moisés. *Chico Science: A Rapsódia Afrociberdélica*. Recife: Editora Comunicarte, 2000.

Nettl, Bruno. *The Study of Ethnomusicology: Twenty-Nine Issues and Concepts*. Urbana: University of Illinois Press, 1983.

———. *The Western Impact on World Music: Change, Adaptation, and Survival*. New York: Schirmer, 1985.

Oliven, Ruben George. "'The Woman Makes (and Breaks) the Man': The Masculine Imagery in Brazilian Popular Music." *Latin American Music Review* 9/1 (1988): 90-108.

Page, Joseph A. *The Brazilians*. Reading, Massachusetts: Addison-Wesley Publishing Company, Inc., 1995.

Pareles, Jon and Patricia Romanowski, ed. *The Rolling Stone Encyclopedia of Rock & Roll*. New York: Rolling Stone Press/Summit Books, 1983.

Parker, Richard G. 1991. "The Carnivalization of the World." Chap. in *Bodies, Pleasures, and Passions: Sexual Culture in Contemporary Brazil*. Boston: Beacon Press, 1991.

Pereira, Carlos Alberto Messeder. "Quem Sabe Faz a Hora... e Espera Acontecer!" Chap. in *Em Busco do Brasil Contemporâneo*, 97-105. Rio de Janeiro: Notrya, 1993.

Pereira, Pereira da. "Folk-lore Pernambucano." *Revista do Instituto Histórico e Geográfico Brasileiro* 70: 3-641. Rio de Janeiro: Imprensa Nacional, 1908.

Perrone, Charles A. *Masters of Contemporary Brazilian Song: MPB 1965-1985*. Austin: University of Texas Press, 1989.

Perrone, Charles A. and Christopher Dunn, eds. *Brazilian Popular Music and Globalization*. Gainesville: University Press of Florida, 2001.

Pinto, Tiago de Oliveira. "Samba: Verbindendes Element." Chap. in *Capoeira Samba Candomblé: Afro-Brasilianische Musik im Recôncavo, Bahia*, 106-159. Berlin: Staatliche Museen Preussischer Kulterbesitz, 1991.

———. "The Pernambuco Carnival and its Formal Organizations: Music as Expression of Hierarchies and Power in Brazil." *Yearbook for Traditional Music* XXVI (1994): 20-39.

———. "Musical Difference, Competition, and Conflict: The Maracatu Groups in the Pernambuco Carnival, Brazil." *Latin American Music Review* 17/2 (fall/winter 1996): 97-119.

Rampazzo, Pedro. "A Influência dos Ritmos Regionais na Música Pernambucana dos Anos 90." Paper for the journalism course of the Universidade Católica de Pernambuco - UNICAP, n/d.

Raphael, Alison. "From Popular Culture to Microenterprise: The History of Brazilian Samba Schools." *Latin American Music Review* 11/1 (June 1990): 73-83.

Ratliff, Ben. "From Brazil, the Echoes Of a Modernist Revolt." *New York Times*, May 17, 1998.

Real, Katarina. *O Folclore no Carnaval do Recife*, 2d ed. Recife: Editora Massangana, Fundação Joaquim Nabuco, 1990.

Risério, Antônio. *Carnaval Ijexá: Notas sobre Afoxés e Blocos do Novo Carnaval Afrobaiano*. Salvador: Corrupio, 1981.

Said, Edward W. *Orientalism*. New York: Vintage Books, 1979.

Sakolsky, Ron and Fred Wei-Han Ho, ed. *Sounding Off! Music as Subversion/Resistance/Revolution*. New York: Autonomedia, 1995.

Schreiner, Claus. *Música Brasileira: A History of Popular Music and the people of Brazil*. Translated from the German by Mark Weinstein. New York: Marion Boyars, 1993.

Science, Chico. "Chico Science Mangue Star." Produced by Carlos Germano, Gilson Martins, and Didier Bertrand. Executive direction by José Mário Austregésilo. TV Viva/TV Jornal, year unknown. Videocassette.

Seeger, Anthony. "Whoever We Are Today, We Can Sing You a Song About It." In *Music and Black Ethnicity: The Caribbean and South America*, ed. Gerard H. Béhague, 1-13. Coral Gables: University of Miami North-South Center, 1994.

Silva, Leonardo Dantas. "Maracatu: Presença da África no Carnaval do Recife." *Folclore* 190/191 (Jan./Feb. 1988). Recife: Editora Massangana, Centro de Estudos Folclóricos, Fundação Joaquim Nabuco.

Skidmore, Thomas E. *Black into White: Race and Nationality in Brazilian Thought*. New York: Oxford University Press, 1974.

———. "Race and Class in Brazil: Historical Perspectives." In *Race, Class, and Power in Brazil*, ed. Pierre-Michel Fontaine, 11-24. Los Angeles: Center for Afro-American Studies, UCLA, 1985.

Skidmore, Thomas E. and Peter H. Smith. "Brazil: Development For Whom?" Chap. in *Modern Latin America*, 3d ed. New York: Oxford University Press, Inc., 1992.

Slobin, Mark. *Subcultural Sounds: Micromusics of the West*. Hanover, New Hampshire: University Press of New England, 1992.
Soares, Karina de Melo, Sandra de Deus Ishigami, and Alba Cristina de Albuquerque Moreira. *Espectáculos Populares de Pernambuco*. Recife: Companhia Editora de Pernambuco, Secretaria de Cultura do Estado de Pernambuco, 1996.
Taylor, Timothy D. *Global Pop: World Music, World Markets*. New York: Routledge, 1997.
Teles, José. *Meteoro Chico*. Recife: Editôra Bagaço, n/d.
———. *Do Frevo Ao Manguebeat*. São Paulo: Editora 34, 2000.
Tinhorão, José Ramos. *O Samba Agora Vai... A Farsa da Música Popular no Exterior*. Rio de Janeiro: JCM Editôres, 1969.
———. *Pequena História Da Música Popular—Da Modinha Ao Tropicalismo*. 5th ed. São Paulo: Art Editora, 1986.
Various. *Som da Nota* (special on the music and culture of the communities of Peixinhos and Alto José do Pinho). Produced by Germana Pereira. TV and Editing Direction by Didier Bertrand and Gilson Martins. Direction by Alexandre Alencar. General Direction by Nilton Pereira. TV Viva, 1998. TV program (SBT channel, Recife) on videocassette.
Vianna, Hermano. *O Mistério do Samba*. Rio de Janeiro: Zahar, 1995.
———. *The Mystery of Samba: Popular Music and National Identity in Brazil*. Edited and translated from the Portuguese by John Charles Chasteen. Chapel Hill & London: The University of North Carolina Press, 1999.
Walser, Robert. "Rhythm, Rhyme, and Rhetoric in the Music of Public Enemy." *Ethnomusicology* 39/2 (spring/summer 1995): 193-217.
Winant, Howard. *Racial Conditions: Politics, Theory, Comparisons*. Minneapolis and London: University of Minnesota Press, 1994.
Wollen, Peter. "Cinema/Americanism/The Robot." In *Modernity and Mass Culture*, eds., James Naremore and Patrick Brantlinger, 42-69. Bloomington & Indianapolis: Indiana University Press, 1991.
Yúdice, George. "The Funkification of Rio." In *Microphone Fiends: Youth Music and Youth Culture*, ed. Andrew Ross and Tricia Rose, 193-217. New York and London: Routledge, 1994.

Index

Abril Pro Rock, 44-45
   musical influences of the bands, 67
"A Cidade" (song), 105-107
Afoxé
   compared to the *maracatu nação*, 81, 81n. 23
   instrumentation, 81n. 25
   in Recife, 20
African diaspora, 9
Afrociberdelia, 107
Alto José do Pinho, 94-95
Antropofagia, 2, 53, 111
Appadurai, Arjun, 12
Averill, Gage, 14-15, 122

Baião, 75
Baile Perfumado (film), 47
Banda de Pífanos Dois Irmãos de Caruaru, 3
Béhague, Gerard, 6
Benjor, Jorge
   influence on Fred Zero Quatro, 45
Bilby, Kenneth, 126n. 47
Blocos afro, 9
Bombo (drum)
   first use on stage by middle class musicians, 56n. 10
   in CSNZ, 2
   popularity of, 60
Brazilian national identity, 113-114
   and bossa nova, 6, 118-119
   and *mangue*, 118-119
   and Rio de Janeiro, 5-6, 118-119
   and samba, 6, 114, 114n. 29, 118-119
   and *tropicália*, 119
Browning, Barbara, 9

Caboclo de lança, 2, 105, 105n. 7
Carnival
   in Bahia, 9
   in Rio, 9n. 14
Carvalho, João Jorge de, 9
Cascabulho, 3, 74
Castro, Josué de, 27, 109, 111, 112
Cavalo-marinho, 74
Chão e Chinelo, 74
Chaos Theory, 112
Chico Science & Nação Zumbi
   formation of, 32-34
   in New York City, 2
   role in the *mangue* movement, 1
Comadre Florzinha, 74

"Da Lama Ao Caos" (song), 112-113

Index

Devotos (do Ódio), 67-68

Erlmann, Veit, 13, 120, 122-123

Feld, Steven, 126
Folklore
    adaptation of, 73
Freyre, Gilberto, 113
Forró, 75
Forró de rabeca, 75

Gender identity, 8-9
Gil, Gilberto
    collaboration with CSNZ, 54
Gonzaga, Luiz, 58, 75
Guerra-Peixe, César, 81
Guillermoprieto, Alma, 9n. 14

Jackson do Pandeiro, 58

Kubik, Gerhard, 6

Lamento Negro, 32-33
Lenine, 56n. 10
Lins, Renato (Renato L.)
    account of origins of the *mangue* movement, 34-35
    "*Mangue Beat*" radio program, 46
Lopes, Nei, 6, 8

Mabuse, Herr Doktor, 29
Mulata, 9n. 14
Mangue
    and Brazilian national identity, 118-119
    and northeastern Brazilian pride, 24-25
    and postmodernism, 103-104
    and postmodernity, 16
    and resistance, 126
    and world music, 12, 12n. 22
    compared with *axé-music*, 25n. 29
    compared with *Rock Brasil*, 64-65
    compared with *tropicália*, 52-56
    crab image, 109
    definition of, 34-36
    "*Mangue Beat*" radio program, 46
    manifesto, 43
    official culture's relation to, 23-24
    style and ideology, 104-113
    swamps, 27
    tradition and modernity, 4
Manifesto Antropófago, 52
Maracatu
    origin of the term, 81-82
    "Maracatu Atômico" (song), 21-22
Maracatu de baque solto, 83
    as played by Nação Pernambuco, 71
    explanation of, 83, 83n. 31
Maracatu de baque virado
    as played by Nação Pernambuco, 70-71
    explanation of, 83, 83n. 31
Maracatu Nação, 80-86
    influence of *Candomblé*, 82-33
    influence of two "nations," 82n. 27
Maracatu Nação Estrela Brilhante, 84-86
    author's involvement with, 19-20
Mestre Ambrósio, 74-79
    in New York City, 3
Mestiçagem, 113-114

Moehn, Frederick, 117-118
Monson, Ingrid, 124-126
Moura, Roberto, 6
MPB
    and *mangue*, 4
    explanation of, 51
Mukuna, Kazadi wa, 6
Mundo Livre S/A
    compared with rock boom of the '80s, 38
    formation and early history, 38-40
Murphy, John, 74

Nação, 70n. 4
Nação Pernambuco, 69-73
    appearance at Abril Pro Rock, 44
    role on the "new music scene," 70, 72
"New Music Scene"
    influence of CSNZ and Mundo Livre S/A, 2
    origins of, 42
    range of music in, 3
    some influential artists, 28
Northeast Brazil
    relation to Brazilian national culture, 25

"O Cidadão do Mundo" (song), 108-111

Pagode samba, 8, 8n. 11, 63, 64
    and Afro-Brazilian identity, 11
Parker, Richard G. 170n. 14
Peixinhos, 94-95
Pernambuco
    expressive culture, 23
    folk heritage, 1
    relation to Brazilian cultural identity, 24
Perrone, Charles, 7

Pinto, Tiago de Oliveira, 7
Pires, Paulo André
    as rock producer, 30
    on Chico Science's influence, 97
    on the origins of the "new music scene," 42-43

Racial classification in Brazil, 114n. 31
Racial democracy, 8, 9n. 14
Racial identity
    Afro-Brazilian, 8-9
    Indigenous Brazilian, 9-10
Racial ideology in Brazil, 114n. 27
Raphael, Alison, 7
Real, Katarina, 81
Recife
    author's impressions of, 22-23
    history, 22-23
    poverty, 23
Ribeiro, Maureliano
    role in the *mangue* movement, 33
Rock Brasil, 63-65

Samba-reggae,
    and racial identity, 9
Science, Chico
    as role model, 97
    cross-cultural identity, 2
    death of, 2
    formative musical influences, 31-32
    importance of, 28
    role in the *mangue* movement, 2
Seeger, Anthony, 9
Slobin, Mark, 12
Soparia (bar), 42, 44
Suassuna, Ariano
    views on *mangue*, 24, 92

Tinhorão, José Ramos, 7
Tropicália, 49-56

Valença, Alceu, 58-60
Veloso, Caetano
    discusses *tropicália*, 49
    views on *mangue*, 54
Vianna, Hermano, 6, 114-115
Via Sat, 96-97

Yúdice, George, 115-117

Zero Quatro, Fred
    early musical experiences, 37-38
    initial impressions of Chico Science, 40